FACTORS INFLUENCE TOURISM AND TRANSPORT

FUTURE CHANGES

JOHN LOK

Copyright © John Lok

All Rights Reserved.

This book has been published with all efforts taken to make the material error-free after the consent of the author. However, the author and the publisher do not assume and hereby disclaim any liability to any party for any loss, damage, or disruption caused by errors or omissions, whether such errors or omissions result from negligence, accident, or any other cause.

While every effort has been made to avoid any mistake or omission, this publication is being sold on the condition and understanding that neither the author nor the publishers or printers would be liable in any manner to any person by reason of any mistake or omission in this publication or for any action taken or omitted to be taken or advice rendered or accepted on the basis of this work. For any defect in printing or binding the publishers will be liable only to replace the defective copy by another copy of this work then available.

copyright

Contents

Preface

Introduction

Nowadays, global tourism industry is experiencing decline stage or decline life cycle stage due to COVID19 human hung disease occurs. It brings many travelers begin to feel fear to catch air planes because any one passenger may be gotten this kind of new disease when one or more than one passenger who had owned this kind of new lung disease and he/she is or they are sitting in the air plane. So, many travelers believed that when one owned COVID 19 lung disease passenger is catching in any one air plane, it will have high chance that they will be contacted to give this kind of disease easily by the air in the closed windows airplane. Due to this reason, this kind of new disease had influenced global many travelers felt fear to catch air planes to go to different countries to travel in these two years, even future. However, whether COVID 19 disease is the main factor to influence global tourism industry decline and oil price changes. It is one interesting question to research.

Hence, this kind of new disease can bring these questions to global tourism industry development and fuel need, such as: Can travelers number influence fuel price whether it raises up or falls down? If it was sure that tourism industry recession or growth up, it can have direct or indirect relationship to cause fuel price increasing or decreasing effect, whether what are the main factors to cause tourism industry development or recession can influence fuel price rises up or falls down? Why and how traveler traveling leisure behavior can influence fuel price increases or decreases or fuel need increases or decreases to airline industry?

In my this book, I shall attempt to apply behavioral economic theory to explain why and how traveler individual catching air planes leisure activities or travelling leisure need or leisure activities, they have direct or indirect relationship to influence future fuel price changes. Readers can attempt to follow behavioral economic view to explain whether traveler individual leisure activities can have any relationship to influence future global fuel need changes or price changes.

Prologue

Table of contents

Whether individual habitual behaviour can influence travelling behaviour: e.g. renting travel transportation tools
How to determine future travel behavior from past travel experience and perceptions of risk and safety for the benefits to travel consumers?

What is push and pull factors to influence any
traveler who chooses where is whose preferable travelling destination.
Why expectation, motivation and attitude factor can influence travelling behaviour.
What methods can predict future travel behavioural consumption
How to use qualitative of travel behavioural method to predict future travel consumption.
How to apply advanced traveler information systems (ATIS) to predict future travelling behaviour.
How does online tourism sale channel can influence traveling consumption of behaviour.
Actively based patterns of urban population of travel behavioural prediction method.
What is trip based versus activity based approaches?
Why senior age will be main travelling target.

Psychological method to predict
travel behavioural consumption.
Reference
Chapter 4
What factors can influence travel behavioural consumption p.61-70
Chapter 5
Oil price changes influences tourism industry experiences growth life cycle stage or decline life cycle stage
● How to develop new economic tourism industry
● How new economic development in oil industry p.71-91
New and old economic theories explain oil is not main factor
to influence tourism income
● Can economic theory explain old price change to influence tourism income?
● How the price of oil changes influences global tourism industry growth or recession?

Chapter 6
International war and illness factors influences tourism industry experiences decline cycle stage
● Can wars impact global tourism development to experience
decline life cycle stage p. 92-110

1.1.1 How did First World War influence
Europe economy and tourism industry declines ?

1.1.2 Can US poor economic consequences of war influence tourism industry growth?

1.1.3 Can economy policy influence peace and
security?

1.1.4 How civil wars influence economic growth and tourism industry declines?

1.1.5 How economic impact of the war and higher military spending? Country itself internal civil war influences

2.1 The relationship between country itself
internal war and traveler lesiure need

2.1.1 How internal war influences human welfare?

2.1.2 Can internal civil wars influence the country's tourism
industry long time decline cycle stage experience ?

2.1.3 How can be stopped the civil internal war to influence decline cycle stage to
gloabl tourism industry?

Bibliography

Chapter 7

Economic recession or boom how influences consumer behavior when the business had been experiencing decline life cycle stage

● COVID -19 disease how influence businesses may experience either growing life cycle stage or decline life cycle stage. p.111-149

● How recession influences the role of advertising changes?

Applying business development strategy to raise the educational robotic manufacturer sale number in recession period

● How to develop organizations in growth stage?

● How to apply business development strategy to help educational robotic manufacturers to enter traditional education market ?

● Future educational robotic are applied on development teaching maths market

Tourism industry life cycle stage strategy

● New and old economic theories explain oil is not main factor to influence tourism income

● What are the characteristics of birth life cycle stage to tourism industry ?

● What characteristics to space tourism growth stage?

Airport service life cycle stage improvement strategy

How can process improvement management strategy influence airport service performance?

Chapter 8

Factors influence oil industry life cycle stage

- Reasons cause oil industry experiences
decline life cycle stage p.150-185
- How to raise global gas users need desire ?
    Electronic vehicle how influences future gas
vehicle market life cycle stage experience changes
HOW DESIGNING UNDERGROUND MASS TRANSIT RAILWAY TO BRING PASSENGERS
    - Designing transportation system advantages
- Underground train transportation needs to
know passenger behaviour reasons
reference
- How to let passengers feel impact of
undergrouund train transport to their working time efficiency
- How underground train MTR can let passengers to feel
catching time reducing .
    Artificial Intelligent In Road Transportation Strategy influences
vehicle oil need
How artificial intelligent vehicle may interact intelligent
transportation tools
- Does oil price sudden high rising factor influence global oil industry rapid reaches decline life cycle stage?

CHAPTER I

Quality of traveler individual leisure need reducing

For environmental quality concept, it concerns with health, safety, wellbeing, residential satisfaction and the physical sustainability can be considered to result from an when live ability can be considered to represent the interaction between the physical and the social domains. As with expenditure on the environment, investment in social capital contributes to quality of life. However, the benefits will again vary amongst individuals, depending largely on the security of their individual circumstance. As with the environment, the government can certainly adopt strategies that provide for public security by taking measures to reduce crime, a measure likely to be appreciated by everybody (except criminal) , at least to one degree or another. In other necessary to enhance social interaction, namely community centers or sports facilities. Furthermore, the creation of social capital has an statement which responds to general social trends to raise Ireland citizen's quality of life.

I shall indicate Ireland to explain whether environmental factor is the main factor to influence our quality of life and economic growth. Is environmental quality higher in the Ireland west regions? And if so, does this compensate for lower incomes in these regions? Is it bad that rural areas are characterized by higher costs of living in areas other than housing by environmental factor? In fact, in Ireland , UK country, population increase has a direct impact on the environment by placing demands on local natural resources, particularly open space and water. It also leads to a sense of crowding that reduces the utility associated with access to the environment. How can environment factor influence economy growth in Ireland? In Ireland, agriculture has gone through a period of significant change that has been accelerated reductions in the amount of mixed cropping and traditional land management. Indeed, changes in the expectations of young farmers will ensure that further change is likely to be characterized by increases in farm size and greater specialization with implications for landscape and wildlife. These characteristics of farm holdings are more familiar in the east regions of Ireland , UK country. As with likely to extend to the west regions as the older generation of farmers retires, although this will probably be accompanied by a trend to more farming of production needs to young farmers. So, good natural environment can provide Ireland young farmers to produce more agriculture to earn income, even who can export more rice, fruits, vegetable etc. agriculture foods to overseas. Hence, Ireland GDP will be raise if it can have good natural resource environment to provide Ireland young farmers to grow foods to sell to domestic and /or foreign agricultural market. Given the rate of economic growth, and its concentration in the east of the Ireland, UK country, it would be easy to presume that the quality of the environment is higher the further away from the mid east one goes. Thus, good natural environment is an important factor to influence the farming industry development in Ireland , UK county to satisfy their needs and to raise their quality of life nowadays.

I shall indicate New Zealand and America two developed countries to explain why which are facing environmental pollution challenge to influence their citizen's quality of life and economic growth nowadays. The first country is NZ, although, New Zealand is a developed and natural environmental country, but it had been envountering air pollution annouance and noise annoyance to influence it's citizen's health-related quality of life. I shall indicate why which has this relationship between of them in New Zealand. Nowadays, New zealand population growth is an increasing demand for consumer products and urbanization have lead to concerns over the lived environments in many of the world's cities, such as Auckland, wellington cities in New Zealand. However, environmental quality is an important determinant of health, such as the bad influence of traffic-related air and noise pollution on health outcomes, specially with respect to at risk groups, both in relation to long term exposure as well as acute effect, from brief exposures. For example, cholesterol levels and in relation to myocardial infaction. Nowadays, New Zealand is encountering the high degree of air pollution and noise annoyance to influence it's citizen's quality of life. Air pollutants can be detected either visually, such as witnessing smoke emanating from a vehicles's exhaust, or by smell, such as when odorants stimulate olfactory receptors. The evidence linking air pollution to adverse impacts on human health.

Many air impacts on human health. Many air pollution health studies have focused specifically on urban area, and vehicle generated pollution in particular, as road vehicles are one of the major sources of pollution across much of the world. Elemental carbon, Nox and ultrafine particles an considered to be pollutants most strongly associated with road traffic emissions. In Auckland and Wellington cities, New Zealand , it has been estimated that 71% of summer and 21% of winter concentrations of fine particulate matter is attributable to motor vehicles. Moreover, poor town planning decisions in Auckland (and in New Zealand in general) over many decedes has meant that may people live in very close proximity to busy road and motorways within " road corridors" and so are the adverse effects of road traffic, including noise and air pollution as well as experiencing on potential for degradation in their quality of life. Such as, New Zealand is highly suitable for studies investigating the impact of roads on the health of its residents. For example, NZ, road traffic noise and aviation noist has been linked to cardiovascular disease, hypertension and ischemic heart disease. It influences NZ resident personal psychological and physical both health challenges. In fact, NZ noise increases morbidity and mortality independently of air pollution exposure, though air pollution constituted a greater burden of disease when arise exposure had a greater impac on quality of life, e.g. NZ road traffic noise and air pollution will be caused from drivers in busy time. Specially in Auckland and Wellington cities. It will influence urban and rural environmental pollution. Some retired old people who will feel annoyance when this road traffic occurs in Auckland or Wellington cities to close to their houses in transportation busy time every day.

Next developed country is America, this country's air pollution is also serious nowadays. Because traffic jam often occurs in New York, Washington, Boston etc. big cities in US. So, U.S. cities' parks and its trees have significant influence to produce fresh air to provide U.S. residents who are living in cities to breach for their body health. David

J. & Gordon , M. (2016) indicated " In U.S. these urban parks are estimated to contain about 370 million trees with a structural value of approximately $300 billion." The number of park trees varies by region of the country, but which can produce significant air quality effects in and near parks, related to air temperatures, air pollution, ultraviolet indication and carbon dioxide (a dominant greenhouse gas related to global climate change). Additional open space and other vacant lands in cities, which may contain trees and other vegatation. Contribute significant additional benefits, effects of parks and open space at the city scale can vary significantly depending on the amount of parkland and amount of tree cover within the parkland.

The reasons why parks can reduce air pollution. Parks generally have lower air temperature than surrounding areas. Temperatures are usually cooler toward the center of a park than around its edges. At night, the center of a large park may be 13 degree cooler than surrounding city areas. The cooler air from parks often moves out into adjacent developed neighborhoods. This cooling of surrounding areas tends to increase with park size and percentage of the park covered by trees. So, cooler air temperature is provided by urban parks can have significant impacts on human health. During heat wave events, which can kill hundreds of people, park areas may provide city dwellers with some respite from high air temperture, particularly in the evening, during hot, sunny days tree shade can greatly increase human comfort. Because park influences on air temperature extend to developed areas outside of parks, local energy use for heating and cooling buildings is also effected. Although, the net around effect of parks on energy costs has been by reducing temperature is difficult to estimate at least in the southern United States the effect will usually be a net annual benefit. Futhermore, large park trees will reduce winds and may provide a benefit of winter heating of buildings near the park. Although, the overall economic effect of urban trees and parks on air temperature reduction is not fully billions of dollars annually at the national scale in terms of improved environmental quality and human health.

In fact, trees and vegetation in parks can help reduce air pollution both by directly removing pollutants and by reducing air temperatures and building energy use in and near parks. There tree effects can reduce pollutant emissions and formation. However, park vegetation can increase some pollutants by either directly emitting volatile orgnic compounds that can contribute to ocone and carbon monoxide formation or indirectly by the emission of air pollutants through vegetation maintenance practices, such as operation of chain and use of transportation fuels. David J. & Gordon , M. (2016) showed "Annual pollution removal and economic benefits by U.S. urbank park trees is estimated at about 75,000 tones ($500 million) or 80 pounds per acre of tree cover ($300 per acre of tree cover). Carton storage and annual removal by urban park trees and soils in the United States is estimated at about: carton storage trees: 75 million tons ($1.6 billion), carton storage (soils) : $102 million tons of carbon removal (trees): 2.4 million tons ($50 million)". Park management is recommended by U.S. environment protection department: considering that most of the effects of trees on microclimate and air quality are beneficial for park users and nearby residents; park designs that include a variety of land cover, areas of dense trees, scattered trees and lawn are likely to provide the greatest opportunities for optimum physical comfort of visitors; increase the number of healthy trees (increase pollution removal and carbon storage); sustain existing tree cover (maintains pollution removal levels) and (carbon storage); maximize use of low volatile organic compound emitting trees reduces ozove and carbon monoxide formation; sustain large, healthy trees (large trees have greatest per tree effcts on pollution and carbon removal); using long-lived trees (reduces long term pollutant emissions from removal; reducing fossil fuel in maintaining vegetation reduces pollutant ans carbon emissions)." So, if US had many green parks, then which can reduce air pollution, also it can assist many travellers who prefer to travel to US to raise GDP travelling income growth generally.

(i) Why environmental pollution and human right abuses has close relationship to influence quality of life and economic growth?

In fact, environment pollution and human right abuses has close relationship. It is clear that poverty situations and human rights abuses are worsened by environmental degradation. The result can influence poor human quality of life to the developing countries' people unfairly. There are these several abvious reasons: firstly, the exhaustion of natural resources leads to unemployment and emigration to cities; secondly, this affects the enjoyment and exercise of basic human rights. Environmental conditions contribute to a large extents to the spread of infections diseases. From the 4,400 million of people who live in developing countries, almost 60% lack basis health care services, a almost a third of these people have no access to safe water supply; thirdly, degradation poses new problems, such as environmental refugees. Environmental refugees suffer from significant economic, socio-cultural and political consequences. And fourthly, environmental degradation worsens existing problems suffered by developing and developed countries. David J. Nowak & Gordon M. Melsler (2016) showed" Air pollution , for example, accounts for 2.7 million to 3.0 million of deaths annually and of these 90% are from developing countries. " Hence, our societies need to concern human right law to protect unfair treatment to developing countries people. Firstly, both disciplines have deep social root, even though human rights law is more rooted within the collective consciousness, the accelerated process of environmental degradation is generating a new " environmental consciousness". Secondly, both disciplines have become internationalized . The international community has assumed the commitment to observe the realization at human rights and respect for the environment. Thirdly, both areas of law tend to universalize their object of protection. Human rights are presented as universal and the protection of the environment appears as everyone is responsibility.

Human right and environment law can raise our quality of life because the first approach is one where environmental protection is described as a possible means of fulfulling human rights standards. Here, environmental law is conceptualized as giving a protection that would help ensure the well-being of future generations as well as the survival of those who depend immediately upon natural resources for their livelihood. So, the end is fulfulling human rights, and the route is though environmental law, the second approach places the two sphere in inverted positions, it states that the legal protection of human rights is an effective means to achieving the ends of conservation and environmental protection. Therefore, the presently existing human right is as a route to environmental protection. The focus is on the connection to influence any economy: health, food supply , housing, fresh natural air supply etc. aspects of quality of life issues. Hence, human right and environment law and human quality of life and economic growth has close relationship . We can not neglect to concern how to achieve human right law to protect our nature environment existing in our societies.

What are environmental factors affect human health in important way, both positive and negative? On positive environmental factor aspect, which can sustain health, and promoting them is preventive medicine. They include : sources of nutrition (farming, oil quality, water availability, bio diversity/bio integrity, genetically modified organisms ; hurting, fishing: wildlife, fish populations; water (drinking, cooking, cleaning,sanitation); air quality; ozone layer (protection from cancers disease etc).; space for exercise and recreation, sanitation/waste recycling and disposal. On negative environmental factors aspect, which are threats to health, and controlling them is public environmental health. They include: environmental conditions favouring disease sectors (endemic and exotic sectors); invasive biota (visuses, bacteria etc.), their hosts and sectors; environmental disruptions: floods, droughts, storms, fires earthquakes, volcanoes; air quality: pollution landing to respiratory disease or cancers; water quality: biotic and abiotic contaminants ; integrity of water transport and intrastructure; monitoring and management of municipal, agricutural, industrial outflows to the environment (gases, liquids, solid waste), human changes of the environment that: create conditions that favour disease; disturb and release noxious levels of previously bound chemicals (e.g. mercury released becomes poison) or bioto (e.g. methane released from thawed peat contributes to climate changes, create temporary, intense, life threatening heat islands (e.g. urban heat waves exacerbated by climate change); result from nuclear; biological or chemical welfare or terrorism, disruption cased by other war and violense.

(ii) What is space and environmental technology?

For example, Cananda is a developed country and it begins to concern environmental pollution challenge to announced $3 million to support the initiative strengthening health and environment linkages: from knowledge to action. The initiative will bring together scientific, technical and socio-economic information on environment and health linkages, and transfer that knowledge to inform decision-making at the local, regional and national levels. Also, Canada is principally concerned with the health of Canadians. This involves health factors in Canada and in biologically shared health regions (shared geography or exposure through trade and travel). Supports international health initiatives, such as determining health risks throught environmental analysis of disease vectors in Africa or Asia.

How can the space and environmental factors affecting health? Environmental information and environmental management contribution to the maintenance and restoration of health. Space based environmental management factors and communications can play roles in: Environmental information is for optimising use of health resources; distribution of and access to health advice and treatment (i.e. to health staff treatment facilities; short range environmental prediction for avoidance of high risk, situations and to guide immediate health system responses. Managing acute risks, adopting to them (e.g. temporary moving of vulnerable elderly monitored; modeling of health impact of environmental parameters; prediction of long term health resource needs and environmental planning and mitigation and adaptation to global changes. Large benefits are possible from attention to environmental factors, e.g. asthma prevention, disease and epidemiology. Benefits need to be quantified. This is of particular interest and relevance to pandemics , such as malasia in underdeveloped countries, potentially saving thousands of lives.

What is space and environmental technology? It can contribute to and keep abreast of environmental health forecasts (using existing models and known parameters); prepare and deliver prospectuses for what space can do in anticipation or response; steer space programs according to real risks and real accumulative health benefits, as long technical investment, don't focus primarily on threats that may have high emotional impact , but are of low actual risk; position space technology and the canadian space program in people's winds, aggressively and realistically, as a first line contributor to foresight and preduction, long term maintenance of well-being and prevention of factors of ill-health ; ongoing delivery of health services and management of current health factors and potentially capable and ready to respond in health emergencies. Finally, making the full business case for investment in space technology and space program contributions relative to the full and public and private cost of health programs. This connects not only to GDP raising, but to indicators of quality of life to any countries.

● Reference

Cornelia, B.F. (1999) Rural development news, the North Central Regional Center For Rural Development vol. no 24 , IOWA.

David J. Nowak & Gordon M. Melsler (2016) " Air quality effects of urban trees and parks." National recreation and park association, USA.

De Hollander, A. E. M., J.M. Melse, Elebret & P. G.N. Kramers (1999), " An Aggregate public health indicator to represent the impact of multiple environmental exposures" Epidemiology: 606-617.

Felce, D. and Perry, J. (1995). Quality of life: A contribution to its definition and measurement, vol. 16, no.1 pp: 51-74.

Los Angeles Country Department Of public Health (2016), Country Health Ranking Model, Retrieved From www.countryhealthrankgings.org/our-approach. USA.

Melse, J.M. & A.E. M. De Hollander (2001). " Human Health And The Environment", background document for the OECD Environmental Outlook, OECD, Paris.

McGregor, S.L. T., & Goldsmith, E.B. (1998). Expanding our understanding of quality of life, standard of living and well-being. Journal of family and consumer science, 90(2), 2-6, 22.

McMichael, A.J. M. Mckee, J. Shkolnikov and T. Valkanen (2004), " Morality trends and setbacks, global convergence or divergence?", Lancet 363, 1155-1159.

Yale Center For Environmental Law And Policy (2006). Environmental Performance Index. Data available on-line at http://epi.yale.edu

Future of sustainable resources

scarcity economic and social loss to oil industry

In economic theory, it indicates two major factors are responsible for the emergence of economic problems. They are (i) the existence of unlimited human wants and (ii) the scarcity of available resources, such as limited numbers of food and natural resource shortage. I feel that human need to solve these two problems before 2050 years. How to balance an optimization approach for human and ecological flow needs ? How to solve climate change environment problem and welfare is for the centrality of human need? Because natural environment factor and natural resource and food shortage and our social economic growth which will have close connection relationship. If natural environment is bad, it will influence a lot of crops numbers can't be grown in farms. The reason of crops shortage will be caused, due to numbers of crops supply to be reduced because bad weather can not grow much crops and overpopulation numbers will increase largely at the same time before 2050 year. It will cause the numbers of demand is more than supply seriously. The result of the prices of foods will be increased by overpopulation and food shortage, so that it will cause every country inflation will be risen, it will occur in developing countries urban areas due to which have , such as India , China, Africa etc. countries have no many farms to provide to farmers to grow foods because air and water pollution and factories are built on farm land , so which need to pay higher price to import crops and foods to provide whose overpopulation to eat from overseas developed countries. Experience of developing countries that have succeeded in the reducing hunger and malnutrition shows that economic growth doesn't automatically ensure success, the source of growth matters too. This isn't surprising since 75% of the poor in developing countries live in rural areas and their incomes are directly or indirectly linked to agriculture. Many countries will continue depending on international trade to ensure their food security. It is estimated that by 2050 year developing countries net import of rice will were than double from 135 million tones in 2008/2009 to 300 million in 2050 year. It seems overpopulation will cause developing countries foods shortages in 2050 years.

Climate change and increased biofuel production represent major risks for long term food security. Studies estimate that the aggregate negative impact of climate change on African agricultural output up to 2080 year to 2100 year could be between 15% and 30%. Agriculture will have to adapt to climate change, but it can also help mitigate the effects of climate change. A recent study estimates that continued rapid expansion of biofuel production up to 2050 year would lead to the number of pre-school children in Africa and South Asia being 3 and 1.7 million higher. Thus, policies promoting the use of food based biofuels need to be reconsidered with the aim of reducing the competition between food and fuel for scare resources. The sharp increases in food price that occurred in global and national markets in recent years, and the resulting increases in the number of hungry have sharpened the awareness of policy makers and of the general public. Hence, different countries governments need to concern safe agricultural system to avoid any foods shortage to supply after 2050 year.

The perspective for 2050 year raises a number of important questions. Are current public and private investments sufficient to ensure adequate agricultural production potential, sustainable use of natural resources, information and communication research for technological breakthroughs to avoid foods shortage for the future? What needs to be undertaken to help agricultural meet the challenges of climate change and growing energy scarcity? What can be done to ensure food security in Africa, India , China etc. developing countries. The facing highest population growth rates,. The severest impacts from climate change and the heaviest burden of HIV/AIDS etc. diseases threats.

Finally, on the changing socio-economic environment hand, the main socio-economic factors that drive increasing food demand are population growth, increasing urbanization and rising incomes. In 2007 year, the USA dept. of Economic and Social affairs indicated that in fact, the developed countries population growth is slower than developing countries. However, all of the growth in the world's population will take place in urban areas. By 2050 year, more than 70% of the world's population is expected to be urban. Thus, scientists need to concern to predict developing countries urban area people foods demand and supply both numbers whether global foods can provide enough supply to urban area people in developing countries after 2050 year. On the other side, human will concern whether there be enough natural resource base of land, water and genetic diversity to meet developing countries needs after 2050 year.

What factors cause the resources scarcity and why human need to solve the resources scarcity before 2050 year

In comparison to the past 50 years, the rate at which pressure are building up on natural resources-land, water, bio-diversity will be increasing during the coming 50 years. An expanded use of agricultural feedstock for biofuels and ongoing environment degradation would work in the opposite direction. Much of the natural resource base already in use worldwide shows degradation . These include capture fisheries and water supply . In addition, actions to other ecosystem services, such as the ecosystem service, food production often cause the degradation of others, soil nutrient depletion, erosion, desertification, deflection of freshwater reserves, loss of tropical forest and biodiversity are clear indicators.

Whether natural resource base should be adequate to meet the future demand at global level. Whether any developing countries should still limit commercial natural resource import capacity to let rural area population to use to protect whose domestic natural industry development when rural area population will be increasing seriously in 2050 year. Biodiversity, another essential resource for agricultural and food production is threatened by urbanization , deforestation, pollution and the conversion of wetlands. As a result of agricultural modernization, changes in diets and population density, humankind increasingly depends on a reduced amount to agricultural biological diversity for its food supplies.Thus major reforms and investments are needed in all regions to cope with rising scarcity and degradation of land, water and biodiversity and with the added pressures resulting form rising incomes, climate change and energy demands.

There is a need to establish the right incentives to protect agriculture's environmental services to protect biodiversity and to ensure food production using new agricultural technologies before 2050 year. For the developing countries, in order to ensure that resources are available in the required quantity and quality and in the urban locations where they are needed, large additional investments need to be made in order to avoid rural people of hunger coincides with resource scarcity before 2050 year. Increased investment incentives and provided stable production growth incentives : land, water and biodiversity of three natural resources. The aim should be to stop over-exploitation, degradation and pollution, promote efficiency gains and expand overall capacities as appropriate . To provide the rural population engaging in ecosystem services with win-win solution to improve the sustainability of ecosystems, mitigate climate change and improve rural incomes. Whether and under what conditions the estimated future food demand can be met and how food security can be achieved. Hence, every country needs to have an effective economy system to attempt to solve the basic economic problems. The function of the economy is to allocate scarce resources among unlimited wants. Moreover, every country needs to have effective economic system to study of its citizen behavior in relation to how scarce resources to allocated and how choices are made between alternative uses of the country government's limited expenditure. Due to our earth has scarce resources, it implies human will scarce natural resources to provide us to use. Our governments need to predict whether what our earth's limited natural resources will be all used in order to solve our natural resources to be used in the short time quickly as well as our governments need to apply effective economic system to design soluble methods to avoid our earth will be not to provide any natural resources to satisfy our daily essential needs in one day.

The average U.S. resident , in a year, consumes 275 pounds of meats, uses 635 pounds of paper and uses energy equivalent to 7.8 metric tons of oil. Before, long years ago, the average American ate 197 pounds of meat, used 366 pounds of paper and used energy equivalent to 5.5 metric tons of oil. In the U.S. there is about one passenger car for every two people. Otherwise, Europeans have about one passenger car for every 3.1 people. On the other side, Developing countries have on average, about one passenger car for every 49 people. What does economics have to tell us about these differences in consumption?

Consume sovereignty means the idea that consumer's needs and wants determine the shape of all economic activities. Is this belief valid? That is are the final goals of economic activity all to be found in the act of consumption. Hence, if one day, our earth scarce any kinds of natural resources to be caused shortage, e.g. water, air, oil, land , gas, solar, gas , unclear , wind energy resources as well as foods e.g. vegetables and meats etc. eating resources. Due to human numbers are increasing, such as China, India and Africa etc. developing countries' people numbers are increasing much than the USA, UK etc. developed countries 's people numbers every year. But, our earth's vegetables and pigs, cows, sheet etc. meats foods numbers are decreasing every year. I believe that our foods and vegetables and natural energy resources prices will be influenced to be rose too much due to human demands (wants) are excessive to compare to our earth natural energy resources and meats and vegetables foods supply numbers. On the other side ,if every country's inflation will be increasing , but our salaries will be decreasing, or our salaries will be kept to stable and no changing, even employers will decide to dismiss employees to cause unemployment ratio rising. In result, global consumers' shopping ability will be falling down and crime numbers will be rising by poor, such as developing countries, e.g. Africa, China, India etc. will have many people feel hungry, or who feel diseases , even who will be sick to die from diseases or will be kill to die by crimes. Also , these other factors include foods scarcity, foods and natural energy prices rising, working and home environment pollution etc. factors , these factors can then cause global economic poor , serious inflation ,unbalance incomes reallocation between rich and poor people, discrimination and unfair threat will be caused between countries, even , the war between countries will be caused.

Hence, our governments need to concern how to solve our earth natural energy resources and foods and vegetables scarcity challenge , due to which will be caused shortage to supply to human to consume to use or eat in the future on day occurrence. Thus, above reasons can be concluded that as below:

Nowadays, the numbers of human (every country people) are increasing more than just the increasing numbers of consumers' consumption activities , such as our daily essential consumption include meats and vegetables etc. foods and natural energy resources, such as lands, water, gas, oil, wind, water, nuclear, electricity etc. energy . Moreover, natural resources and foods numbers are decreasing due to overpopulation are increasing in developing countries and the numbers of emigration are rising to developing countries, such as UK, USA, France, Germany poor people numbers are increasing due to war or poor issues occur in the developing countries. Moreover, due to the provision consumption activities are most directly address living standard (or lifestyle) goals, which have to do with satisfying basic needs and getting pleasure through the use of natural resources energy provision service demand and vegetables and foods tasty demand by the developed countries' people needs . Also, these poor issues will occur in the developing countries possibly in the future. Due to these factors, I predict our essential consumption , such as foods, vegetables and natural energy resources service provision price will be increasing in global competitive market due to foods and vegetables and energy shortage will be caused by the overpopulation demands rising up and foods and natural energy resources supply numbers falling down factors. Hence, our governments must need to find methods to solve the problem of our essential natural resources shortage and foods scarcity issues occurrence in the future.

Suggestions to solve resources scarcity methods
- Estimation of growth of rural population and income and expected changes of natural resources supply numbers

I recommend developing countries need to estimate growth of rural population and incomes numbers and expected changes numbers in consumption patterns . Taking into account developing countries' known resource capacities and projected development of yields, input use and technologies and making assumptions about their future trading capacity, estimates are also make of future food production level, land use and natural resource numbers import trade demand of developing countries estimation before 2050 year.

Estimation of water natural resources, such as water scarcity agreement on key definitions, the conceptualization of water scarcity in ways that are meaningful for policy development and decision making, the quantification of water scarcity, policy and technical response options available to ensure food security in conditions of water scarcity, criteria and principles that should be used to establish priorities for action to response to water scarcity in agriculture and ensure effective and efficient water scarcity copying strategies. Thus, developing countries will concern to reduce water resources shortage risk. Why is predict water supply important?

During the twentieth century, large multi-purpose dams have served the needs of agriculture, energy and growing cities, and helped protect population from flood hazards. On farm water conservation, particularly the adoption of agricultural practices that reduce runoff to increase the infiltration and storage of water in the soil in rained agriculture is the most relevant local supply enhancement option that farmers have to increase foods production by increasing water availability and decentralized water harvesting conveniently in rural areas for farmers needs. For example, ground water exploitation has grown or in scale. Ground water's capability to provide flexible, on demand water in support of irrigation has been as a major advantage by farmers in rural areas. Thus, farmers need to learn how to reduce water losses increase water productivity and water re-allocation to avoid natural resource of water shortage after 2050 year.

● Renewable natural resources and foods planting sustainability development

The concept of sustainability has become the current answer to absolving our earth of its environment and economic crises in the 21 ST. century. On the one side, the pessimists, usually ecologists and other scientists, who are convinced the earth can't forever support the different countries' demand of renewable and non renewable resources. On the other side, are the optimists, the economists, who are equally convinced that the earth, with market incentives, appropriate public policies, material substitution, recycling and new technology can satisfy the needs and improve the quality of human welfare. Both views are supporting arguments are explored used and sustainable development. Thus, renewable old energy natural resource can keep old energy natural resource to renew to use or research other new energy resource to substitute old natural resource, it will reduce the risk of energy resource shortage if the other new natural resource can be substituted to the old natural energy resource to use in our daily life , such as inventing one kind of new energy resource can be used to substitute gas to drive cars or drive boats or plans or the old gas can be renewed or cycled to use to drive cars or boats or the oil can be renewed or cycled to use to cook. Also, our earth foods, e.g. fruits, vegetables or meats etc. foods if which can be recopied to grow many numbers planting foods from any one kind food or many kinds of foods, such as one meat can be copied to manufacture two to three same kind tasty meats or unlimited same kind tasty meats. I believe the renewable natural resource energy or recopied foods can reduce our foods or energy shortage after 2050 year.

The application of sustainable strategy
between local and national and regional
of international countries

A redefined concept is of the society as whole system, made up of three concentric circles: the economy is found within the society, and both the economy and society exist within the environment. Sustainability indicators are therefore said to attempt to measure the extent to which these boundaries are respected.

I think sustainability measure as a whole concept environment, society and economy. At the bottom of the triangle is the environment or the ultimate means which represents natural resources as a precondition for decent human life. The economy (which includes technology, politics and ethics) is on the next, is not independent but serves as a vehicle for achieving ultimate ends. At the top is equity or society or ultimate end which refers to the wellbeing of the human being.

According to Daly(1990) who indicated "that the economy therefore succeeds to the extent that it conserves and restores ultimate means the environment, and enables the achievement of ultimate ends society equity. This is the application of sustainable strategies to local, national and regional issues, as well as the role of international agencies in local /national strategies." Our earth occurs issues of overpopulation, diseases and political conflict, developed countries also have to deal with problems, such as pollution and unlimited urban expansion with limited resources. Sustainability is the process suggested to improve the quality of human life within the limitations of global environment. It involves solutions for improving human welfare that doesn't result in regarding the environment. We(human) need to concern living within certain limits of the earth's capacity to maintain life, understanding the interconnections among economy, society and environment and maintaining a fair distribution of foods and vegetables and natural energy resources and opportunity for this generation and the next. Thus, on the one side, our governments need to concern three categories: Social/ political, environmental and economic issues are interconnection. Social issues include poverty, consultation, empowerment and culture. Environmental issues include pollution, natural resources and biodiversity/ resilience and economic issues include efficiency, growth and stability. It seems our governments need to considerate social and environment and economic issues to reduce our natural energy resources and foods and vegetables to allocate to let every country people to use fairly.

Reducing global warming and biodiversity
issue occurrence

It seems that we need to know our society will influence our natural environment good or bad. If our society damaged our natural environment, then it will be possible to influence our foods supply of decreasing numbers. e.g. fishes, pigs, cows, sheep and vegetables and fruits etc. foods . Due to bad climate and air and lands and ocean pollution can influence foods can not be grown easily and successfully in farms or fishes can not be lived healthy in ocean. Then, it will cause our meats, fruits and vegetables etc. foods supply shortage. Even, our gas , oil, water etc., natural resources will cause our oceans and lands pollution if human pollute our oceans and lands. In result, our natural resources used numbers will be reduced due to clean lands and oceans are polluted for long time. Finally, natural resources and meats and vegetables and fruits , rice etc. foods prices will be risen due to which are shortage to supply and developing countries' population numbers are increasing which will cause more demand.

Finally, it shall cause many developing countries' poor people who can't eat enough meats, fruits, rice vegetables etc. foods as well as who can't use enough natural resources to attempt to adapt whose past normal daily life, such as lacking enough oil to help them to cook foods to be heat to eat at home or lacked enough water to be boiled to drink. Even, whose health will be poor , then who get diseases to cause die easily when there is no enough oil to buy or enough water to drink. Hence, these developing countries governments need to concern foods and natural resource scarcity problems which will be occurred if who do not find methods to reduce this issue to be occurred after 2050 year.

As Erekson et. al.(1999) concerns about'' loss of resources, such as biodiversity or global weather (climate) warming are pacified with the potential of new technology which will lead to greater investments to the future generations for alternative resources and welfare.''

Hence, I recommend our governments need to concern global warming or biodiversity issue because of our foods and vegetables and natural resources, such as water, air will be possible polluted to be caused shortage quickly if our earth's global warming or biodiversity issue occurrence to cause our earth's large oceans or lands areas to be polluted. Our governments can attempt to control natural resources , such as oil, gas, water supply into the market and not though the political special conditions to keep them, without considering the political and social standings, which rule the control power and the use of those resources. Such as developed countries can be able to minimize the impact of foods or/and natural resources production and consumption over the natural resources, they are only mechanisms built within an economic rationality, which should be possible to control its people's demand of natural resources, e.g. oil, gas, water and supply of natural resources get more balance. Then these natural resources sale price won't be raised more every year. When there developed countries' people , such as American and Britain who can control to reduce to spend to use the excessive natural resources too much in any time and any place habitually. Then , I believe the developing countries' governments e.g. Africa, China, India, which can buy those developed countries governments' excessive natural resources to raise those developed countries' natural resources supply numbers to provide to whose people to use as well as the most important benefit is that developed countries can gain foreign income from excessive natural resources expectation. Then, these governments will raise GDP economic growth. Hence, if developed countries could control whose people consume natural resource numbers and they could also control to produce natural resource supply numbers . Then, they can gain more excessive natural resources export chance to achieve to raise GDP economic growth aim for long term. As Kirkby et al., (1995)explained ''the complexity of sustainable development our natural environment. If our governments can let our earth natural environment gets creation to maintenance, then our natural environment will be reduced the time to degradation. In the long time result, our society rural and urban economy will be growth , then our different countries' global growth will be caused diversity.'' Hence, it seems different countries' governments need to concern sustainable development to our natural environment .

How to apply agricultural green bio-economy
concept to solve control sustainable food
consumption and production in a resource-
constrained world

Nowadays, challenges for the global food supply have never been so complex. Between now and 2050 year, it has been predicted that growth in the global population and changing diets in developing countries, special in India and China and Africa etc. developing countries which may lead to an increase of around 70% in food demand. At the same time, depletion of fossil hydrocarbons will increase the demand for biomass for biofuels and industrial materials. Hence, developed and developing countries' governments ought need to coordinated to reduce air and water pollution and approached to lands use planning and oceans use planning to supply enough farms to grow potatoes, vegetables, tomatoes, fruits and let cows, pigs, sheep etc. animals can have comfortable and clean farm to live to produce good tasty meats to provide human to eat as well as to reduce pollution to supply fresh and clean water to let fishes to be lived and provides to human to drink clean water. Due to overpopulation will be predicted by scientists after 2050 year, so it will be caused foods and energy shortage possibly. Hence, different countries' governments need have long term perspectives to prepare to have enough foods and energy supply to provide us to eat and use for our earth with resource constraints and environmental limits, and which includes guideline on agricultural research to achieve foods supply aim.

On the one hand, I believe the knowledge-based bio-economy can play in realizing there challenges in particular the balance demand between foods, feed and fuel and the strategic role new technologies can have upon developing a sustainable an green bio-economy. On the other hand, I also think production of the presently high resource dependence and to build more environmentally begin sustainable agriculture system able to feed 9 billion people by 2050 year. I recommend global governments need to concern all aspects of food security including the total food chain and impacts of other land-use and management as well as non food areas, research areas which can be closed to free resources for new priorities, research to manufacture more new unique natural resources, due to gas, oil etc. resources will be used all in one day. On the energy shortage aspect, Substitution of these oil, gas etc. natural resources are needed . For example, nuclear energy is a kind of new natural resource, it can be used to push machines of rockets to be moved in space. In the future, I hope that nuclear energy can be used to drive cars or ships or trains etc. transportation tools in land. Hence, new natural resource research is essential and valid investment to be improved by scientists in the future.

On the global food supply interconnected challenges hand, including climate changes, energy and water supply are further encountered by the financial and economic changes in an increasingly globalized world. As a result, it is unclear how the growing demand for food and bioenergy (both biomass and biofuels) within a wider bio-economy can be met without further compromising ecosystem services on which all economic activities and social depend. I shall emphasizes the interaction of the economic, social and ecological components of our food systems at various levels, with feed backs increasingly the uncertainty and risks relating to future developments.

We need to face the food requirements of a growing world population have to be satisfied and we also need to the face of increasing resource scarcities, such as water, energy and land and foods etc. with the situation further exacerbated by climate change. Thus, we need to focus on our reducing demand through food consumption behavioral changes and structural changes in food systems and food chains change. Due to some developed countries people often to choose to buy these foods to eat excessively e.g. cow meat and pig meat and drink excessive soft drinks, e.g. man-made color juice. So, these developed countries consumers will feel these excessive foods and soft drinks can be rubbish if these developed countries consumers often drink these man-made color juice and eat pig and cow meats often excessively. It seems who ought to change their diet behavior and food consumption to avoid to spend too much money to buy excessive foods and drinks and who often shall not decide to eat and drink them when who feel not hungry habitually . Hence, changing human diet habit is one important psychology factor to reduce water and foods shortage, due to the meats and juices can be reduced to be rubbish if human can learn how to control their diet habit to reduce to consume excessive meats and vegetables and rice and soft drinks etc. kind of foods and drinks. Then, I believe that food and water drinking numbers will be reduced too much in the future. Hence, different countries' governments need to educate whose people to know that why who will face foods and water scarcity possibly and to let who to know how the issue can be avoided to cause by the changing of their diet habit and consumption behavior. Teaching includes, such as let who to learn why resources scarcities are expected to reduce and defining food security concept, the need is for a better understanding of complexity of vegetable systems, the need to improve the diversity and response capacity of food systems to enhance resilience, the need to address both food consumption and production, knowledge generation and innovation through cross-sector approaches is essential and the need for agricultural knowledge and innovation systems that are fit for farming purpose. After developed countries' people are educated to let who to know why who need to reduce to consume excessive foods and soft drinks habitually to aim to avoid the chance of foods and water supply shortage will be occurred after 2050 year.

On the other side, in the case of biodiversity, the loss of functional biodiversity destabilizes ecosystems and weakens their ability to deal with natural disasters or human induced stresses, such as pollution and climate change. Hence, scientists need to research how to reduce new diseases to cause foods and water pollution, even new diseases cause to influence human health. Due to unpredictable new diseases will be caused foods, fruits, vegetables etc. can't be grow easily , even cows, pigs, sheep etc. animals are not health to cause diseases to be died easily. Then, those new diseases will be decreases our foods supply numbers seriously.

Resources scarcities are expected to define future food security. The predominant form of agriculture, food processing and retailing relies heavily on cheap inputs and the potential impact on this of long term resource scarcity trends has been largely overlooked. Scarcities are either biophysical limits, such as resource supply and availability or environment limits relating to pollution and its impacts on ecosystems and the global climate system. Hence, every country's government ought to educate to let whose citizen to discuss how to protect future food security topic to avoid resource scarcities occurrence after 2050 year. We need to know we are facing pollution (e.g. land, water, energy) and related to environmental limits e.g. climate change, ocean acidification and biodiversity loss. They represent a real threat, not only to future food supplies, but also to global stability and prosperity, through increasing poverty to developing countries and impacts on international trade, finance and investments.

Hence, pollution and environmental limits will have direct relationship to influence every countries' foods supply numbers , then it will influence every country's gross domestic product income if the consumption is reduced by foods inflation. For example, the combined effect of climate change and bio-diversity which makes the food production systems poorly due to a reduced resilience to shocks and changes over the long term , such as the limited availability of ore resources, soil degradation to loss of biodiversity. Both of these require a long term strategic approach to research and an openness to new research directions. These will need to help provide solutions towards more sustainable food consumption and production, some of which will need to break with current farmers or food manufacturers way of producing food methods. For example, research into ecological approaches: foods nutrient and water clean management and replacement of energy intensive inputs are priorities. Research to support energy efficient technologies for use in the food chain is also needed. Industry should assist in tackling the forthcoming challenges with new business models that can support the decoupling of resource use and changing consumption excessive foods behaviors and improving health foods production methods. For instance, changing the foods supply chains) e.g. more local purchasing) may have huge impacts on costs and also on creating closer links and confidence between producers and consumers.

In conclusion, different countries need find methods to solve foods and energy scarcity problem before 2050 year. I recommend that who can attempt to solve earth warm climate, innovate agricultural production and supply system, change human diet habit and food consumption of behavior, co-operate the trade of foods and energy demand and supply between countries fairly and reasonably, reduce food and natural resource waste, renew and recopy new kind of foods, research new natural resource substitution etc. different methods. However, if every country government can attempt to find any one or more of these methods to solve food scarcity to avoid to occur before 2050 year. I believe that the food scarcity challenge won't be occur after 2050 year in the future.

Reference

Erekson, O.H., Loucks, O.L. Strafford, N.C. 1999.
The context of sustainability . In: Sustainability
perspectives for resources and business
USA, p. 3-21.

Daly, H.E. 1990, Towards some operational
principles of sustainable development,
ecological economics, 2(1), 1-6.

Kirkby, J; O' Keefe P., Timberlake, L. (eds.) 1995.
The earthscan reader in sustainable development.
Earthscan Publications Ltd., London, 1-14p.

4.1 Suggestions to solve resources scarcity methods to oil supply

I. Estimation of growth of rural population and income and expected changes of natural resources supply numbers

I recommend developing countries need to estimate growth of rural population and incomes numbers and expected changes numbers in consumption patterns . Taking into account developing countries' known resource capacities and projected development of yields, input use and technologies and making assumptions about their future trading capacity, estimates are also make of future food production level, land use and natural resource numbers import trade demand of developing countries estimation before 2050 year.

Estimation of water natural resources, such as water scarcity agreement on key definitions, the conceptualization of water scarcity in ways that are meaningful for policy development and decision making, the quantification of water scarcity, policy and technical response options available to ensure food security in conditions of water scarcity, criteria and principles that should be used to establish priorities for action to response to water scarcity in agriculture and ensure effective and efficient water scarcity copying strategies. Thus, developing countries will concern to reduce water resources shortage risk. Why is predict water supply important? During the twentieth century, large multi-purpose dams have served the needs of agriculture, energy and growing cities, and helped protect population from flood hazards. On farm water conservation, particularly the adoption of agricultural practices that reduce runoff to increase the infiltration and storage of water in the soil in rained agriculture is the most relevant local supply enhancement option that farmers have to increase foods production by increasing water availability and decentralized water harvesting conveniently in rural areas for farmers needs. For example, ground water exploitation has grown or in scale. Ground water's capability to provide flexible, on demand water in support of irrigation has been as a major advantage by farmers in rural areas. Thus, farmers need to learn how to reduce water losses increase water productivity and water re-allocation to avoid natural resource of water shortage after 2050 year.

II. Renewable natural resources and foods planting sustainability development

The concept of sustainability has become the current answer to absolving our earth of its environment and economic crises in the 21 ST. century. On the one side,
the pessimists, usually ecologists and other scientists, who are convinced the earth can't forever support the different countries' demand of renewable and non renewable resources. On the other side, are the optimists, the economists, who are equally convinced that the earth, with market incentives, appropriate public policies, material substitution, recycling and new technology can satisfy the needs and improve the quality of human welfare. Both views are supporting arguments are explored used and sustainable development. Thus, renewable old energy natural resource can keep old energy natural resource to renew to use or research other new energy resource to substitute old natural resource, it will reduce the risk of energy resource shortage if the other new natural resource can be substituted to the old natural energy resource to use in our daily life , such as inventing one kind of new energy resource can be used to substitute gas to drive cars or drive boats or plans or the old gas can be renewed or cycled to use to drive cars or boats or the oil can be renewed or cycled to use to cook. Also, our earth foods, e.g. fruits, vegetables or meats etc. foods if which can be recopied to grow many numbers planting foods from any one kind food or many kinds of foods, such as one meat can be copied to manufacture two to three same kind tasty meats or unlimited same kind tasty meats. I believe the renewable natural resource energy or recopied foods can reduce our foods or energy shortage after 2050 year.

III. The application of sustainable strategy
between local and national and regional
of international countries

A redefined concept is of the society as whole system, made up of three concentric circles: the economy is found within the society, and both the economy and society exist within the environment. Sustainability indicators are therefore said to attempt to measure the extent to which these boundaries are respected.

I think sustainability measure as a whole concept environment, society and economy. At the bottom of the triangle is the environment or the ultimate means which represents natural resources as a precondition for decent human life. The economy (which includes technology, politics and ethics) is on the next, is not independent but serves as a vehicle for achieving ultimate ends. At the top is equity or society or ultimate end which refers to the wellbeing of the human being. According to Daly(1990) who indicated "that the economy therefore succeeds to the extent that it conserves and restores ultimate means the environment, and enables the achievement of ultimate ends society equity. This is the application of sustainable strategies to local, national and regional issues, as well as the role of international agencies in local /national strategies." Our earth occurs issues of overpopulation, diseases and political conflict, developed countries also have to deal with problems, such as pollution and unlimited urban expansion with limited resources. Sustainability is the process suggested to improve the quality of human life within the limitations of global environment. It involves solutions for improving human welfare that doesn't result in regarding the environment. We(human) need to concern living within certain limits of the earth's capacity to maintain life, understanding the interconnections among economy, society and environment and maintaining a fair distribution of foods and vegetables and natural energy resources and opportunity for this generation and the next. Thus, on the one side, our governments need to concern three categories: Social/ political, environmental and economic issues are interconnection. Social issues include poverty, consultation, empowerment and culture. Environmental issues include pollution, natural resources and biodiversity/ resilience and economic issues include efficiency, growth and stability. It seems our governments need to considerate social and environment and economic issues to reduce our natural energy resources and foods and vegetables to allocate to let every country people to use fairly.

IV. Reducing global warming and biodiversity
issue occurrence

It seems that we need to know our society will influence our natural environment good or bad. If our society damaged our natural environment, then it will be possible to influence our foods supply of decreasing numbers. e.g. fishes, pigs, cows, sheep and vegetables and fruits etc. foods . Due to bad climate and air and lands and ocean pollution can influence foods can not be grown easily and successfully in farms or fishes can not be lived healthy in ocean. Then, it will cause our meats, fruits and vegetables etc. foods supply shortage. Even, our gas , oil, water etc., natural resources will cause our oceans and lands pollution if human pollute our oceans and lands. In result, our natural resources used numbers will be reduced due to clean lands and oceans are polluted for long time. Finally, natural resources and meats and vegetables and fruits , rice etc. foods prices will be risen due to which are shortage to supply and developing countries' population numbers are increasing which will cause more demand. Finally, it shall cause many developing countries' poor people who can't eat enough meats, fruits, rice vegetables etc. foods as well as who can't use enough natural resources to attempt to adapt whose past normal daily life, such as lacking enough oil to help them to cook foods to be heat to eat at home or lacked enough water to be boiled to drink. Even, whose health will be poor , then who get diseases to cause die easily when there is no enough oil to buy or enough water to drink. Hence, these developing countries governments need to concern foods and natural resource scarcity problems which will be occurred if who do not find methods to reduce this issue to be occurred after 2050 year.

As Erekson et. al.(1999) concerns about" loss of resources, such as biodiversity or global weather (climate) warming are pacified with the potential of new technology which will lead to greater investments to the future generations for alternative resources and welfare." Hence, I recommend our governments need to concern global warming or biodiversity issue because of our foods and vegetables and natural resources, such as water, air will be possible polluted to be caused shortage quickly if our earth's global warming or biodiversity issue occurrence to cause our earth's large oceans or lands areas to be polluted. Our governments can attempt to control natural resources , such as oil, gas, water supply into the market and not though the political special conditions to keep them, without considering the political and social standings, which rule the control power and the use of those resources. Such as developed countries can be able to minimize the impact of foods or/and natural resources production and consumption over the natural resources, they are only mechanisms built within an economic rationality, which should be possible to control its people's demand of natural resources, e.g. oil, gas, water and supply of natural resources get more balance. Then these natural resources sale price won't be raised more every year. When there developed countries' people , such as American and Britain who can control to reduce to spend to use the excessive natural resources too much in any time and any place habitually. Then , I believe the developing countries' governments e.g. Africa, China, India, which can buy those developed countries governments' excessive natural resources to raise those developed countries' natural resources supply numbers to provide to whose people to use as well as the most important benefit is that developed countries can gain foreign income from excessive natural resources expectation. Then, these governments will raise GDP economic growth. Hence, if developed countries could control whose people consume natural resource numbers and they could also control to produce natural resource supply numbers . Then, they can gain more excessive natural resources export chance to achieve to raise GDP economic growth aim for long term. As Kirkby et al., (1995)explained "the complexity of sustainable development our natural environment. If our governments can let our earth natural environment gets creation to maintenance, then our natural environment will be reduced the time to degradation. In the long time result, our society rural and urban economy will be growth , then our different countries' global growth will be caused diversity." Hence, it seems different countries' governments need to concern sustainable development to our natural environment .

V. How to apply agricultural green bio-economy
concept to solve control sustainable food
consumption and production in a resource-
constrained world

Nowadays, challenges for the global food supply have never been so complex. Between now and 2050 year, it has been predicted that growth in the global population and changing diets in developing countries, special in India and China and Africa etc. developing countries which may lead to an increase of around 70% in food demand. At the same time, depletion of fossil hydrocarbons will increase the demand for biomass for biofuels and industrial materials. Hence, developed and developing countries' governments ought need to coordinated to reduce air and water pollution and approached to lands use planning and oceans use planning to supply enough farms to grow potatoes, vegetables, tomatoes, fruits and let cows, pigs, sheep etc. animals can have comfortable and clean farm to live to produce good tasty meats to provide human to eat as well as to reduce pollution to supply fresh and clean water to let fishes to be lived and provides to human to drink clean water. Due to overpopulation will be predicted by scientists after 2050 year, so it will be caused foods and energy shortage possibly. Hence, different countries' governments need have long term perspectives to prepare to have enough foods and energy supply to provide us to eat and use for our earth with resource constraints and environmental limits, and which includes guideline on agricultural research to achieve foods supply aim.

On the one hand, I believe the knowledge-based bio-economy can play in realizing there challenges in particular the balance demand between foods, feed and fuel and the strategic role new technologies can have upon developing a sustainable an green bio-economy. On the other hand, I also think production of the presently high resource dependence and to build more environmentally begin sustainable agriculture system able to feed 9 billion people by 2050 year. I recommend global governments need to concern all aspects of food security including the total food chain and impacts of other land-use and management as well as non food areas, research areas which can be closed to free resources for new priorities, research to manufacture more new unique natural resources, due to gas, oil etc. resources will be used all in one day. On the energy shortage aspect, Substitution of these oil, gas etc. natural resources are needed . For example, nuclear energy is a kind of new natural resource, it can be used to push machines of rockets to be moved in space. In the future, I hope that nuclear energy can be used to drive cars or ships or trains etc. transportation tools in land. Hence, new natural resource research is essential and valid investment to be improved by scientists in the future.

On the global food supply interconnected challenges hand, including climate changes, energy and water supply are further encountered by the financial and economic changes in an increasingly globalized world. As a result, it is unclear how the growing demand for food and bioenergy (both biomass and biofuels) within a wider bio-economy can be met without further compromising ecosystem services on which all economic activities and social depend. I shall emphasizes the interaction of the economic, social and ecological components of our food systems at various levels, with feed backs increasingly the uncertainty and risks relating to future developments.

We need to face the food requirements of a growing world population have to be satisfied and we also need to the face of increasing resource scarcities, such as water, energy and land and foods etc. with the situation further exacerbated by climate change. Thus, we need to focus on our reducing demand through food consumption behavioral changes and structural changes in food systems and food chains change. Due to some developed countries people often to choose to buy these foods to eat excessively e.g. cow meat and pig meat and drink excessive soft drinks, e.g. man-made color juice. So, these developed countries consumers will feel these excessive foods and soft drinks can be rubbish if these developed countries consumers often drink these man-made color juice and eat pig and cow meats often excessively. It seems who ought to change their diet behavior and food consumption to avoid to spend too much money to buy excessive foods and drinks and who often shall not decide to eat and drink them when who feel not hungry habitually . Hence, changing human diet habit is one important psychology factor to reduce water and foods shortage, due to the meats and juices can be reduced to be rubbish if human can learn how to control their diet habit to reduce to consume excessive meats and vegetables and rice and soft drinks etc. kind of foods and drinks. Then, I believe that food and water drinking numbers will be reduced too much in the future. Hence, different countries' governments need to educate whose people to know that why who will face foods and water scarcity possibly and to let who to know how the issue can be avoided to cause by the changing of their diet habit and consumption behavior. Teaching includes, such as let who to learn why resources scarcities are expected to reduce and defining food security concept, the need is for a better understanding of complexity of vegetable systems, the need to improve the diversity and response capacity of food systems to enhance resilience, the need to address both food consumption and production, knowledge generation and innovation through cross-sector approaches is essential and the need for agricultural knowledge and innovation systems that are fit for farming purpose. After developed countries' people are educated to let who to know why who need to reduce to consume excessive foods and soft drinks habitually to aim to avoid the chance of foods and water supply shortage will be occurred after 2050 year. On the other side, in the case of biodiversity, the loss of functional biodiversity destabilizes ecosystems and weakens their ability to deal with natural disasters or human induced stresses, such as pollution and climate change. Hence, scientists need to research how to reduce new diseases to cause foods and water pollution, even new diseases cause to influence human health. Due to unpredictable new diseases will be caused foods, fruits, vegetables etc. can't be grow easily , even cows, pigs, sheep etc. animals are not health to cause diseases to be died easily. Then, those new diseases will be decreases our foods supply numbers seriously.

Resources scarcities are expected to define future food security. The predominant form of agriculture, food processing and retailing relies heavily on cheap inputs and the potential impact on this of long term resource scarcity trends has been largely overlooked. Scarcities are either biophysical limits, such as resource supply and availability or environment limits relating to pollution and its impacts on ecosystems and the global climate system. Hence, every country's government ought to educate to let whose citizen to discuss how to protect future food security topic to avoid resource scarcities occurrence after 2050 year. We need to know we are facing pollution (e.g. land, water, energy) and related to environmental limits e.g. climate change, ocean acidification and biodiversity loss. They represent a real threat, not only to future food supplies, but also to global stability and prosperity, through increasing poverty to developing countries and impacts on international trade, finance and investments. Hence, pollution and environmental limits will have direct relationship to influence every countries' foods supply numbers , then it will influence every country's gross domestic product income if the consumption is reduced by foods inflation.

For example, the combined effect of climate change and bio-diversity which makes the food production systems poorly due to a reduced resilience to shocks and changes over the long term , such as the limited availability of ore resources, soil degradation to loss of biodiversity. Both of these require a long term strategic approach to research and an openness to new research directions. These will need to help provide solutions towards more sustainable food consumption and production, some of which will need to break with current farmers or food manufacturers way of producing food methods. For example, research into ecological approaches: foods nutrient and water clean management and replacement of energy intensive inputs are priorities. Research to support energy efficient technologies for use in the food chain is also needed. Industry should assist in tackling the forthcoming challenges with new business models that can support the decoupling of resource use and changing consumption excessive foods behaviors and improving health foods production methods. For instance, changing the foods supply chains) e.g. more local purchasing) may have huge impacts on costs and also on creating closer links and confidence between producers and consumers.

In conclusion, different countries need find methods to solve foods and energy scarcity problem before 2050 year. I recommend that who can attempt to solve earth warm climate, innovate agricultural production and supply system, change human diet habit and food consumption of behavior, co-operate the trade of foods and energy demand and supply between countries fairly and reasonably, reduce food and natural resource waste, renew and recopy new kind of foods, research new natural resource substitution etc. different methods. However, if every country government can attempt to find any one or more of these methods to solve food scarcity to avoid to occur before 2050 year. I believe that the food scarcity challenge won't be occur after 2050 year in the future.

Environment Economy-Pollution and illness influences oil consumer behavior

How the economic consequences of outdoor air pollution influences consumer behaviors ? Air pollution can increase number of respiratory and cardiovas cular diseases. How they can impact economic growth, e.g. on human health, mortality and morbidity and agriculture aspects ? Whether when this diseases are caused from outdoor air pollution, why it can influence consumer behavior or brings negative consumpton emotion?

The macroeconomic costs of these impacts of outdoor air pollution that are linked to economic activity, and it raises welfare costs related to activity morality and pain and suffering from illness to consumers. For example, market costs are those that are associated with biophysical impacts that directly affect economic activity, e.g. lower crop yields affect agricultural production . Non market costs may also include the monetised welfare costs of morality (premature deaths) , and of the disutility of illness (pain and suffering).

Raising emissions reflect the assumptions on economic growth with increasing GDP and energy demand, especially in fast growing economies, such as the high population countries, India and China. These large changes are due to the increase in the demand for agricultural products and energy (include transport and power generation). For continuousing increase in energy demand to China and India car drivers, when they need to drive their cars to go to anywhere often. The higher emission will bring serious pollution. The environment protecting householders will decrease to use emissions from energy demand for, with reflects technology improvement in energy efficiency, the use of cleaner fuels, and biomass in open fire to cleaner energy sources including LPG, ethanol or enhanced cooking stoves. Hence, when many people get the diseases from air pollution. It will increase the medical (healthcare) cost to governments or when government needs to give welfare assistance to patients.

The three different market impacts of air pollution may include: reduced labor productivity, increased health expenditures and crop yield losses. They may reduce the GDP pollution feedback on the economy. At the global level, the consequences of labor productivity and health expenditure may impact to market cost increases,because increases expenditure to labor productivity, health expenditure and value added generated in agriculture from low productivity changes in crop yields.

What is the welfare costs of mortality and illness ? It is possible to attribute a cost to non-market impacts, such as the premature deaths and the costs of pain and suffering from illness . The welfares cost of the premature deaths caused by air pollution are calculated using the value of a statistical life to any one. Large costs can also associated with the pain and suffering from illness. So, pollution causes diseases to bring welfare cost increases, they include hospital living day to every patient when he is caused illnesses from air pollution. Moreover, it will impact government pollution expenditure to raise welfare cost to assist the low income level pollution illness patients' hospital living welfacre cost when they need to live long days in hospitals.

How does air pollutin impact on consumer automobile choices ? Air pollution levels can bring negatively affect the sales of fuel inefficient cars to China or India car drivers. They will choose to buy electronic cars to drive to replace fuel cars, because electronic cars only need to charge battery and it can reduce air pollution. When China or India their big city people's income level is rising, they will have more money to buy electronic cars to drive to reduce air pollution. Moreover, they believe that electronic cars can have better car quality and reduced air pollution need to charge battery fuel efficiency to compare fuel cars, when they need to often drive cars on roads. Som electronic cars demand will be the preference choice battery fuel efficiency or green driving tools to compare general fuel cars to satisfy China and India car purchasers when they are living in serious air pollution environment cities.

When the high environment protection awareness car buyers number is increasing in the countries, environment protection awareness will influence their car choice decison on which car to buy , when they are living in more heavily polluted cities tend to buy less fuel-inefficient cars. So, the electronic cars number need will increase in China and India both car market, because these two countries have similar characteristics, they have high population and gardens and farms number is less and there are many people are living in cities and many people are high income level , they usually have one car at least. So, they must feel cities are serious polluted by their diving behaviors. So, their environment protection awareness are ususally higher to compare other countries , they have less cities. So high air pollution to cities can excite the environment protection awareness to China and India car purchasers as well as they will prefer to choose to buy electronic cars to replace fuel cars to drive in possible, because they do not hope to live a high car dirty cities to cause their poor health when they have high income level. Also, it implies that it has direct relationship between China and India cities have high income level people number increases and air pollution level increases and electronic car demand number increases and fuel car demand number decreases in China and India car market in micro economic China and India electronic car and fuel car demand and supply market.

I assume that each China and India car consumer makes a relatively fuel or electronic car choice among possible car transmissions, between the option of buying no car and buy car or between the option of buying electronic car and fuel car. However, air pollution will be one major factor to influence China and India car purchase demand number on electronic and fuel car supply number. If china and India's air pollution can reduce, then car purchase number will increase, as well as the fuel car demand number will also increase ,because China and India have many cities are polluted serious. It can influence car purchase buyers how to decide car choice to make car or no car purchase decision, even purchase either fuel car or electronic car decison.

● How consumer decisions are impacted on environment?

Environmental impacts may occur on households, when they need to buy food, mobility, house, household goods and appliances for home use in household consumer behavior view. It can bring direct impacts, that occue because of the use of householder products and services during householders are staying at home. When householders feel need to raise living quality, they will considerate how they use services and related household products. When minimizing the use of natural resources and toxic materials as well as the emissions of waste and pollutants over the life cycle of the service or household product, e.g. using electricity or fuel time at home, cooling time and bathing time at home activities. So, for on householder who has high environment protection awareness and energy protection awareness, he will reduce long time to use electricity or fuel use time for cooking, bathing, watching television, listening radio time activities at homes, because he does not hope energy waste and protect air fresh at homes.

So, consumption is concerned by environment factors, such as demographics, technology, income and prices, psychological, social , cultural environments, e.g. consumers economic behavior is influenced by habt, routines, conventions etc. different environment factors influence. So, economic assumptions of rational and regular behavior is based on long-established principles, such as utility maximization. For example, when one country is encountering serious air or water pollution, then consumers will spend long time to search any data (marketing research activities) when they need to make purchase decision on pollution environment as well as pollution environment is dependent on (e.g. attitude, intention to the consumers).

Because when pollution environment will influence consumption behavior, such as behavioral and experimental economic to consumers. It implies on pollution environment's psychological assumptions on individual consumption motives, such as on the role of mental habits, loss confidence. So, consumers usually feel to spend long time to make purchase choice or decison on pollution environment, exaggerated optimism, expectatons, avoiding miscalculation,short-sightedness more enjoyment etc. psychological factors. When they need to make purchase decision on pollution environment, e.g. when one car consumer will need to make choice to buy one car, when he is living in China city, city is polluted serious. So, he will need to spend long time to gather any car model and brand and quality and fuel quality air polluted level to achieve to choose to buy the most clean fuel and the most least air polluton car to avoid to cause air polluton when he is driving the car in the China's city. So, air pollution way causes the China environment protection awareness car consumers to spend long time to gather any less use fuel car information to avoid to cause air pollution when he needs often to drive the car on the city roads in the China cities. Hence , air pollution may cause the China car purchasers feel need to spend more time to gather car information in order to decide whether he ought to buy one car or no car purchase choice on the air pollution environment. So, the car must use less fuel to avoid air pollution easily when he drives the car on the China's cities' roads.

Reference

Erekson, O.H., Loucks, O.L. Strafford, N.C. 1999.
The context of sustainability . In: Sustainability
perspectives for resources and business
USA, p. 3-21.

Daly, H.E. 1990, Towards some operational
principles of sustainable development,
ecological economics, 2(1), 1-6.

Kirkby, J; O' Keefe P., Timberlake, L. (eds.) 1995.
The earthscan reader in sustainable development.
Earthscan Publications Ltd., London, 1-14p.

CHAPTER II

Terrorism attack and fuel price raising influences tourism industry to experience decline life cycle stage

Nowaday, airline industry is entering global competition. So, any some less positive or negative social environment changing which will influence any airlines' passenger behavioral consumption change. For example, air ticket price rises or fuel price rises or the country's season is bad or the global economy is bad or the country has terrible death threat etc. different negative social environment change fastors which will influence any country passenger individual travel consumption desires.

In Special, business class airline transportation demands are also increasing, due to many business travelers need to catch planes to go to any different countries to do business as well as many cargoes need to be carried from planes to transport to different countries to sell. So, business class traveler target group behavioral consumption is difficult to influence travelling consumotion desires from external environmental factors because business class traveler target group concerns to need to catch planes to go to another country to discuss business co-operation with the country's businessmen. So, their business travel desires won't easy to be influenced more than individual entertainment travel consumer's desire.

It seems cargo and business aim of aviation transportation industry has less chance to be influenced to reduce businessmen traveler or cargo transportation numbers to compare to entertainment traveler numbers by external environment change influences, due to the business travelers and cargo transportation travelling desires is difficult to reduce travelling or transportation needs to reduce the " doing businesses to earn profit chance with another country's businessmen". However, ignorance of internal or external market dynamics, catching entertainment travelers business can be detrimental to airline profitability more than carrying cargoes or business travelers business. Because the demands of travelling different countries' travelers' consumption are still more than the demands of businessmen carrying cargoes in any countries every year. So, the global GDP of travelling income sector is still have the important position to any country nowadays.

How can positive or negative social environment change influence any airlines' air ticket prices to be risen or fallen as well as how can these social environment change influence passenger consumption desires ? For example: What is the petroleum price change influence ?In fact, the increase in petroleum price can have chance to affect every airlines passenger has a negative manner to reduce travel consumption because increased oil prices have resulted in the reduction of airline services operations, the number of airline schedules flights, even airline bankruptcies. Whether global economic inflation or deflation, terrorism threats to the country, oil shortage or oil price rising or fallening, bank interest rate increasing or decreasing etc. external factors which have the most influential causes to bring the bad or good effects to cause airline industry share price reducing or increasing or increasing or reducing air ticket price. In result, these external environmental changes will influence the global traveler numbers to be increased or decreased at the time.

To support this hypotheses, this are my research first question, such as : Does a combination of terrorism and price of petroleum significantly influence airline profit changing mostly? The alternative hypothesis was my research second question, such as: Whether a significant relationship exists between terrorism, price of petroleum and airline profitability more than other factors, such as inflation, bank interest rate or air ticket price changing of these factors to influence passenger consumption desires change. I shall indicate that the first assumption was that terrorism has a negative effect on airline profitability and another assumption was that only external factors as oil prices or terrorism affect airline profitability. Finally, the terrorism and oil shortage and oil rising price factors can influence every passenger travel consumption desire to be reduced mainly.

Terrorism attack influences traveller need

However the effects of oil price and terrorism on airline profitability was limited to a regional perspective, so oil price and terrorism external environmental change will only influence some countries' airline traveler numbers to be decreased, e.g. the terrorism attack of plane crash event to USA on 11 Sept. After the terrorism attack happened on USA 11 Sept. incident of terrorism attack was restricted to events of skyjacking, attacks on oil production, refinery and distribution. Then, due oil shortage will be caused due to reducing oil production, refinery and distribution as well as it will influence oil price is risen and airline ticket price is also risen. It will reduce travel consumption desire to some countries if their airlines' ticket prices are also increasing. Other types of terrorist activities, such as attacks on financial targets or senior government officials could have an adverse effect on the petroleum and airline industry. I think the disruption of the production or distribution of petroleum because of incidents of terrorism was costly in terms of loss of business and the inflationary effect on fuel dependent products or services.

In fact, some airlines have adopted more fuel saving technology, so whose fuel consumption would not use more than other non fuel saving technology airlines. It seems fuel price increasing will not be the only factor to influence the airline industry's traveler numbers decreasing due, the owning more fuel saving technologic airlines which air tickets prices won't influence to be risen , due to reducing oil production and shortage influences . However, due to some airlines which have fuel saving technology, so which can avoid to use more fuel to provide planes to use and which fuel costs will be reduced, then which can provide cheaper air ticket fare prices to compare the non fuel saving technology airlines. The result will cause some not owning fuel saving technological airlines which will lose travelling customers in this global airline travelling market, also the not fuel saving technological airlines need to renew their fuel technology if which want to keep their competitive abilities to avoid to close down their businesses. So, what factors will influence the not owning fuel saving technological airlines profitability to be reduce if the oil shortage factor can not influence their planes energy supply to be reduced to cause air ticket prices to be increased? To answer this question, I shall indicate another financial risk factor how it influences airline industry behavioral change.

Also, I shall indicate the financial risk of airline industry evidence from Cathay Pacific airways and China airlines against key determinants of which include interest rate, exchange rate and fuel price risk for the period of January 1996 year to December 2011 year. During this period, these key external factors which were the most serious influence to cause these two airlines choose to change their strategic behaviors. Due to any these financial risks is difficult to predict and it was also changing often, these factors will also affect any airlines stock returns which arise from changing economic conditions, e.g. fuel price movements and fluctuations in exchange rates. These external unpredicted changing factors will attribute to the air tickets cyclical demand, capital investment, fixed costs of labor and landing rights to this global airline industry. Finally, it will cause some airlines need to rise air ticket prices to reduce expenditures increasing.

However, the relationship between fuel price and stock prices varies across economies which will influence travel passenger consumption of desires. For example, the effects of oil price changes in sub-sector indices, such as wood, paper and printing, insurance and electricity. In the past, on global stock exchange market was positively significant in 2011 year. Otherwise, with respect to the U.S.A. aviation industry, some economists suggested that global airlines stock returns were negatively to percentage change in fuel prices related to any airline firm value, e.g. Qantas and Air New Zealand were negatively share price growth to fuel price risk in the short term in the 2011 year. Thus, due to these two airlines share price went down, it will influence investors who loss confidence to buy their shares as well as it will influence travelling passengers who choose to buy other airlines' air tickets to go to travel because they will feel these two airlines have business challenges, e.g. bad service quality and food quality and uncomfortable airline seat environment and poor management style. etc different bad feeling. So, these two airlines' share prices went down, it will influence every travel passenger's confidence to choose to buy their air tickets to sit their planes to go to travel.

Airlines fuel manufacturing supply strategy

However, there are some airlines which are the characteristic of self organization . It means that they are present in that both of oil fuel production and providing flights service in airline industry. So, these self organization airlines can control the oil fuel price by themselves. However, any self supply airline organization is also evident in efforts by businesses acts of terrorism against economic targets by adopting proactive steps, such as airline and airport security. So, it seems any self suply airline organization can reduce the risk to avoid oil price raising and terrorism attacks in airline industry risk management sector because oil shortage won't influence their air ticket prices need to be raised. Beside, these self supply airline organizations which have high technology of fuel efficient aircrafts, the use of one aircraft model, the adoption of direct routes versus customer loyalty programs and other operational cost reductions are strategies for increased profitability.

To solve oil price, terrorism etc. external risk to airline industry. Instead of high technology of fuel efficient aircrafts and self supply airline organization methods can solve terrorism attacks and oil price rising risks. However, I believe that there are other risks will threaten to airline industry. This risks concern traveller individual psychological factors influence, so it means that any airlines can apply psychological methods to predict which airline passengers' travel consumption desires. The risks include such as (1) user factor, such as : the travel country culture and tradition difference will influence the traveler chooses to prefer to go to the country to travel , the traveler's education level is high , who will choose to go to developed countries to travel, e.g. USA, UK. Otherwise, if the traveler's education level is low, who will choose to go to developing countries to travel, e.g. China, India etc. (2) economic factor, such as air tickets and airline fuel costs, (3) human resources and macro economic factor, such as political stability, economic development, educational policy, health policy, environmental policy. However, these risks occurrences are resulting in the relationship of cause and effect events. These events are not directly observable.

Such as, the complexity of relationship between terrorism and airline profitability. Hence, if global airline industry can predict when those risks occur to do protective strategic behavior. It is possible that which can understand why these risk events will occur and their protective strategic behaviors also influence their outcomes to be positive to avoid any external risk threats on the long term. However, I think hierarchy, self supply airline organization efficiency methods which are as possible predictors of user preferences to avoid risk threat events to cause whose airline businesses failure occurrences in airline industry because it can reduce oil shortage factor which causes their air ticket prices need to be rised to keep their planes can have enough fuel supply.

● Why tourism and airline industries have close relationship to influence their profitability between of them.

In my study, I suppose terrorism, profitability and the price of petroleum which had properties of distinct and interrelated close relationship. Moreover, these variables (terrorism, profitability and the price of petroleum) displayed differentiation, self replication, efficiency and hierarchy which can cause risk events to airline industry. However, I also think the other internal and external threat factors of airline industry, such as inflation, bank interest rate, business model, service quality, airline fuel or plane engine technology, air ticket pricing, brand loyalty, airline strategic management, government policy and fuel hedging of these factors which can also raise the risks to threaten any airlines existence in airline industry.

There are two basic business models in airline industry. They are network (full service) and low cost (discount) carriers. The network carrier model employs diversification strategy by increased domestic destinations, serving international routes, providing diverse seating arrangements (business, economy and first class), maintaining a complex system of offering high quality service. Otherwise, low cost (discount) airlines focus on lower air fares. To keep operating costs down, discount airlines offer shorter routes and provide point-to-point destinations rather than through sophisticated flights are primarily in domestic destinations. So, discount airlines operate a common model aircraft fleet, offer a single seating arrangement and cheaper flight services offered to compare network airlines. However, these two basic business models have their unique competitive abilities to provide any airlines existence in airline industry nowadays.

In fact, natural resource of oil is decreasing in our earth. But as the same time, human demand is increasing and oil supply is decreasing, so it also causes the oil fuel price is increasing to supply to airline industry. It influences not only to airline industry, it also impacts of higher oil fuel price to tourism, such as expansion of airports are made based on expected demand increase.

Tourism has been proven to many adverse events, including terrorism, flight disruptions. Beside, the bad natural climate change influences, such as the volcanic ash cloud event occurred in April 2010 year. So, airline industry need to concern climate change because it will cause high fuel prices indirectly. For example, the event occurred the extreme increase in operating costs for airlines in 2008 year, due to unprecedented prices for aviation fuel also meant, that despite the introduction of fuel charges, so this event causes the global airline industry recorded losses seriously. Even if alternative fuels become commercially available for airlines which are still likely to be more expensive than present aviation fuel. Thus, it seems that poor tourism will influence poor travel consumption and low airline tickets sale.

Higher airfares in the future are likely to lead to reduction in travel and cause tourists to shift from more distant to closer destination. When some of the economic responses to higher oil prices are obvious assessing the overall economic impacts on tourism is difficult. However, long term changes in global oil price rises will be similar to global changes in other commodity prices, exchange rates and income. It is therefore important to consider the impact of high oil prices on tourism from a general equilibrium perspective rather than relying only on bottom partial equilibrium. However, I believe tourism and airline industries have close relationship, such as tourism and airline industries are likely to suffer in an environment of high oil prices. Given that tourism destinations receive tourists from a range of origins, it would be useful to understand of some countries are increasing oil prices than others. Such as the net oil importing countries are selling higher oil prices than oil exporting countries generally. For example, New Zealand is an oil import country to provide planes for international visitor arrivals, so its oil fuel price is usually higher to charge to NZ airlines because any NZ airlines need to pay to foreign countries to buy any oil more expensive price. So, NZ airlines usually charge higher airfares to its visitors to compare the other exporting oil countries' airlines.

In economic theory, on income effects indicate negative impacts on tourism demand, the exact effects of higher oil fuel prices for specific destinations are far from clear. However, airline industry's different market segments show different sensitivities to air ticket fares changes. On the first hand, if the visitors are long destinations generally wealthier than average and therefore potentially less affected, as energy costs would be a smaller proportion of their income compared will be those from less wealthy groups. On the second hand, oil prices don't translate into higher transport costs especially not on air routes that are highly competitive and that are maintained for strategic reasons. On the third hand, many other factors shape tourists' decision making, including emotion drivers or those related to images, fashions and perceptions.

Increasing environmental protection awareness of tourists could also be an important factor to influence tourism consumption, instead of oil fuel price raising causes air ticket fares raising factor to reduce traveler numbers. However, oil price raising reason causes also due to high use of cars, vans and domestic air transport in some countries, e.g. Hong Kong, China countries, there are many people like to buy cars to drive. So, the private driver numbers are increasing demand to cause these countries' oil fuel prices raise in the short time suddenly. It will influence HK and China air tickets prices need to be risen , due to there are many cars, vans and domestic air transport tools need to use oil to supply energy to cause oil import numbers will increase to HK and China and HK and China airlines need to pay higher price to buy oil to use. In the result, HK and China airlines air ticket prices will also need to rise and it will influence HK and China travel consumption desire.

Fuel raising price solve methods

● Why oil fuel raising price factor can cause risk to airline.

In long run, implications of changes to supply and demand side conditions of oil fuel energy may differ qualitatively. For example, due to investment responses of producers, consumers and governments in alternative energy sources and more energy efficient plants, vehicles are supplied in order to achieve oil fuel price can't be risen seriously.

However, I believe oil fuel rising charge will be an important factor to influence global airline ticket fares to be also increased. Firstly, on the bank interest changing factor, e.g. bank interest rate rising which only attract more bank saving. But it can not influence the bank savers who choose to reduce relax time to go to other countries travelling. Otherwise, when the bank savers can save more money to earn higher interest in banks, who will prefer to choose to use their saving to consume travelling. Due to who can earn higher interest rate after a period of saving time. So, I believe whose behavioral travelling consumption will be raised when the banks will raise interest rate, then the bank savers won't choose to save more money in banks. So it is possible that who will withdraw more money to consume to go to travelling from their bank saving. It seems bank interest rate changing won't influence bank savers' behavioral travelling consumption to be reduced. Secondly, on the exchange rate changing factor, although any country's exchange changing will cause other countries' money value to be fallen down or risen up. However, it won't influence any travelers' behavioral consumption to be reduced seriously. Although, it is possible that the traveler won't spend too much to go to shopping when who travel to the another country and arrive the country. But, it is not possible to influence the traveler decides to reduce consumption to buy any air ticket to go to travelling. Thirdly, any country inflation also can not reduce travelers' travelling consumption easily because inflation can influence consumers who choose to buy cheaper foods and clothing and reduce entertainments in their every day life. But, one country's inflation can not influence it's citizen do not spend much travelling expenditure because travelers only spend one time or two times of travelling every year usually. So, the travelling expenditure rate of any households is not too much to compare daily essential expenditure. So, it seems that bank interest rate and exchange rate changing and inflation factors won't influence any travelers' travelling consumption of decisions to be reduced easily. Otherwise, if the oil fuel price raises too much, then global airlines' cost will be raised. So, the airlines only choose to increase their air fare prices to aim to avoid loss possibly. It seems that oil fuel price has direct influence airline income.

● Methods to solve rising air fare prices demand.

I. Why will biofuels energy be demanded ?

I suggest these methods how to avoid the oil raising price factor to cause airline air fare prices to be risen to lead the risk of traveler numbers to be reduced.

The first method: Whether aviation fuel markets will have what benefits from biofuels supply to planes. I shall refer the scope includes trends in jet fuel price, airline response to fuel price, increases and volatility and environmental goals for aviation. The aviation fuel supply industry includes production, distribution and consumption of aviation fuel and it outlines players in the aviation fuel supply chain. For example, at each airport, fuel supply chain organization and fuel sourcing could differ with regard to the role of oil companies, airlines, airport owners and operators and airport service companies. However, major jet fuel purchasers are airlines, general aviation operators, corporate aviation and the military, with most of the jet fuel in global different countries demanders being used for domestic commercial and civilian flights carrying passengers, cargos or both. Commercial aviation fuel efficiency has improved dramatically over time, largely due to aircraft and engine upgrades and operational and air traffic control improvements. So, it seems that fuel supply factor can influence airline fare prices majorly.

However, jet fuel prices generally correlate with prices of crude oil and other refined petroleum products, such as diesel. So, increasing prices and the persistent price volatility of jet fuel markets import airline industry finances in any countries. However, airlines use various strategies to manage aviation fuel price certainty, including financial hedges, increased vertical integration and adjustments in aircraft utilization and size to avoid the jet fuel raising price risk. Investments in alternative aviation fuel could be a mechanism to diversity expose to the price of petroleum. It seems the use of alternative aviation fuel would serve to diversify the fuel mix to reduce the risk of jet fuel monopoly raising price threat. If a diversified fuel mix were to avoid either fuel raising price in short term or to avoid fuel raising price in long term. Potential benefits include reduced actual fuel costs from only choice of jet fuel supply increased price certainty and lessened fuel costs. This diversify could allow airlines to become more consistently profitable and to make other investments in their businesses.

So, biofuels have potential to meet aviation industry needs, possibly including managing risks of upward fuel price trends and fuel price volatility and avoid risks with greenhouse gas emissions. So, the aviation fuels market could use biofuels to reduce greenhouse gas emission and mitigate long-term upward price trends, fuel price volatility or both.

What are the challenges of high priced oil for aviation? In fact, nowadays not the resources of oil as such, but much more the insecurity of supply, due to geopolitical instability in combination with a tight oil market makes a scenario with much higher oil prices than the world is currently experiencing not unlikely. Aviation is completely dependent upon oil as its fuel source. Since no practical energy substitute is readily available for commercial aviation, a scarcity of petroleum relative to demand will present a major aviation policy. In addition, efficiency gains, due to operational measures and new aircraft medium term. In particular, it has been demonstrated that the annual reduction rate in fuel consumption traffic unit is not a constant, but is itself also falling, in contrast to past estimates.

So, a high-priced oil scenario will have severe consequences for demand, airline revenues, the competitive position of airports and eventually airline networks, strategies and fleet development. In particular, transfer demand, short-haul and leisure traffic can be expected to be heavily affected by high oil prices, due to their relative high price sensitivity. So, different countries' governments or/and airlines are valuable to research another new and potential biofuel energy to substitute oil energy to supply our planes to reduce the threat of oil monopoly supply to influence the cause of air fare raising prices. Because the elasticity is very high to travelers, when the travelers feel air fares are rising high or even low level to influence travelers who will choose not to buy the air tickets to go to travel easily.

Will the fuel (oil based inputs) risk be higher to compare other costs to cause air ticket prices to be increased?, e.g. engineering maintenance, employees salaries, general cleaning, security office expenses etc. expenditures to airlines? If the probability-weighted upside effect on firm value when a risk is resolved favorably is greater the risk than the probability-weighted downside effect if the risk is resolved badly, then expected value work not be enhanced by hedging. So, the risk will be resolved badly to any commercial airlines. Airlines are an interesting case because the direct effect of source of risk resides squarely within the no offset in revenue functions (unlike for oil producers, for example), so value effects from costs feed directly into equity value. Most directly, the risk source is fuel costs to commercial airlines. Jet fuel is of course, a mix product of crude oil, so airlines indirectly face oil price risk. There are reasons to expect that airlines' fuel costs might to convex in oil price (i.e. absent any hedging). For example, oil prices, being generally pro-cyclical in recent times, tend to be highest when airline demand is strong. Airlines are therefore apt to use more high priced fuel than low-priced fuel over time. Airlines can raise air fare benefit is limited by the elasticity of demand. Also, cost functions could be influenced from fuel cost corresponds to upturns in economic activity overall (due to demand pressures on oil related prices), so it causes that airline's capacity delivers their services given their level of fixed capital. The essence of airlines basis risk in the case of jet fuel is essentially the time profile of the refining margin between crude and jet fuel, or the time profile of the price differential between other refined distillates and jet fuel. Thus, it is far from clear that risk management with oil is sure to add value to any airlines. It seems the impact of airline energy and any countries' domestic or foreign airline passenger travel numbers which have direct close relationship.

II. Whether the relationship between terrorism and oil prices has close relationship.
Whether the relationship between terrorism and oil prices has close relationship. It needs to judge to determine if a combination of terrorism and the price of petroleum significantly predicted airline profitability and which variable whether the further period was the most significant between the terrorism occurrence and the price of petroleum influence. So, different countries' governments or airlines need to collect samples of financial records from which country's any airline commercial passengers and cargo airlines on costs of fuel and any airline profitability. Also, gathering the terrorism data were comparison of terrorist attacks on petroleum in oil-producing nations, and incidents of high jacking aboard any country's aircraft. When any countries' airlines or governments can judge whether the impact of airline energy and terrorism risk level is high or middle or low level. Then, which can use this sample data to measure how to do positive social change to whether to increase or reduce employment in commercial aviation industry, or ought need to invest other higher commercial activity in tourist and other travel related service businesses and when is the most right time to adopt of green technologies by the civil aviation manufacturing

industry after the terrorism attacks occurrence to any country. It seems that any countries' governments or airlines which ought concern that the event of when the terrorism attacks will occur and gather past sample data to predict when the next time terrorism attacks event will be occurred and the risk will be high or middle or low level to influence global airline industry development.

III. What factors will influence airline industry's price elasticity of supply and demand?
In fact, the airline industry is largely dependent on the supply of the oil industry. Otherwise, the oil industry is inelastic. However, the increase or decrease of the price of airfare is directly related to the increase or decrease of the oil's price to fuel the aircrafts because there has no any new energy which can be substituted to oil fuel to airline industry. So, it seems oil fuel producers are monopolies to control its sale price to be raised easily.

Another factor that can affect airline industry to be directly targeted by a tragedy brought about by terrorism. The past four years, from 2001 year to 2005 year, there had been at least $40 billion worth of losses in the airline industry because of the September 11 date terrorism attacks in 2000 year. There had been an expected and significant decrease in the demand for the airline industry services because of the attacks that involved planes hijacking and crashing into key locations like the World Trade Center and the Pentagon in USA. Although, terrorism attacks can bring risk to influence fuel price rising in airline industry. However, this risk occurrence to airline industry is only that after the terrorism attacks occurred. It is possible that terrorism attacks won't occur again in the future.

Otherwise, our concerning ought be the greenhouse emissions and how it affects global warming. The air quality would be better once this new regulations are adopted. However, it would affect large airlines. So, it would increase the price of airfares because of economic fees that airline companies have to cover. Air pollution can give a negative impact on the domestic or oversea owned airline companies for long term. If airlines' planes can use clean fuel to fly, e.g. biofuel, then it will bring benefits to global airlines for long term. On the positive side, the environment would be healthier as the earth's temperature would rise, and greenhouse effect would be dramatically reduced. This positive effect can come at a cost that is greater than most people perceive. So, the environment protection travellers who will reduce travelling times to avoid air pollution is caused to influence human health. It seems that airlines need to concern to apply psychological method to predict whose travelling consumption of behavior which is more suitable than behavioral economy method.

On the psychology view point on travelers, who will be more preferable to catch planes to go to different countries to travel, due to the chance of air pollution and global environmental warm issues will be reduced to low risk to influence our health if planes can use biofuel to be energy to fly in the future one day. It seems that spending expenditure to research other non polluted biofuel new energy is one solvable method to global airline industry in the future. To solve, any airlines or countries' governments or oil producers ought choose to spend more time to research new biofuel. Otherwise, the predicting when terrorism attacks event will be occurred, it is more difficult to predict the time more than researching to produce new biofuel energy method in the future.

So, I recommend that researching the new biofuel energy or other kinds of energy to substitute the oil energy and air pollution risk these two factors are the urgent behavioral economy method is used to solve this challenge which the airlines or oil producers or different countries' governments which need to concern nowadays. Because these two negative environment factors are the most influential to cause traveller individual travelling consumption desire to be fallen among of other negative environment factors.

CHAPTER III

Tourism strategy influences tourism industry reaches growth to mature life cycle stages

The main cost related factors to offline or online travel agents

Nowadays,many online or offline travel agents have interest to find what the main factors that can affect their strategies to reduce airline costs. The main factors include route structure, type and characteristics of the aircracft, cost of labor and management quality, which will influence whether which airline routes are the most suitable to let online travel agents or offline travel agents to help them to sell paper air tickets or electronic air tickets to attract travel consumption more easily.

Thus, a cost-related strategy is the main important factors to influence travel consumption choice between online or offline travel agents. For example, considering that advantages in costs is an important strategy for carriers to remain in travel transportation market.

The deregulation process of travel markets and increasing opportunities for competition have created excess capacity in many markets that causes lower rates, even with its rising costs. Thus, the travel strategic costs management as well as travel consumers that their behavior under different influences can bring competitive advantages over travel players.

Cost reduction in the travel market -based industry is a very important way of being competitive between offline and online travel agents, when facing travel air ticket prices decreasing for every trip. So reduce to total travel cost, e.g. fuel, maintenance, labor etc. is relevant, but the influence of each component on every total trip cost depends on factors that are related or not to airline operation. For example, some airline can adopt the lowest cost model to sell air tickets from offline or online travel agents which compete for travel passengers with traditional modes as self driving road transport trip in large areas of countries domestic travel market, such as US, UK domestic travel market. However, the decision about the relevance of one cost is not a simple matter. The effectiveness of reduction of each item that comprises the total cost of airline can change over time, depending on both the business model and the scope of the airline company or online /offline travel agent company as well as external factors.

However, there are three types of competition advantage between online and offline travel market: They are such as agility, differentiation cost and the differentiation may be related to a product of superior quality, higher value f the brand or the company's positive reputation. Such as the online travel agent's providing the different airline cheap air ticket price and kind of trips to provide to travel consumer consumer comparison or the offline travel agent's famous brand or positive reputation to let travel consumers feel travel agents can provide many actual trip package to let them to compare by oral clearly. Thus, the online travel agent's weakness is lack of travel agent individual exploration to let every travel consumer to understand every trip package more clearly.

But online travel agent's strength is it can provdide one website to let travel consumer attempt to compare different trip air ticket and/or hotel price to make personal travel pre-booking decision at home. The another advantage is related to techniques that reduce production cost, making it is possible to offer cheaper air ticket, or hotel room rents, or cheap trip package, than the competition. Such as online travel agent can sell more cheape electronic air ticket price to compare traditional offline travel agent's paper air ticket price.

Finally, agility refers to the speed which the company responds to market demands. For example, if the online travel agent can make statistics to analyze how many online travel consumers to choose to buy which airlines' electronic or paper air tickets, e.g. which airline trip destinations and trips and hotels choices are the most popular attraction to them. Then, the online airline has possible to respond to provide to the most popular airline trips choices, electronic air ticket price comparison choices and hotel rooms prices choices to attract many online travel consumers to enter their online travel websites to choose different airline electronic tickets to buy or pre-book hotel rooms from travel agent websites. Also, if the traditional offline travel agents can attempt to gather every travel consumer's destination trips, hotels , airline paper or electronic ticket prices enquires to make statistics to make which travel trip journeys or destinations and airline paper travel ticket prices are the most popular. Then, it is possible that they can respond to every travel consumer individual demand more to attract whose travel agent choice more easily.

Airline travel agency AirAsia in the domestic airline low cost strategy

There are three major characteristics of the airline industry namely is product nature, its expenditure structure and its market entry conditions. Airline agent's product is homogeneous or undifferentiated , causing significant competition in airline domestic travel or foreign travel both markets, which are free from regulations and economic barriers. However, high capital and operating expenditure is another important characteristic of the airline industry. Aircrafts, airlines' major capital expenditure are very costly to acquire . For operating expenditures, aviation fuel and labor make up the two major costs in the industry.

Another important characteristic of the airline industry is the conditions for market entry, which differs between international and domestic airline markets . In the international travel market, airline travel agency entry is very difficult as international flights and routes are the results of regotiations between governments . On the other hand, in the domestic and regional travel market, travel agency entry depends on the level of deregulation or liberalisation.

More and more countries, however are opening up their domestic travel markets for more competition. In addition, government plays an important role to regulate the travel markets and existing players may significant influence over now travel agent entrants.

In fact, the mjor factors influence to international or domestic travel consumption increasing numbers are the global economy and safety issues, instead of other different economic factors, such as travel destination choice, electronic air ticket or paper air ticket price, hotel price , the country's political change, e.g. war occurrence, bad weather , e.g. very cold or very hot etc. different factors infuence. Because generally , the world or any region of it is in an economic crisis or depression , the demand for airline services will fall. The late 1990 year Asian financial crisis for example, resulted in minimal increase in the number of worldwide airline passengers incrased only minimally from 1997 to 1998 year. Another factor of influencing the travel passenger number to be decreased, it concerns safety issues are also an important driver of the travel industry, which is subject to very safety standards to influence travel passengers' travel choice to the country. In addition, they are also unexpected safety related events, such as the 11 Sept. 2001 year tragedy in the US, which caused reduction in passengers . The increasing popularity of low cost airlines is the newest trend in the airline industry if which hope many passengers choose to buy whose electronic air ticket or paper air ticket to catch which planes to fly from online travel agent or offline travel agent channels.

The rise of low cost airlines, such as AmericaWest, JetBlue and Airtran in US, Ryanair and EasyJet in Europe and Vigin Blue in Australia. The share of low cost airline strategy is popular in the US and European airline market. For example, the Southwest airline low cost strategy is the basis of most low cost airlines operations. The key of the strategy is to reduce costs when at the same time offering low prices to passengers. History showed that the low cost airline strategy is easy to replicate , but difficult to implement successfully.

However, I suggest airlines need to know what functions which can attract passengers to chose to catch their planes to fly if they expect to rise passenger numbers. For example, the critical function of the Malaysia airline travel is to connect the major towns and remote interior areas within East Malaysia, which has poor road systems and limited availability of other significant means of transportation . In contrast, West Malaysia has more developed and extensive rod and railway systems.

Therefore, airline travel is not the main mode of long distance transportation. It implies Malaysis airline ought concentrate on focusing short distance transportation strategy for passenger beneficial choice function. For example, a new small Malaysia airline serving one or two routes may enter easily. Otherwise, a larger airline servicing multiple routes may be harder to enter Malaysis airline market. It also means access to capital and labor are the major obstacles for new airline entrants to Malaysia airline market. Thus, small airlines into a larger airline is probably more likely to be successful as in Air Asia's case to Malaysia airline market.

Thus, the airline low cost strategy competition positions include very low or minimal pressive from other airline similar service substitute products, low or medium power of airline similar input suppliers. In conclusion, low cost airline strategy is a god method to be attempted to win competitors in airline market.

How consumers select travel service between online and offline mode in travel industry

Nowadays, the travel industry is operating through two different modes, online and offline respectively. It involves the identification of the competitive strategies adopted by the tour operators. For example, it was found that e-retil travel is platform that is bringing two market forced the demand and supply tour operators and the customers together, and both parties and more inclined towards online mode in near future. Tour operators are gaining by operating at low cost and increasing their business reach when customers get what they desire as per their convenience. For example, many tour operators had promoted tourism destination through website that allow user to use interface for booking transporttion, foreign exchange etc. However, the role of travel operators (agents) should be assisted any airlines to promote their travel package service by internet more easily , such as tourism destination , arrangement of hospitality, restaurants, transportation tools during their trips.

The reasons why consumers choose online travel service include:

Firstly, it is online researching hospitality service. Online travel websites can provide many different accommodation furniture, such as seeking hotel locations, rooms prices comparison, prepaid hotel rooms by visa card payment transaction method, range from luxury five stars deluxe category hotels to small guest houses. The primary need of tourist is to find a place for residing in foreign country or domestic country to ensure whose safety and relaxing needs. Online travel website channel can help whom to find a place , according to his/her needs and paying capacity in the most shorten times.

Secondly, it is online restaurant (food and beverages researching) service. Full service restaurants are divided into two categories, fine dining and casual dining restaurants . Fine dining restaurants are usually located in the premises of luxury hotels, provide high quality food at premium price with good ambience and highly trained professionals. Thus, travel consumers can also compare the different restaurant food price and seek where is the restaurant and find.

What food taste of food supply from the travel agency or travel operator website easily 250 + tour operators are registered with the ministry of tourism (website of tourism ministry) , and the major players in the industry are dealing online and are dominating the travel industry. The major online travel players are Thomas cook, Cox and Kings, make any trips, clear trip, gatra.com and Expedia.

The tour operators whether online or offline offers a large number of services to the tourists including customized package where the customer selects each element of the tour package, specialized tourism package and complete tour guide package.

Nowadays, the tour operational travel (agents) are working through two different modes: offline online . Big brands with luge investment are dealing online and enjoying low cost benefits and huge profit margins. When the small tour operators have their market niche and managing have their market niche and managing their profits by dealing offline.

It is generally prefer offline mode that is the opportunity for small capital investment or employee number for tour operators. But the large scenario is changing as with the usage of internet by the tour operations have given convenience to the customers and now the customers of modern age have started developing preference for online modern. Thus, internet technology change any countries' travel agents or tour operators' air ticket sale method. So, it brings electronic ticket sale method is more popular to compare to traditional travel paper air ticket sale method.

However, online electronic ticket sale method has its disadvantages such as online transaction is unsafe, if the consumer 's name and address and visa card number is stolen to let any internet users to know to be used to buy any products from internet channel easily. Otherwise, traditional walk in offline travel paper ticket sale method is more safe, because the travel consumers can pay cash to the travel agents directly.

However, offline travel agent disadvantages include that the research identified that information communication and technology has very crucial role for tourism industry. Tourist can access any kind of information about tourism destination and tourism products from any part of the world. Tourism comprehends with social media. For example, it was found that (ICT) is bosting up tourism industry. (ICT) helps in searching the location, search for information on tourism products, and e-booking of airline tickets and hotel reservation.

The online travel sale service attraction is that the recent development in the field of information communication and technology and its practical application in tourism and hospitality industry. Generally , online travel sale service must have consumer side and the supplier side.

The decision making prcess of consumer was analyzed and it was found that travel information search and traveller individual electronic ticker pre paid to prebook any plane seat, hotel rooms and restaurants prices comparison to prebook service of traveler individual purchase behavior are corresponding with the usae of (ICT).

What is the online travel sale service strategy?

The two most important things for travel operators (agents) are online travel marketing and strategic management. Former can enhance business operations. Use of (ICT) develops financial capabilities , however, it depends on management choice, financial condition and position. Some researchers recommended that the usage of IT should not be restricted at operational level, however it should be extended up to senior level and should be used for decision making. Social media is regarded as a platform where the tourists and travel operators/agents (suppliers) of tourism industry cross each other. Thus, the role of social media has been directed for future research in tourism industry. Hence, it seems online travel sale service has these features to attract travel consumers to choose to use this online mode to buy electronic air ticket. Such as, airline electronic air ticket price comparison, pre-booking plan seats to avoid full seats flights to delay consumer individual trip plan, pre-booking hotel rooms and prices comparison as well as prebooking restaurant seats and food price and taste comparison, travel destination easy search. Otherwise, these features to attract travel consumers to choose to walk in to travel agents to buy paper air ticket directly. They include: safe cash or visa card payment to avoid personal information is stolen by website payment channel, e.g. via card number, address, name , birth date personal information. Also the travel consumer can enquire any questions from the travel agent and gets individual feedback from the travel agent by oral before who ensure to choose to buy which kind of travel package for whose travel destination. In special, when the travel consumer has much time to spend to enquire any travel trip question, walk in travel agent is the best enquire methods to let the travel consumer to know the trip information clearly.

- Online/offline travel operators (agents) maketing strategies

Offline walk in travel unique segment service strategy

Nowadays, online and offlce travel operators competitions are serious. In fact, tourism marketing , there will be more need for online travel operators in the future, due to online travel sale service is popular to be accepted by online travel consumers. Thus, I recommend walk in offline travel agents need to concentrate on focusing some unique travel service to attract new or old travel consumers if who hope to survive.

I recommend that they can focus on specific specialized services, such as travel consultation (specialization) hypothesizing that systematic differences exist between the usage of travel agents for different travel contexts and travel agents can survive if they focus on specific segments of the market, such as older travelers (segmentation; hypothesizing that systematic differences exist between the usage of travel agents depending on the personal characteristics of travellers). The unique travel needs include: specific services related to package holidays, transport services, beach on city holidays, as well as destinations travellers are not familiar with.

I shall give my opinions to provide insight into alternative strategies for travel agencies in a matured travel market with a high internet penetration as below:

The internet online travel sale service is a reality of popular to let travel consumers to feel convenient to pre-book air seat, hotel rooms , air electronic ticket prices comparison. In order to make final purchase decision very easily in the shortest time. Consequently , it has penetrated the decision making process of travel to attract them to choose to buy electronic air ticket, prebooking hotel rooms or restaurant seats from online travel agent channel more than walk in offline travel agent channel. This is especially true in the tourism business where consumption to consume (booking) and the purchase-related information search (Bieger & Lasesser 2004; Crotts 1998).

In fact , apply website to provide travel sale method has these good consequence. From travel operator (agent) supplier's perspective, the success potential derived from operating a website consist of lower distribution costs, higher revenues and a larger potential market share (due to the ubiquitous access). From traverler's perspective, the internet allows direct communication with tourism suppliers facilitatinf requests for information and allowing services and travel related products, e.g. prebooking hotel rooms, restaurant seats , electronic or paper air tickets, travel trip arrangement package products to be purchased at any time and any place from online travel agents /operators conveniently.

Offline / online travel agency (operator) business depends on earn commissions on behalf of airlines. Thus, offline walk in travel agency (operator) business model that would extend existence as a booking agency (thus focusing on consultation and interpersonal contact) strategy.

As a matter of fact, commission -cutting , which began in the US well ahed of Europe, has had a profound effect specially on business travel agents . Consequently , many of them have re-invented themselves as " travel managers", instead of selling tickets and making arrangements, they charge consultancy fees for reducing the amounts client companies spend on travel (Daneshku, 1999).

● Systematic differences strategy applies to offline walk in travel agent

Thus, I recommend systematic differences strategy can be applied offline walk in travel agent (operator). It means that walk in travel agents could reorient their offline walk in travel agent business to focus on contexts that are less substitutable by other channels and media . Factors hypothetically attributing to the delineation of travel contexts include: helping travellers to choose best travel destinations, helping travellers to attempt to find the number of previous trips (indicating the familiarity with a destination) for their travel reference, helping them to find the cheapest, the most convenient and the most close transportation to ctch during their trips, helping them to find the different types of accommodation and rooms price comparison , nature/type of the trip comparison , arrangement of time of booking (as indicator of spontneous / planned travel) nd helping them to budget overall travel expenditure .

Systematic differences in travel agent use exist in dependence of personal (characteristics with with tourists. Walk in offline travel agents could benefit from a travelling client segmentation strategy and customize and target their services to those travellers that are most likely to be and remain their customers.

Factors hypotheticlly attributing to the traveller segment include: travel expenditure per day, useful travel information as indicator for perceived risk and socio-demographic (age, gender, highest completed and education, professional positions) . Generally, the role of walk in offline travel agent with regard to the travel infrrmation search and booking behavior have take an incoming perspective. Such as looking at visitors from different travel markets at a similar destinations. The comparison of central importance in determining whether specialization of travel contexts or market segments is the more promising strategy for walk in offline travel agents.

However, travel package tours strategy must b offline walk in travel attraction . Due to some walk in travellers target segmentation market has still needs. Generally, this travel package tours of travel segmentation consumer who like to enquire the travel agents to concern what the hotel rooms price are the cheapest to provide to them to live, what transportation tools the travel agent can arrange to them to catch anywhere the country destination, the travel agent can provide them to visit during their tour journey. Thus, the travel trip package service is still popular need to offline walk in travel agent (operator). This market is only belonged to offline walk in travel agents (operators) nowadays.

Service fees and commission cuts strategy

The reduction or removal of airline commission continues to challenge travel agencies' profitability It is crucial to understand what trends travel agencies need to be aware of to ensure how to profitability and increase travel agencies' revenues with service-fee models.

Service fees are not only a way to compensate for the loss of airline commission but also a way to generate new revenue sources for travel agencies that guarantee their long term profitability. Many travel agencies are expanding their service fee models, both in terms of the mounts changed and the number of service to airline.

However, if travel agent charge too much service fee to exceed the general airline travel market service fee reasonable or standard level. It will influence many airlines do not choose to find the travel agent to help them to sell air tickets. Travel agents apply fees most often for airline related services. They charge differentiated fees depending on the destination, type of reservation (e.g. frequent flyer), number of tickets sold or type of airline (e.g. full service versus).

However, service fee increases can raise customer loyalty and satisfaction. It won't reduce client numbers or result in a lose in clients.. The reason is that service fees can be tailored to suit individual customer. This helps travel agencies target their clients, with tailored services based on their past purchasing patterns and identity services for which clients' willingness to pay is greater , such as trip planning identity service for which pay , such as hotel only or special promotion.

To revenue mix for travel agencies is increasingly shifting to service fes as airlines have lowered or cut commissions. Successful travel agencies in many European countries are fast adopting, and constantly upgrading , their service fee schemes. Thus, it seems reasonable service fee level is one important factor to influence travel agents and airlines good relationship. In fact, even travel agents raise service fee, it won't influence travel consumer number to be reduced , even they raise air ticket price. It they can provide the informations concerning the reasonable hotel rooms prices and food quality comparison to satisfy travel consumers' living arrangement or helping them to find the reasonable restaurants' food prices and where are their location arrangement or providing the reasonable airlines' electronic air tickets or paper air tickets sale service, even arrangement any high entertainment quality of travel destination trips to let travel consumers to feel satisfactory.

However, I believe the raise air ticket price factor won't influence the travel consumer number to be decreased. Any offline or online travel agents will encounter this crisis. By cutting travel agents' commission. Airlines decreased their dependence on travel agencies as a distribution channel. In fact, three key variable factors will influence travel agents' commission income to be decreased. They include below:

● The unsustainable or no change financial losses by airlines , due to the growth of low cost carriers, leading to an increase in the number of bankruptcies.

● No negative consequences from previous commission cuts: airline had progressively lowed the commission payments.

● No effective resource for travel agencies to satisfy airlines needs.

● The appearance of now airlines and air routes to provide to travel agencies to fall down air ticket price to attract consumers' choices, due to who don't feel to spend much money to go to this new air routes or catch new airline plans , whether these new air routes are excite to entertainment or whether they are safe planes to catch.

● An increase in the number of bankruptcies to cause travel comsumption desire to be reduced.

● New competition forced down air fares.

● The necessity to cut production costs, especially with low cost meaning low production costs and low fares, even if the two are closely linked.

Internet negative influences to travel agents

Although, on the one hand, internet creates offline travel agents to use websites to help them to sell electronic air ticket or travel related products, such as prebooking hotel rooms , restaurants, transportation tools etc. travel service. However, on the other hand, internet also brings travel agencies competitive disadvantage with regad to suppliers' direct websites , when airlines are able to control seat availability and prices. Indeed internet cause the decision is made by the airlines to reduce and/or eliminate travel agency commission has led them to use technology that many of their distrust or are not inclined to use, and to compare prices and travel schedules constantly.

As a result of this travel sale service environment, traditional offline travel agencies are at a competitive disadvantage with regard to online travel agencie and to airline carriers, which have developed their own direct websites where they are able to control seat availability and prices.

Nevertheless, travel agents' pay programmes remain. From some airlines, travel agents receive negotiated incentive commission closely linked to their performance as incentive . However, airlines still need travel agents' assistance to help them to promote air tickets to sell, due to travel agents can provide trip packages, transportation tools, prebooking hotel rooms, restaurants and air tickets arrangement and they can give any enquiries to every individual travel consumer. It is free charge travel professional enquiry service for travel agency's competitive features.

Consequently, how agencies can reduce their reliance on airline commission payments. I recommend these following strategic options to them to apply as below:

● Streamlining operations, controlling staff costs, when ensuring the client feels as little impact as possible.

● Expanding or moving into the leisure business, where commissions on ono-air products remain high (cruise, hotel, railway travel)

● Specializing in geographic areas or becoming niche players for specific leisure products, e.g. destination weddings, student travel group cultural travel, cruises only, cruise and railway travel etc.

● (d) establishing a service fee driven business model.

Concentrating on business travel marketing strategy

The certain characteristics to the business travel market allowed this sector to adapt more easily to the disappearance of commission. Business travel systems have always had different relationship with different customers. They usually have long term buyer relationships, set up long before the commission cap. Some of them quickly renegotiated their contracts to include a transaction or management fee, knowing that the majority of these fee arrangements are specific the need of the client.

The reasons why airlines reduce commission to paid to travel agents. They include petrol costs increasing, e.g. indirect and by pass the established distribution chain by developing airlines' their own websites; reducing or removing commission paid to travel agencies. Consequently, the decision to cut travel agencies' commission clearly shows that airlines wanted to decrease their reliance and dependence on travel agencies as a distribution channel. Thus, the internet appears to be an efficient and cost-effective distribution channel. Also, by creating airlines' own websites and setting directly to their clients, airlines are also to control seat availability to their clients and prices to their websites.

What an e-commerce strategy is used by internet travel websites?

Nowadays, the commercial use of electronic travel ticket travel is common, the most purchased online products include, for example, the name brands in online travel Epedia.travel .com and cheap tickets have been or are being integrated in large online travel firms.

Generally, online travel websites apply these strategies to attract travel consumers as below:

Firstly, shopping mall strategy, means to conduct a comprehensive factors for e-commerce. The online service provider needs to organize catalogs of services, take orders through their websites, accept payments securely, send service or related document, such as airline tickets to consumers and manage client data , such as client profiles.

Secondly, portal strategy, portal websites , such as yahoo give visitors the chance to find almost everything , they are working for in one place. Websites , such as Altavista.com and yahoo.com provide users with a shopping page that links them to many sites carrying a variety of products. Once a client is familiar with a website, who will be more likely to use the online service.

Thirdly, pricing strategy, low price is as a major competitive weapon. It includes a comparison pricing on discount price or price negotiation to let online travel consumers to get the best electronic travel ticket price choice to buy any airline tickets.

Travel agents vs online booking: Tackling the shortcomings and strengths

Consequently, however, one travel consumer who chooses either online booking sale service or traditional walk in offline travel agent to enquire travel service. These both of travel sale methods have shortcomings also. Such as it is possible that online electronic travel ticket purchase has personal data ,e.g. visa card, name, birth data, address, which will be stolen by online crime internet users more easily, who can not enquire any travel questions to get clear travel information concern whose travel destination package service choice or hotel room choice or transportation tool or restaurant choice and airline choice by travel agent. Also, it is possible that walk in travel agent paper travel ticket purchase shortcomings include that the travel consumer can not check any airlines' seat and pre book hotel room or transport tool or restaurant in the shorten time if who needs to fly immediately. Thus, it seems that online travel agent's client group is business travel intention, who does not need to enquire travel agent and has desire to per book airline seat in the short time. Otherwise, the offline walk in agent's client group is entertainment intention , who need to walk in to travel agent to enquire whose travel package and has no desire to pre book airline seat in the short time. Thus, online travel agent ought concentrate on design good travel package for the business travel consumers. Otherwise, offline travel agent ought concentrate on design good travel package for the entertainment travel consumers. Thus, they can have themselves unique travel target package to adopt to their different travel need. Such as business travel consumers need to live cheap and comfortable hotels, catching cheap and fast transportation tools in their business trips, eating in cheap and good taste food in restaurant and spending the less time to catch the airline plan to arrive the destination and cheap and comfortable business class plan seat. Such as entertainment travel consumers need the travel agent can help them to design cheap and enjoyable travel package, includes living comfortable hotel room, exciting and enjoyable trip, good taste food and railway, travel bus, cruise and plane provision in trip.

In conclusion, In fact, tourism is a quite unique area of business in a sense that is a travel sale service product and it can't be observed or manipulated through direct experience prior to purchase . Instead clients have to purely rely on indirect or virtual experience. Thus, every online or offline travel agent ought attempt to design different travel package to attract every business traveler or entertainment traveller trip need because every traveler will have personal unique trip need in this competitive travel sale service market in the future.

Reference

Bieger. Th., and Ch. Laesser (2004). " Information sources for travel decisions: Toward a source process model," Journal of travel reserch, 42(4): 357-371.

Daneshku, S. (1999). " Unwived travel agents unworried bi internet, " Financial Times , London. June 16, 1999:10.

Foucault, B. Lery, N. Rifkin, A. & Silfies , 2000.

" Comparision of textbook prices by retailer and by college" working paper. Cornell University, Ithaca, Ney.

CHAPTER IV

What factors can influence travel behavioural consumption

Prediction travel behavioral consumption from traditional human's mind of tourism market research method

How to predict travel consumption? It is one question to any travel agents concern to use what methods which can predict how many numbers of travelers where who will choose to go to travel more accurately. I think that who can consider how to predict travel behavioral consumption from psychology view and computer science view both.

On the psychology view, It has evidence to support the relationship between self-identify threat and resistance to change travel behavior to any travelers, controlling for whose past travelling behavior, resistance to change if a psychological phenomenon of long standing interest in many applied branches of psychology. Past travelling behavior has been acknowledged as a predictor of future action. Such as travelling behavior that is experienced as successful is likely to be repeated and may lead to habitual patterns. Some psychologists differentiate habit between two concepts, such as goal oriented and automatic oriented both. Although repeated past travelling behavior is addition goal oriented and automatic oriented. Further non-deliberative nature of habit may make appeals to judge and to predict future individual traveler's behaviour accrately. However, repeated travelling behavior without a necessary constraint of goal orientation and automatic oriented both. So, it seems that psychological factor can influence any individual traveler why and how who choose to decide whose travelling behaviour.

On the computer statistic view, structural equation modeling is an extremely flexible linear-in-parameters multivariate statistical modeling technique. It has been used in modeling travel behavior and values since about 1980 year. It is a software method to handle a large number of variables, as well as unobserved variables specified as linear combinations (weighted averages) of the observed variable.

Whether climate change can influence travelling behaviours.

The flexibility of human travelling behavior is at least the result of one such mechanism, our ability to travel mentally in time and entertain potential future. Understanding of the impacts is holidays, particularly those involving travel. Using focus groups research to explores tourists' awareness of the impacts of travel own climate change, examines the extent to which climate change features in holiday travel decisions and identifies some of the barriers to the adoption of less carbon intensive tourism practices. The findings suggest many tourists don't consider climate change when planning their holidays. The failure of tourists to engage with the climate change to impact of holidays, combined with significant barriers to behavioral change, presents a considerable challenge in the tourism industry. Tourism is a highly energy intensive industry and has only recently attracted attention as an important contributions to climate change through greenhouse gas emissions. It has been estimated that tourism contributes 5% of global carbon dioxide emissions. There have been a number of potential changes proposed for reducing the impact of air travel on climate change. These include technological changes, market based changes and behavioral changes. However, the role that climate change plays in the holiday and travel decisions of global tourists. How the global tourists of the impacts travel has on climate change to establish the extent to which climate change, considerations features in holiday travel decision making processes and to investigate the major barriers to global tourists adopting less carbon intensive travel practices. Whether tourists will aware the impacts that their holidays and travel have on climate changes.

When, it comes to understand indvidual traveler's behavioral change, wide range of conceptual theories have been developed, utilizing various social, psychological, subjective and objective variables in order to model travel consumption behavior. These theories of travel behavioral change operate at a number of different levels, including the individual level, the interpersonal level and community level. Whether pro-environmental behavior can be used to predict travel consumption behavior in a climate change. However, the question of what determines pro-environmental behavior in such a complex one that it can not be visualized through one single framework or diagram. Despite the potentially high risk scenario for the tourism industry and the global environment, the tourism and climate change ought have close relationship. Whether what are the important factors and variables which can limit tourism? e.g. money, time, family problem, extreme hot or cold weather change, air ticket price, journey attraction etc. variable factors. Mention of holidays and travel were deliberately avoided in the recruitment process, so as not to create a connection factor to influence traveler's individual mind. However, the dismissal of alternative transportation modes can be conceived as either a structural barrier, in the sense that flying is perhaps the only realistic option to reach long-haul holiday destination, or a perceived behavioral control barriers in that an individual perceives flying as the only option open to whom. The transportation tool factor will be depend to extent on the distance to the destination. This can also be interpreted in a social perspective as an intention with the resources available where much international tourism is structured around flying. To increase the availability of different transportation modes, tourists could choose holiday destination closer to home.

Finally, also how to predict future travel behavioural consumption. I feel that travel agents need to predict whether any country's random daily variation of weather factor is also important to influence travel behaviour. e.g. in weather, temperature, rainfall adn snowfall with traffic accidents factors will have relationship to cause travel demand. Some scientists estimate suggest that when warmed temperatures and reduced snowfall are associated with a moderate decline in non-fatal accidents, they are also associated with a significant increase in fatal accidents. Thus increase in fatalities and temperature. Half of the estimated effect of temperature on fatalities is due to changes in the exposure to pedestrians, bicyclists and motorcyclists as temperature increase. So, if any countries have rainfall, snowfall and low temperature to cause traffic accidents, whether this accident occurrence will influence the travelers who liking climb snow hills, riding bicycle, running sports who will avoid to travel to these countries' bad weather after occurs. So, why I feel that this natural climate factor will also be one serious factor to influence travel behavioral consumption.

Market method predicts future travel consumption behavior

Whether individual habitual behaviour can influence travelling behaviour : e.g. renting travel transportation tools

Whether habit can be intended to predict of future travel behavior to people are creatures of habits. Many of human's everyday goal-directed behaviors are performed in a habitual fashion, the transportation made and route one takes to work, one's choice of breakfast. Habits are formed when using the some behavior frequently and a similar consistency in a similar context for the some purpose whether the individual past travel consumption model will be caused a habit to whom. e.g. choosing whom travel agent to buy air ticket or traveling package; choosing the same or similar countries' destinations to go to travel ; choosing the business class or normal (general) class of quality airlines to catch planes. Does habitual rent traveling car tools use not lead to more resistance to change of travel mode? It has been argued that past behavior is the best predictor of future behavior to travel consumption. If individual traveler's past consumption behavior was always reasoned, then frequency of prior travel consumption behavior should only have an indirect link to the individual traveler's behavior. It seems that renting travel car tools to use is a habit example. So, a strong rent traveling car tools useful habit makes traveling mode choice. People with a strong renting of traveling car tools of habit should have low motivation to attend to gather any information about public transportation in their choice of travelling country for individual or family or friends members during their traveling journeys.

Even when persuasive communication changes the traveler whose attitudes and intention, in the case of individual traveler or family travelers with a strong renting travel car tools habit. It is difficult to change whose travel behaviors to choose to catch public transportation in whose any trips in any countries. However, understanding of travel behavior and the reasons for choosing one mode of transportation over another. The arguments for rent traveling car tools to use, including convenience, speed, comfort and individual freedom and well known. Increasingly, psychological factors include such as, perceptions, identity, social norms and habit are being used to understand travel mode choice. Whether how many travel consumers will choose to rent traveling car tools during their trips in any countries. It is difficult to estimate the numbers. As the average level of renting travel car tools of dependence or attitudes to certain travel package policies from travel agents. Instead different people must be treated in different ways because who are motivated in different ways and who are motivated by different travel package policies ways from travel agents.

In conclusion, the factors influence whose traveler's individual behavior either who chooses to rent traveling car tools or who chooses to catch public transportation when who individual goes to travel in alone trip or family trip. It include influence mode choice factors, such as social psychology factor and marketing on segmentation factor both to influence whose transportation choice of behavior in whose trip.

How to determine future travel behavior from past travel experience and perceptions of risk and safety for the benefits to travel consumers?

How to determine future travel behavior from past travel experience and perceptions of risk and safety for the benefits to travel consumers? Why does individual traveler avoid certain destination(s) is(are) as relevant to tourist decision making as why who chooses to travel to others. Perceptions of risk and safety and travel experience are likely to influence travel decisions. If travel agents had efforts to predict future travel behavior to guess whether travelers will feel where is(are) risk and unsafe to cause who does not choose to go to the country to travel. Then, the travel agents will avoid to choose to spend much time to design the different traveling package to attract their potential travel consumers to choose to travel. The reason is because in the case of individual traveler's tourism experience, the traveler whose past disappointment travel experience (psychological risk) will be a serious threat to the traveler's health or life (health, physical or terrorism risk). The past safety or unhealthy risk to the country(countries) will influence the traveler decides to choose not to go to the countries(country) to travel again in the future.

What is push and pull factors to influence any traveler who chooses where is whose preferable travelling destination

How to predict individual traveler's behavioral intention of choosing a travel destination. Understanding why people travel and what factors influence their behavioral intention of choosing a travel destination is beneficial to tourism planning and marketing. In general, an individual's choice of a travel destination into two forces. The first force is the push factor that pushes an individual away from home and attempt to develop a general desire to go somewhere, without specifying where that may be. The other force is the pull factor that pull an individual toward in destination, due to a region-specific or perceived attractiveness of a destination. The respective push and pull factors illustrate that people travel because who are pushed by whose internal motives and pulled by external forced of a destination. However, the decision making process leading to the choice of a travel destination is a very complex process. For example, a Taiwanese traveler who might either choose new travel destination of Hong Kong or another old travel Asia destinations again or who also might choose any one of Western country, as a new travel destination. The travel agents can predict where who will have intention to choose to travel from whose past behavior and attitude, subjective and perceived behavioral control model.

The factors influence where is the traveler choice, include personal safety, scenic beauty, cultural interest, climate changing, transportation tools, friendliness of local people, price of trip, trip package service in hotels and restaurants, quality and variety of food and shopping facilities and services etc. needs. So, whose factors will influence where is the individual travel's choice. It seems every traveler whose choice of travel process, will include past behavior. e.g. travelling experience, travelling habit, then to choose the best seasoned travelling action to satisfy whose travel needs. This process is the individual traveler's psychological choice process, who must need time to gather information to compare concerning of different travel packages, destination scene, climate change, transportation tools available to the destination, air ticket price etc. these factors, then to judge where is the best right destination to travel in the right time.

Why expectation, motivation and attitude factor can influence travelling behaviour.

Social psychology is concerned with gaining insight into the psychological of socially relevant behaviors and the processes. For instance, on a global level bad influence to global warming, it influences some countries extreme cold or hot bad climate changing occurrence, then it ought influence some travelers' behavioral decision to change their mind to choose some countries to go to travel at the moment which do not occur extreme hot or cold climate (temperature). e.g. above than 40 degree in summer or below than 0 degree in winter. Due to the extreme climate changing environment in the countries, it will cause them to feel uncomfortable to play during their trips. So, the global warming causes to climate changing factor will influence the numbers of travel consumption to be reduced possibly. This is global climate changing environment factor influences to bad or uncomfortable social psychological feeling to global travelers' mind of traveling decision. What is individual traveler expectation, motivation and attitude? Tourism sector includes inbound (domestic) tourism and outbound (overseas) tourism both incomes to any countries. According to recent article, a tourist behavior model has been developed, called the expectation, motivation and attitude (EMA) model (Hsu et al., 2010).

This model focuses on the pre-visit stage of tourists by modeling the behavioral process by incorporating expectation, motivation and attitude. Travel motivation is considered as an essential component of the behavioral process, which has been increasing attention from the travel; industry. The economic approach defines "tourism" is an identifiable nationally important industry. It includes the component activities of transportation, accommodation, recreation, food and related service. So, tourism behavioral consumption is concerned the individual tourist's usual habituate of the industry which responds to whose needs, and of the impacts that both the tourist and the tourism industry have on the socio-cultural, economic and physical environment.

However, travel motivation means how to understand and predict factors that influence travel decision making. According to Backman and others (1995, p.15), motivation is conceptually viewed as " a state of need, a condition that services as a driving force to display different kind of behavior toward certain types of activities, developing preferences, arriving at some expected satisfactory outcome." So, motivation and expectancy which has close relationship to any tourist before who decided to do any tourism of behavior. Some economists confirmed motivation and expectancy which has relations, such as expectation of visiting an outbound destination has a direct effect on motivation to visit the destination; motivation has a direct effect on attitude toward visiting the destination; expectation of visiting the outbound destination has a direct affect on attitude toward visiting the destination and motivation has a mediating effect on the relationship in between expectation and attitude.

What methods can predict future travel behavioural consumption

How to use qualitative of travel behavioural method to predict future travel consumption?

I also suggest to use qualitative of travel behavioural method to predict future travel consumption. Methods such as focus groups interviews and participant observer techniques can be used with quantitative approaches on their own to fill the gaps left by quantitative techniques. These insights have contributed to the development of increasingly sophisticated models to forecast travel behavior and predict changes in behavior in response to change in the transportation system. First, survey methods restrict not only the question frame but the answer frame as well, anticipating the important issues and questions and the responses. However, these surveys methods are not well suited to exploratory areas of research where issues remain unidentified and the researched seek to answer the question "why?". Second, data collection methods using traditional travel diaries or telephone recruitment can under represent certain segments of the population, particularly the older persons with little education, minorities and the poor. Before the survey, focus group for example can be used to identify what socio-demographic variables to include in the survey, how best to structure the diary, even what incentives will be most effective in increasing the response rate. After the survey, focus, focus groups can be used to build explanations for the survey results to identify the "why" of the results as well as the implications. One Asia Pacific survey research result was made by tourism market investigation before. It indicated the travel in Asia Pacific market in the past, had often been undertaken in large groups through leisure package sold in bulk, or in large organized business groups, future travelers will be in smaller groups or alone, and for a much wider range of reasons. Significant new traveler segments, such as female business traveler. The small business traveler and the senior traveler, all of which have different aspirations and requirements from the travel experience.

Moreover, Asia tourism market will start to exist behaviors in the adoption of newer technologies, a giving the traveler new ways to manage the travel experience, creating new behaviors. This with provide new opportunities for travel providers. The use of mobile devices, smartphones, tablets etc. and social media are the obvious findings to become an integral part of the travel experience. Thus, quality method can attempt to predict Asia Pacific tourism market development in the future.

However, improving the predictive power of travel behavior models and to increase understanding travel behavior which lies in the use of panel data(repeated measures from the same individuals). Whereas, cross-sectional data only reveal inter-individual differences at one moment in time, panel data can reveal intra-individual changes over time. In effect, panel data are generally better suited to understand and predict (changes in) travel behavior. However, a substantial proportion was also observed to transition between very different activity/travel patterns over time, indicating that from one year to the next, many people renegotiated their activity/travel patterns.

How to apply advanced traveler information systems (ATIS) to predict future travelling behaviour?

Nowadays, information can impact on traveler behavior and network performance. For example, when steadily growing levels of vehicle ownership and vehicle miles traveled information has been identified as a potential strategy towards man aging travel demand, optimizing transportation networks and better utilizing available capacity. Toward, this goal to predict further tourist behavioral consumption. Many countries, government tourism development institutes has applied advanced traveler information systems (ATIS) which travel behavior models and high-fidelity network performance models made increasingly feasible through the rapid advances in computer power. Crucial components of this problem domain are the modeling of individual tourist drivers' response to travel information and the development accurate guidance of relevance to real would trip makers. So, this advanced traveler information systems (ATIS) can assist the tourist who like to rent travelling car tools to travel in any countries own free traveler information systems service conveniently. Also, this travel information system can be intended to assist travelers to make better travel choices. e.g. this system can improve the decision making of individual traveler rather than improvements of network performance overall. So, we need to understand how tourists make their travel plans. Also, understanding decision process that lead to booking of the trip is equally important, as it allows of a potential behavior.

How does online tourism sale channel can influence traveling consumption of behaviour?
Nowadays, internet is popular, it seems that booking air ticket behavior of using internet is predicted to influence overall tourism air tickets payment method. Tourism industry has grown in the previous several decades. Despite its global impact, questions related to better understanding of tourists and whose habits. Using online travel air ticket booking benefits include booking electronic air tickets can be made from entering any electronic travel agents websites in the short time and electronic travel ticket payers do not need leave home, who can pay visa card to pre booking any electronic travel ticket from online channel conveniently.

How to analyze activity based travel demand ? Nowadays, human are concerning the traffic congestion and air quality deterioration, the supply oriented focus of transportation planning has expanded to include how to manage travel demand within the available transportation supply. Consequently, there has been an increasing interest in travel demand management strategies, such as congestion pricing that attempts to change aggregate travel demand. The prediction aggregate level, long term travel demand to understanding disaggregate level (i.e. individual levels) behavioral responses to short term demand policies, such as ride sharing incentives, congestion pricing and employer based demand management schemes, alternate work schedules, telecommuting limitation of travel agent traditionally work nature shall influence oriented trip based travel modelling passenger travel demand indirectly.

Finally, online travel purchase will be popular to influence the number of travel behavioural consumption nowadays. Any travel package products can be sold from websites to attract travellers to choose to prebook air ticket for any trips conveniently. In the past ten years, the internet has become the predominant carrier of all types of information and transactions. Regarding travel decisions, internet has also become an important sales channels for the travel industry, because it is associated with comparably lower distribution and sales costs, but also because ir adapts to hign supply and demand dynamics in this industry. Consequently, the travel and tourism industry tries to increase the internet sale specific share of sales volumes. So, internet sale channel has changed travel consumption behavioural pattern and characteristics and travel experience. For example, Switzerland has one of the highest population-to-computer ratio in Europe. It is also one of the most highly internet penetrated countries in terms of use of the WWW on a day-to-day basis, with more than 75 percent of the population older than 14 years using the WWW daily (ICT, 2005).

The reason of booking online tourism may include: convenience, fast transaction, finding traveling package choice easily, more airline seats available. So, online booking tourism will influence the traditional tourism agents visiting of sales and air tickets and travelling package numbers to be decreased. Finally, the online booking tourism market shares will be expanded to more than traditional tourism agents visits sale market in the future one day. So, the travel agents who still use the traditional tourism visiting sale channel which ought raise whose features to compare to differ to online tourism sale channel if these traditional touriam agents want to keep competitive ability in tourism industry for long term.

Actively based patterns of urban population of travel behavioural prediction method.

Actively based patterns of urban population. It is a method of motivational framework means in which societal constraints and inherent individual motivations interact to shape activity participation patterns. It can be used to predict one city or urban the numbers of travel demand in the year. It has two elements: First, capability constraints refer to constraints are imposed by biological needs, such as eating and sleeping and/or resources, such as income, availability of cars etc. to undertake the urban or city's family activities in the year. Second, coupling constraints define where, when and the duration of planning activities that are to be pursued with other individuals. So, this method needs to gather information (data) to get the relationship between activities, travel and spending work time and space time to evaluate whether there are how many families who have real needs to spend time to go to travel in the year.

What is trip based versus activity based approaches?

What is trip based versus activity based approaches? The fundamental difference between the trip-based and activity based approaches is that the former approach directly focuses on trips without explicit recognition of the motivation or reason for the trips and travel. The activity based approach , on the other hand, views travel as a demand derived from the need to pursue travel activities. So, it is better understand the individual or family behavior basis for individual or family travelling decision regarding participation in travelling activities in certain places or cities or countries at given times and hence the resulting travel needs. This behavioral basis includes all the factors that influence the why, how, when and where of performed activities and resulting individuals and household, the cultural/social norms of the community and the travel surrounding environment.

Another difference between the two approaches is in the way travel is represented. The trip based approach represents travel as a collection of trips. Each trip is considered as independent of other trips, without considering the inter-relationship in the choice attributes , such as time, destination and mode of different trips. As tours are chains of trips beginning and ending at a same location , say home or work. The tour based representation helps maintain the consistency across and capture the interdependency and consistency of the modeled choice attributed among the trips of the same tour.

In addition to the tour based representation of travel, the activity based approach focuses on sequences or patterns of activity participation and travel behavior, using the whole day or longer periods of time is the unit of analysis. Such as approach can address travel demand management issues through an examination of how people modify their activity participation, for example, will individuals substitute more out-of-home activities for in home activities in the evening of who arrived early form work due-to a work schedule change?

The major difference between trip based and the activity based approaches is in the way, the time dimension of activities and travel is considered. In the trip based approach, time is reduced to being simply a cost making a trip and a day's viewed as a combination, defined peak and off peak time periods. On the other hand, activity based approach views individuals' activity travel patterns are a result of their time use decisions with a continuous time domain. As individuals have 24 hours in a day or multiples of 24 hours for longer periods of time and decide how to use that travel among or allocate that time to activities and travel and with who, subject to their socio-demographic, transportation system and other and scheduling of trips. So, determining the impact of travel demand management policies on time use behavior is an important step to assessing the impact of such policies on individual travel behavior. The final major difference between this two approaches relates to the level of aggregation. In the trip based approach, most aspect of travel, e.g. number of trips etc. are analyzed at an aggregate level.

Consequently, trip based methods accommodate the effect of socio-demographic attributes of households and individuals in a very limited fashion, which limits the activity of the method to evaluate travel impacts of long term socio-demographic characteristics of the individuals who actually make the activity travel choices and the travel service characteristics of the surrounding environment. So, the activity based models are better equipped to forecast the longer term changes in travel demand in response composition and the travel environment of urban areas. Also, using activity based models, the impact of policies can be assessed by predicting individual level behavioral responses instead of employing trip based statistical averages that are aggregated over defined demographic segments.

Why senior age will be main travelling target?

In the past, Germany government had established tourism survey analysis to analyze survey data in order to arrive at reliable conclusions on future trends in travel behavior. To aim to find how demographic change will influence the tourism market and how the industry can adapt to those changes. The travel analysis provided data on tourism consumer behavior, including attitudes, motives and intentions. Since, 1970 year, it is based on a random sample, representative for the population in private households aged 14 years or older. Then, a continuous high scientific standard combined with a national and international users makes the travel analysis a useful tool and reliable source for tourism industry and policy decisions. It aimed to gather statistical data. e.g. on the age structure and on demographic trends, quantitative and qualitative analysis with time series data from the travel analysis. It shows e.g. not only the future volume , quite different from today's seniors, or how who will travel of family holidays will change, e.g. single parents of low, but grandparents of growing significance for tourism.

Demographic change is said to be one of the important drivers for new trends in consumer traveling change behavior in most European countries (e.g. Lind 2001). Because the growing number of senior citizens in the European Union and other industralised countries, such as the USA and Japan, looks to become one of the major marketing challenges for the tourism industry. United Nations statistics predict that the share of people being 60 age or older will grow dramatically in the coming future, and is expected to rise from 10 percent of the world population in 2000 year to more than 20 percent in 2050 year (United Nations Population Division, 2001). From its statistic, some data showed that travel propensity increased throughout life until the age of about 50 years of age and was then kept stable until very late in life 75 age. The most important results is that the travel propensity when getting older is not going down between 65 and 75 age of course, the overall development of this variable is influenced by a lot of other factors which are rsponsible for quite a variation over time. It is now possible to suggest that the general pattern of travel propensity is one of the key indicators for holiday life cycle travel behaviour, includes three stages. The growth stage tends to increase from early aduithood until 45 age old or when reaching some 80%. The next stage is stabilisation from the ages of around 50 age,until 75 age old, starting with a lower increase. Finally, the decrease stage is a slight decrease occurs once people reach the more advanced age of 75 age to 85 age old (Lohmann & Danielsson 2001).

So, it seems Germany government tourism prediction to future travellers' behaviour indicated these findings, such as on how future senior generations will travel, who had used survey data to examine the patterns of travel behaviour of a generation getting older and applied the findings to draw conclusions on the future. Also, it predicted that on the future of family trips, family semgmentation will be the travel behaviour patterns in the future. These findings together with the statistical data on demographic change allowed for a better understanding of the coming tends in family holidays. It's aim developed in consumer behaviour related to demographic change and predicted what will happen future of tourism one had to consider other influences and drivers as well, for example, trends on the supply side. e.g. low cost airlines or in travelling consumption behaviour in general whether how the past may provide a key to predict travel patterns of senior sitizens to the future.

Given the projected growth of the senior citizens market, designing specific marketing strategies to meet the prospective needs of elderly tourists will become increasingly important. It has been an implict assumption that it will be a close relationship between the travel behaviour of today's senior citizens and the those of future ones. The growing number of senior citizens in the world. e.g. China, Hong Kong, Japan, USA etc. countries. Global senior citizen tourism market will be based solely on demographic predictions about the future of the population's age structure. However, many of these seniors won't only live longer but will be fitter and more active until later in life. Many of the will also have plenty in life. Many of them will also have plenty of time and money to spend on travel. So, will these new seniors behave like today's senior citizens? Will they adopt the same travel behaviour as the previous generation or become a new market of oldies for the leisure and tourism indudtry? However, to determine the actual number of senior citizens who will be travelling and to sought to evaluate and specify certain difficult to predict the actual numbers of senior citizen to any country. However, they can be based on the implicit assumption that there is a close relationship between the travel behaviour of past, present and future seniors. But is this a valid assumption? As the reiseanalyse travel analysis survey, which was conducted in Germany every year, offered some interesting data possibiltieis. It was designed to monitor the holiday travel behaviour, opinions and attitudes of Germans and has been carried out since 1970 year, questions in the questionnaire. Data are based on face to face interviews, with a representative sample of more than 7,500 repondents, the interviews being carried out in January each year. All results refer to the average for the defined generated, which ranges generally over ten years. The group of people then at the age of 60 to 69 age is described. This corresponds to the same generation ten years ago, when they had an age of 50 to 59 age. When this methodological approach is not necessarily very sophisticated, it does have the important advantages of being cost effective.

Psychological method to predict travel behavioural consumption.

On the psychological view point, I think individual traveler's character will have those kind of personal characteristics. First, simplicity searchers value above everything ease not transparency in their travel planning and holiday making, and are willing to avoid having to go through extensive research. Second, cultural purists use their travel as an opportunity to immerse themselves in an unfamiliar looking to break themselves entirely from their home lives and engage. Sincerely with a different way of living. Third, social capital seekers understand that to be well travelled is a personal quality, and their choices are shaped by their desire to take maximum of social reward from their travel. They will exploit the potential of digital media to enrich and inform their experiences, and structure their adventures always keeping in mind they are being watched by online audiences. Finally, reward hunters seek a return on the investment who make in their busy , high-achieving lives. Linked in part to the growing trend of wellness, including both physical and mental self improvement who seek truly extraordinary and often indulgent or luxurious' must have experiences.

Why needs to know the personal character of individual traveler's characteristics? Because if travel agents could feel which kinds of individual traveler's character, then who can predict which kind of travel package to design to them more easily. For example, how to determine future travel behaviour from past travel experience and perceptions of risk and safety? We need to concern that the influences of past international travel experience, types of risk associated with international travel and the overall degree of safety feeling during international travel on individual's travelling experiences likelihood of travelling to various geographic regions on their next international vacation trip or avoidance of those regions, due to perceived risk. Because individual traveler's experience of safety risk degree to the countries, it will influence who chooses to go to the countries/country to travel again.

Why do travellers avoid certain destinations are as relevant decision making? Why do they choose to go to the country(countries) to travel? Perceptions of risk and safety and travel experiences are likely to influence travel decisions; efforts to predict future travel behaviour can benefit to individual tourist's decision making. As Weber & Bottorm (1989) defined risky decision is as "choices among alternatives that can be described by prodability distributions over possible outcomes" (p.114). Some psychologists judge subjective perceptions of physical reality, i.e. image of a particular tourist destination, whereas value judgement refers to the way individual rank destinations according to whose attributes. i.e. attractiveness, safety, risk etc. factors to form on overall image. So, if the individual traveler had unhappy and worried and unsafe experiences to go to where the place(country) to travel during whose vacation time before. Then, this negative travel experience will influence who is afraid to go to the place (country) to travel again. Risk of place, country, destination or region means the danger is relatively high to the place, ie.

increasing in airplane accidents, crime or terrorist activity targeting citizens of potential traveler's nationality or the probability of occurrence is great , ie. recent occurrences involving travel regions/destinations under consideration or effective actions to control consequences exist. i.e. selecting safe regions and destinations, taking extra precautions when traveling to risky destinations. These risk factors will influence the individual traveler who chooses to cancel travel plan to go to the country again.

Another interesting research, how to predict behavioural intention of choosing a travel destination, which has focus of toursm research for years, but the complex decision making process leading to the choice of a travel destination has not been well researched. The planned behaviour model using its core constructs, attitude, subjective norm and perceived behavioural control, with the addition of the past behavioural variable on behavioural intention of choosing a travel destination.

Understanding why people travel and what factors influence their behavioural intention of choosing a travel destination is beneficial to tourism planning and marketing. Understanding travel motivation is the push and pull model. The idea of the push and pull model is the decomposition of an individual's choice of a travel destination into two forces. The first force is the push factor that pushes an indvidual away home and attempts to develop a general desire to go somewhere else, without specifying where that may be. The second force is the pull factor, that pulls on individual toward a destination, due to a region specific travel location or perceived attractiveness of a destination. The respective push and pull factors illustrate that people travel because who are pushed by their internal motives and pulled by external forces of a destination. Nevertheless, how push and pull factors guide people's attitude and how these attributes lead to behavioural intentions of choosing a travel destination have rarely been investigated. The decision making process leading to the choice of a travel destination is a very complex process. The planned behaviour model is as a research framework to predict the behavioural intention of choosing a travel destination. The model based on the three constructs of attitude, subjective norm, and perceived behavioural control (Fishbein & Ajzen, 1975).

In conclusion, the factors can influence travelers who decide to choose to travel the country, which include personal safety was perceived to the highest motivation factors among the important factors which include, scenic beauty, cultural interests, friendliness of local people, price of trip, services in hotels and restaurants, quality and variety of food and shopping facilities and services. The factors include both push and pull. Push factors include knowledge, prestige, and enhancement of human relationship etc., whereas, the most significant pull factors include high technologic image, expenditure and accessibility etc. For example, Japanese travelers visiting Hong Kong. Push factors are such as exploration dream fulfillment and pull factors are such as benefits sought, attractions and good climate city. It will be the factor of future travel patterns and motivations of sub-cultural and ethic groups for Japanese choice to go to Hong Kong travelling.

Bibliography

Backman, K., Backman, S., Uysal, M. And Sunshine, K. (1995). Event Tourism : An Examination Of Motivations And Activities. Festival Management And Event Tourism, 3(1), 15-24.

Fishbein, M., & Ajzen, Z. (1975). Belief, Attitude, Intention And Behaviour: An Introduction To Theory And Research, Boston: Addison Wesley.

Hsu, C.H.C., Cai , L.A., Li, M(2010). Expectation, Motivation And Attitude: A Tourist Behavioral Model. Journal Of Travel Research, 49(3), 282-296. http://dx.doi, org/10.1177/004728750 9349266.

ICT Information And Communication Technology Switzerland, 2005. ICT Fakten (ICT facts). Available from http://www.ictswitzerland.ch/de/ict%2fakten/factsfigures.asp(retrieved Dec.12, 2005) in German.

Lind, (2001): Befolkningen, Familjen, Livscykeln- Och Ekonomisk Tillvaxt. Institutet For Tillvaxtpo-litiska studier/ Vinnova/Nutek.

Lohmann, Martin (2001): The 31 st. Reiseanalyse-RA 2001. Tourism: vol. 49, no.1/2001;pp.65-67, Zagreb.

United Nations Population Division (2001). World Population Prospects: The 2000 year Revision, New York.

Weber E.U., & W, P.Bottom (1989). "Axiomatic Measures Of Perceived Risk: Some Tests And extensions." journal of behavioral decision making, 2 (2): 113-31.

CHAPTER V

Oil price changes influences tourism industry experiences growth life cycle stage or decline life cycle stage

Why is economic theory, a worthwhile thing to do ? e.g. helping organizations to solve challenges, helping society to solve challanges in macro economic view, part of the attraction and the promise of economics is that it cliams to decribe policies that will improve people's lives. This is unlike most other physical and social sciences. Sociology and political science have a policy component, but for the most part, they are concerned with understanding the function of standards of living, but this is really a by-product of science as an intellectual activity matters, physical science, has the potential to improve people standards of living.

What is the role of theory in a policy science? When my view that economic is a policy science. I mean that however either old or new economic theories one useful in policy. Theory is as a substitute for data. For example, we want to determine how a market price will respond to a tax, we could estimate this effect by running a regression of market price, against tax rates, controlling for as many other variable as possible. This would give us an equation that we could use to product how prices respond to change in taxes of one country has many unemployment people, then if it's government change a little 2 to 3 % import tax to private cars. Then, it may cause the country's car buyers number to import car demand decreases. The elastic to car import tax is high because the country has many people are unemployment. Hence, society is continue changing. So, some economists will research how to apply old economic theories to change other new theories to attempt to solve social and organizational challenges.

In new economic theories, they are applied new modelling techniques to old real world problems, they add something to economic knowledge to the extent that we accept formalisation as a source of progress in economic. Some economists focus new economic theory on the dynamic of regional growth and economic activity aspect. When the former foucs on long-run regional growth and later is linked to the " new growth theory". For example, the traditional trade theory is unable to explain the existence of different production structures , e.g. the country's geographical positions in similar regions. Also, trade should lead to conflice face greater market competition and loose incomes. Finally, countries having complementary factors were the best condidates to the formation of trading, so that they will specialize in different commodities. In addition, the traditional trade theory performs poorly when there is high mobility of production factors.

I shall indicate what the difference between new and old economic theories below:
In old economic theories, they may include: Scarcity means that the condition in which our wants and greates

than our limited resources. So, we must make choices on how we will use resources. Hence, economic-social concerned with the efficient use of limited resources to achieve maximum satisfaction of economic wants; micro-economic studies such as individuals, firms and industries (competitive markets, labour markets, personal decision making etc.) Otherwise, macro-economics studies the large economy as a whole or in its national economic growth. Government how spends, inflation, unemployment etc. Marginal analysis involves making decisions based on the additional benefits vs. the additional cost.

- Old economic theory
- production possibilities curve

Everyone acts rationally by comapring the marginal costs and marginal benefits of every choice. For example, if you decide to go to college, the opportunity cost of going to college may include work to earn money, production possibilities have four assumptions: Only two goods can be produced, full employment of resources, fixed technology, resources. For example, when one firm produces two products . One is pizza food, another is robots. It produces many robots, then it will produces less pizzas. If it hopes to involve to produce pizzas, but it won't reduce to produce robots. It must need to improve technology in order to improvements in pizza ovens, but robots producing number won't be reduced . If the country has mad cow disease kills 85% of cows, then it will influence the demand for pizza decrease. Then, it may avoid to improve technology to produce many pizza, it can concentrate on applying technology to produce new robot making technology.

In the production possibiliteies curve and efficiency refers this firm can have productive efficiency when robots are being produced in the least costly way, due to pizzas produced number is reduced, this is any point on the production possibilities curve as well as allocative efficiency, when this firm's robots being produced are the ones most desired by society. This optimal point on the ppc depends on the robotic products desires of society.So, the less demand to pizzas, it will influence it applies less technology to produce pizzas, but more technology to be improved to concentrate on producing robotic products.

- Specialization of trade theory

Specialization of trade explains one country can earn comparative advanage when the producer will be lowest opportunity cost to produce. So, countries should trade if they have a relatively lower. For example, US specializes and makes only wheat. Brazil makes only sugar. So, US can export wheat and Brazil can export sugar to earn comparative advantages . When there two countries only concentrate or producing on kind of food in order to earn specialization trade advantages. Free market means little government involvement in the economy, (laissez faire), individuals own resources and the opportunity to make profit gives people incentive to produce items efficiently, wide variety of goods available to consumers and competition and self-interest work together to regulate the economy keep computers and only one company is making them, other making computers to earn profit.

- Invisible hand

This lead to more competition, which means lower prices, better quality, and more product variety. Consequently, most efficient production of the goods, that consumers want, produced at the lowest prices and the highest quality.

What does invisible hand mean? It is the concept that society's goals will be met as individuals seek their own self-interest. For example, when society wants fuel efficient cars. Profit seeking producers will make more, then competition between firms results in low prices,high quality and greater efficiency . Consequently, the government does not need to get involved since the needs of society are automatically met. Thus competition and self-interest act as an invisible hand that regulates the free market.

I shall indicate some new economic theories as below:

● Organizational behavioral economic theory

In new economic theories, it may include behavioral economics, it explains how has changes views of consumer theory and finance, hoe to deal climate change and analyze new ways to deal with international environmental problems, farm economy how to raise crop, vegetable, food productivities, how farmers' agriculture growing behavior can achieve crop, raising productivites aim more easily, e.g. predicting climate when is bad change time.

In new miceo economic theory, economists have recommended new economic theory to help organizations to solve problem effectively and efficiently. The problem solving steps include as below:

Identifying the problems, identifying current successes and strengths, analyzing the causes of the problems, identifying the factors that enable our success, envision our desired future, treating the problems, innovating to build more support for those factors that enable success and move us toward the future we desire. For example, whether or not a team is able to sell the big picture and engage in effective strategic planning depends on members' feeling hoping and looking toward a positive future. By appropriate , they mean information that is realistic and timely information that is true and relevant to the situation. Negative information is approriate when it provides the specific boundaries within which a challenge must be met.

In an economic tightening scenario, for example, appropriate negativity might include a target budget reduction amount and time frame. It might also include recognition that staff and elected officials will have to make hard decisions. Hence, in new micro economic theory, it mains to help organizations to find to avoid target budget exceeds to any projects implementations and avoid prolong time to finish any projects for any organizations, less spending and time reducing or raising efficiency and effective achievement will be applied new nicro economic theory to help any organizations to be applied new micro economic theory to help any organizations to achieve benefits (intangible , i.e. reducing time and raising efficiency, tabgible , i.e. less salaries spending and project team members number to any projects).

Hence, new micro economy theory aims to research new organizational behavior can achieve raising efficiency and improving productivities aims. For graphic organizers theory aims to help organizatins to enhance any organizations members' thinking skills by encouraging brainstorming, generating new ideas, connecting parts to the whole, drawing sequence, analyzing causes and effects etc. There are exactly important traits of economic students to make sense out of economic phenomena and to make effective decisions about economic issues. Thus, in new micro economy view to organizations. It explains that every organizational member ought be independent graphic organizer:

They will ought need to be enhanced skills to help that organizations to achieve any aim easily. They may include : organizations show events in chronological orders multiple timeline (sequential organizers), or hierarachy diagram (hierarchical organizers), such as organizers showing the relation between a concept and its subordinate levels of characteristics, ccyclical organizers (organizers showing the sequence of events in a process , e.g. circle organizer), conceptual organizers . (organizers showing how a mian concept is supported by facts, evidence and characteristics, e.g. concept definition map).

So, new micro economic thoery explains that every organizational memeber may explain that every organizational memeber may have different organizer role when they need to cooperate with other members in themselves organizations any time. When they know whether what their organizer role is in the time. They can make thinking strategy skill more easily in short time , it will bring any organizations much intangible economic benefits, such as reducing meeting time, avoiding over-spending and prolonging time to finish any projects for the organization efficiently.

● Division of labor theory

The another new micro economy theory is divison of labor, organizational coordination and market mechanisms in collect time, problem solving skills. It is a view of economic organizations as problem-solving driven by trial -and error learning and collective selection. It assumes any one economic organization ought produce " well constructed" goods and services, achieves productivity among workers and solving problems by technological search and economic production activities raising skills, the most cheap and the most useful function in order to raising the product productivities and quality improvement.

● Logical process theory

For logical process theory , it implies that most technologies and industries and born with a highly vertically-integrated structure, undergo a distintegration process as the industry grows in the expansion phase, and then re-integrate in the maturity phase, but often along integration proles that differ signicantly from those of the original infant industry. Thus, the degree of vertical integration of an industry undergoes major changes along its life cycle. For IBM computer company example, its needs to find any new product to make new market share, such as IBM electronic book publish will be on new technological product market. Due to ecommerce is popular, many readers began to accept to apply internet technological tool to read any books. So, IBM had attempted to sell electronic books in this new ecommerce e-book publishing market. So, IBM needs to expand its traditional computer sale market to (AI) artificial intelligent mobile and electronic book publish both markets. IBM's computer products has reached maturity phase, it needs to change its another new technological products market. It ought not follow its old logical process to continue research how to invent new computers. It ought change to research how to invent new (AI) mobiles and innovate its electornic book reading platforms to attract many electronic books attractively as well as invent new (AI) mobiles to attract many (AI) mobile users. If it still hopes to continue to win its computer competitions in technological product industry.

● Managerial economics

Another new economic theory is managerial economics, it means tha application of economic methods to the managerial decision making process. It is a fundamental part of any business. It is more attention in business as mergers become more aware of its potential as an aid to decision making, and this potential is increasing all the time. For example, global warming challenge will riase cost to our socity, how governments assess the possible scale of cuture green-house gas emissions, and hence of man-made global warming, involves economic forecasts and economic calculations. Those forecasts and calcualtions will provide the basic for poicy on environment pollution issue how to avoid future social cost raises in possible.

Hence, managerial economics may mean how managers find the most efficient way of allocating scarce resources ans reaching their objectives. It aims to predict and compare the cost and benefit may occur when the manager chooses to do the action. In a neoclassical framework, it treats the individual elements within the economy (consumers, firms , workers) as rational agents with objectives that can be expressed as quantitative functions (utilities and profits) that are to be optimized, subject to certain quantitative constraints.

What is the relevance of the managerial economic theory? For example, protesting against global capitalism that economics is of no use in answering the fundamental questions involving value judgements, like reducing pollution, indeed, economists themselves often admit that their science can only make positive impression of the limitations of economics. Hence, in managerial economic view, government should make use of market forces in order to achieve a more efficient solution.

In the terms of reducing pollution, would governments aim to reduce pollution by 90% in the next ten years? But rich and poor countries would suffer overall from a policy of reducing pollution by 90% and that future generations might not benefit either. So, managerial economic theory aims to let policy maker how to make the more reasonable analysis to conclude and to solve any issue for organization leader or government leader, even individual consumer.

● Social entrepreneurship theory

The final new economic theory is social entrepreneurship for each country, regardless of its socio and economic development, one of the main key indicators of success is the social stability of society. Impossibilty of market and government, are the factors that contribute to the need of social enterprise that provides partical and dynamic solution for local social problems. This social innovation form an environment that promotes scientific, technical , technological and informational innovations increase efficiency of new techniques and technologies reduce innovation costs. So, the new economic theory explains society needs to change. So, social entrepreneurship is needed because society is needed to innovate that serves to adopt social changes and development.

Some economists believe that social enterprise is a new way to solve social and economic problems and focus of social innovation and brings positive change to society. In any one social entrepreneurship, it needs coordinational strategy for the development of social entrepreneurship .So, every one is stakeholder to the social entreprenership. Thus, today a significant theoretical basis for this new economic theory , " social entrepreneurship" concept in the new economic model is formed . Consequently, social entrepreneurship is an innovative form of business, which successfully combines social aims and commercial practice .

Consequently, social entrepreneurship is a innovative form of business, which successfully combines socail aims and commercial practice. Social entrepreneurship ought may solve these social challenges, such as unemployment, poverty, skillful workers number shorten . However, socail entrepreneurship works where the government can not work , due to the lack of funding, and the business does not want to become of low profit ability.

Hence, social entreprensurship is a charity and business approaches to solving social problems. Also unlike traditional business that works for the seeking profit only , social enterprise, performs social functions and works where the government can not work , due to the lack of funding , and the business does not want to become of low profitability. Social enterprise changes the traditional economy model, it does not depend on external sources (donors, grants and donations) , the necessary start up capital , receives income from its own activities. It carries on non-profit activities. It includes socio-oriented structure, the goal of activity is to mitigate or solve the specific social problems. Consequently, profits are reinvested in activity expansion or for social purposes in case of charity organization there is no profit and in traditional business the profits share between shareholders.

New economic development in Tourism and oil industries

● How to develop new economic tourism industry

How to develop tourism industry in new economic environment? Any examination of the new economic development of travel and tourism requires definitions of the subject and its components, which are suitable for economic analysis. However, in new economic development to tourism industry, it is also important to look at tourism conceptually, in order to set the scene for a deeper understanding of the future new tourism industry development.

Tourism is neither a phenomenon nor a simple set if industries, however, in new or old economic development environment. It is a human activity which encompasses human behavior, use of resources, and interaction with other people, economies and leisure enjoyment environment. It is also involved physical movement of tourists to locales other than their normal living places.

In future new economic environment, traditional travel needs to include these element in order to satisfy traveler enjoyment and leisure feeling: They may include: Tourist needs and motivations, tourism selection and behavior and constraints , travel away from home , market interactions between tourists and those supplying products to satisfy tourist needs and impacts on tourists , hosts, economies and environments.

In new economic environment, the tourism products may include: carriers, in any forms of transport for tourist travel accommodation, man-made attractions, which could also include the managed areas of natural attractions, private sector and public sector support services, middlemen, such as tour wholesalers and travel agents.

The tourism resources may also include: Natural resources, lands , minerals, water and biological; labor resources, human work, and enterprise; capital resources, manmade enhancement and other resources. The travel and tourism resources problems may include: As there is frequently a mismatch between producer and consumer perception of what constitutes the tourism product , there may be conflict in ideas of which resources are properly involved as well as many of the resources likely to be in demand for tourism are public goods , or even free resources.

In new economic development to tourism industry view, we need to consider that tourism and travel has the reputation of being a relatively clean and pleasant industry in which to work or invest in order to attract a greater number of resource suppliers than as less well-perceived industry, which therefore keeps rewards prices down by competition, how to attract those retiring from or travel business for example, if their finances are already sound, income from travel is not expected to be optimal , travel and tourism is frequently highly seasonal , offering rewards that are competitive with other industries only some of the time, destination products are often in locations which are of little use to other industries, so that competition for resource use if minimal and hence rewards are low.

In general, tourist purpose may include: recreational purpose : holiday, health and sport and religion as well as business purpose: company business , e.g. conventions and sales trips. So, in new economic tourism development aim, tourism industry need consider hoe to achieve incentive trips to let these both tourists to feel. For example, the overall type of tourism required, destination arrangement, travel mode, accommodation and attraction visiting and purchasing method or distribution channel. The purchasing method choices may include: whether to buy an inclusive package or separate service, whether to buy direct from suppliers, such as airlines or hotels or use an agent , which tour wholesaler or operate or agent to use.

I predict the tourism development in new economic view, it may have these characteristics: Few enterprises in travel and tourism are large, highly cashed-up and have a large asset base, enterprises within travel and tourism that are not in a financial position to diversify, and those do well success to the above —average growth obtainable in travel and tourism compared with many other industries, they would therefore tend to expand within the sector. The result of individual enterprise growth and integration within travel and tourism is an increase in the concentration of that industry. The degree to which output is produced of fewer and fewer enterprises. This can be only be accounted for realistically with the context of an individual economy, Levels of concentration in any part of travel and tourism in the future are likely to depend on two opposing factors: The constant demand by many tourist market segments for new experiences and products, which encourages the development and survival of more and diverse enterprises, and therefore leads to the reduction of concentration as well as technology, which in travel and tourism frequently calls for large capital outlays and requires mass markets for efficient use, promotes integrations and large scale enterprise, especially in air travel and non-personal services (marketing and information communication, travel insurance , tourism payment methods). IN these areas, concentration will undoubtedly increase in future new economic development environment.

● How new economic development in oil industry

The future global economic growth, it will influence personal incomes and GDP rise. They would carry different weight in different countries at different times. Starting from low levels of incomer and economic development. Household consumption will change from being dominated by basic heat to rapidly rising energy use for higher levels of comfort in space heating and cooling (and large dwellings), and greater use of electrical appliances, finally to a degree of saturation influenced by the income distribution patterns of the country concerned. Income distribution typically .changes very slowly, so that the technical market for heart will never be saturated because there will always be a proportion of poor people living in small spaces less comfortably than the average. Industrial energy consumption will be influenced by technical efficiency within each sector, and by changes in the structures of the economy, e.g. changing proportions of agriculture, heavy and light industry, and services. One may eventually see evidence of diminishing marginal returns to additional energy inputs compared to other inputs. Energy consumption in the energy transformation sector may be influenced by income, which drives the demand for electricity to influenced by income, which drives the demand for electricity to grow faster than the demand for heat, but is also subject to the chosen technology of transformation, which is influenced by the cost and availability of primary energy inputs (fuels) in new economic development environment.

IN new economic development environment, it will influences that fuels do not compete in all sectors; for example, the transport sector is dominated by oil. Nuclear and hydroelectric power (and most renewables) reach the user through electricity; electricity itself competes with the direct burning of fossil fuels. Electricity provides the means by which other fuels can compete with oil and gas in sectors, such as space heating and process heat. It also is the only means of powering applications such as motors, computers and lighting: these subsectors are difficult to analyze. However, there is strong evidence that higher incomes do not weaken the demand for electricity so much as the demand for energy in total (in contrast to the effect on the demand for non-electric energy forms).

Econometricians look at the historical record of change in fuel prices and quantities to distinguish several factors between the new economic development and old economic development to oil industry in the future. An income effect. Increasing (reducing) fuel prices reduces (increases) the purchasing power of consumers' income: higher incomes caused by lower prices will increase energy consumption; the consumers' allocation of the increased income to energy purchases may reduce as income rises. Thus income may be heading in a different direction from fuel prices that the effect of fuel price changes when incomes are rising means simply that rising incomes have increased demand. Reducing the cost of using energy through win-win efficiency measures causes a similar problem . On the consequence, in future new economic development environment, it may influence in both cases demand will be less than if the future oil price or efficiency has not changed. The other effect is that an efficiency or substitution effect. An increase in fuel prices may cause consumers to spend more on new equipment, building materials and management operations, which will reduce the amount of fuel required to give the same energy result to the user. The extent of the efficiency effect depends on what happens to the price of the new equipment or building: if those price s rise in line with the fuel price, changes in the balances between fuel and capital or management will not occur. A new user technology , such as the development of the combined cycle gas turbine generator may increase efficiency and thus greatly reduce the quantity of primary fuel needed to produce the required output in this case electricity. If electricity prices had remained sticky, and the electricity and gas markets were not competitive, some of this advantages could have accrued to the gas suppliers in the form of an increase in price, because th4 unit of gas produces more output of electricity, it would have a higher value. In reality, the development of new economic competitive environment in both gas and electricity has tended to ensure that the benefits of such technical advanced accrue to the consumer through lower final prices. The same many apply in the case of improved efficiency in future non-manual driving auto vehicle development: the consumer's cost of motoring is reduced in new economic non-manual driven auto vehicle (Artificial intelligent vehicle) can replace manual driven vehicle , even electricity battery can replace oil energy to be used in vehicles. So, oil price may be influenced to reduce in future new economic development environment.

New and old economic theories explain oil is not main factor

to influence tourism income

● Can economic theory explain old price change to influence tourism income?

I shall attempt to apply old and new economic theory to explain whether oil changing price has direct relationship to influence global tourism indusry development or tourism income as below:

Is oil changing price the main to influence tourism income or tourism development or economic growth ? If oil price rises ar falls, it will or won't cause tourism income decreases or increases? If they have cause and effect relationship, what are the main factors to influence tourism income changes by oil price rises or falls ?

I aim to investigate how any why among oil price shocks will influence tourism income variables. We may distinguish between these oil price shocks: Supply-side , aggregate demand and oil specific demand shocks. I assume that oil specific demand shocks affect inflation and the tourism sector equity index. By constrast, I also believe that aggregate demand oil price shock exercisr an effect, either directly and indirectly tourism generated income and economic growth. So, in old economic theory, supply-side , aggregate demand view to oil specific demand shocks will influence tourism income varies. So, governments ought implement strategies against future oil price movements or plan for economic policy development.

In fact, instead of oil price changes will influence tourism income, it could also harm economic growth and tourism activities, due to the effect they expert on transporation, production cost, economic uncertainty.Because tourism activities is one important sector to influence any country's leisure consumption GDP income source. So, sudden fluctuations in oil prices may also influence economic growth. It is based a hyphthesis known as the tourism led economic growth. So, it seems that they have direct or indirect relationship to case effect between oil price and tourism activities and development. So, increase on tourism income, the called " economic-driven tourism growth". In addition, high oil prices are affecting certain tourism industry segments , e.g. airlines, cruises lines, hotel, rent travelling car services etc. for oil, importing countries example, with reference to macro economic effects, higher oil prices generally lead to higher inflation, when they negatively influence to country's income.

Hence, from a micro-economic perspective, positive oil price shocks lead to a decline in disposable income. for low income people, it will bring an immediate and negative impact on tourism, mainly due to they feel tourism leisure is regarded as a luxury good, when oil price shocks to rise suddenly . It influences any airline or cruise entertainment service providers' costs are influenced to raise. Then, they need to increase air ticket or cruise ticket price. It will bring on negative tourism leisure demands-side the oil price increases low income group, potential tourism leisure consumers. Hence, it seems that oil price may have indirect relationship to influence tourism leisure consumers' needs.

● How the price of oil changes influences global tourism industry growth or recession?

In macro-economic view, sudden mid and long term oil price shock can influence global torusim industry growth or recession. For example, a oil price of US$180 per barrel was considered only a few years ago, now this has a realistic scenario to which all plaers in the T&T sector have to adapt. At such a high level, the price of oil will become even more critical to almost every part of the tourism value chain. Although, weak global demand, caused by global economic recesson, resulted in a steep oil price decline to US$45 per barrel by the fourth quarter of 2008 in the past low oil price occurrence history, this won't change the mid to long -term oil forecast.

In fact, the past oil price occurrence history of the dramatic structural had changed a high price imposed on airlines, travelers, and destination countries, all of which will have to navigate through times of shifting or even declining travel demand. I assume that a high oil price scenario is assumed in the long term in order to highlight the changes , such a senario would mean for consumer behavior and the competitiveness of several destinations.

Low oil price in the 1970 and early 1980 did not bring significant growth of international air travel, but its growth has been strongest between 1980 and 2004, a period with stable and relatively moderate oil prices. Also, the rapid development of the low-cost carrier business model in the 1990s further fueled air travel growth by capturing tourism leisure demand , such as weekend leisure travel to cities using mostly secondary airports in any big area countries, such as UK, US . However, the tourism growth is whole influenced by high oil prices, due to oil price had been continue rising in possible.

Basis of oil is shortage supply product, oil is assumed to be the main energy source for the aviation sector for the nest 30 years. Although, second-generation biofuels seem to be on the horizon, the economics as well as the production scalability and aviation biofuel shortage will be a main challenge to airline industry. So, I assume that oil price will continue rise up, if there have none any aviation biofuel can be reflected to oil to use for air plane energy.

Until 2004, the only factors to have affected air travel growth, negatively were in external shocks , such as 9/11, causes catching air plane crisis or US regional geopolitical conflicts. It brings some travelers feel fear to go to US travel, as well as until recently 2019, human mouth disease can influence air to have disease to anyone from mouth. So, global travelers number had been continue decreasing, because they are fear to get disease by air when many themselves every stranger travelers are sitting on the without windows air planes. Although, mouth human and air disease and US 9/11 air attack both matters may influence oil price falls effect, because air planes flying times will reduce. They won't need frequent to fly, to cause aviation oil energy need reduce. Consequently, oil price will decrease, due to travelers number reduces and air planes flying times are also influenced to reduce. (oil demand decreases cause oil price decrease). Although, air lines ' cost will also be influenced reduce, but oil price decrease can not bring travelers number increase , when air ticket price reduce because global many leisure and business trip travelers feel fear to catch air planes frequently when human mouth air disease occured in 2019. So, oil price decreases can not grow up tourism industry growth or rise tourism income.

However, the obvious impact of a high oil price is an increase in the operating costs of airline. Moreover, fuel cost as a percentage of airline operating costs vary significantly based on the length of the flight. The longer the flight, the higher the fuel costs as a percentage of the airline operating cost. So, from an online's perspective, long -hauel flights represent the most criticial challenge to profitable operation because the share of fuel on these flights, compared with other cost items, is largest, because of the unfacorable fuel economics, due to fuel costs even at high-load factors. For example, Thai airways dropped its non-stop Bongkok to US flights in the summer of 2008 for commercial reasons, because fuel reached operating cost levels of 55 percent on this route, a cost burden that could not be passed on to their customers. So, the estimated price elacticity of passengers demand at this Bongkok to US flights route is high, if Thai Airways rises less air ticket price, it will influence many travelers to choose other airlines to catch air plan to fly. Hence, due to Thai Airways can not make decision to rise air ticket price, because it believes that it will lose many travelers, so it only chooses to drop this non-stop Bongkok to US flights to avoid fuel cost rising economic loss.

However, although micro and macro economic theories may also that oil price variable or change, it may influence global tourism income. But, recently, on 2019, human mouth and air diseases, it can influence global individual leisure and business trip travelers feel fear to catch air plans to avoid their bodies get this kind of death sickness when they sit in the no fresh air supplying air planes. They feel that they reduce leisure travelling flying times or business trip flying times with strange travelers to sit in crowd air planes together. Then, they must many avoid human moth and air disease to avoid death crisis. Hence, in this global human mouth and air diseases threat environment occurrence, even oil price sudden reduces to low price, it brings airline's cost reduces and air ticke price reduces. However, when air ticket price reduce to be very cheaper, it can not still attract global many leisure or business trip travelers to buy air tickets to fly frequently. Why does air ticket reduction, it can not attract many leisure or businee trip travelers to buy air ticket to fly ? The main reason is because human mouth and air disease influences global many travelers feel fear to catch air planes frequently. In psychological view, this kind of human mouth and air sickness will bring long time negative influence to global traveles do not want to catch air planes for business trips or travelling leisure frequently. So, it implies that oil price changing to influence air ticket price reduction factor ought not main factor to influence tourism income. It may include traveler individual negative emotion psychological factor, such as human mouth and air disease or 2019 9/11 attack both cases, they can influence global travelers feel fear to catch air planes to fly to avoid death threat. So, oil changing price ought not be only one absolute main factor to influence global tourism income significantly.

On conclusion, in economic view, it seems that oil chang price may have indirect or direct relationship to influence tourism income, instead of some unpredicted external environment factors influence, such as US 9/11 attack crisis and human mouth and air disease factors, they may be main factors to influence travellers number to reduce in non-economic external unpredicted environment view.

International war and illness factors influences tourism industry experiences decline cycle stage

1.1 Can wars impact global economy threat?

    1.1.1 How did First World War influence Europe economy and tourism industry declines ?

Can wars bring either advantages or disadvantages or both to impact our economy growth ?In history, I feel that international war can influence any country's economy development has either positive or negative impact in possible.

On the inflationary hand, for the First World War economy growth influence example, in the First World War and since most notably the German hyperinflation of the 1920 year, this type of monetary regime shows a far smaller tendency towards inflation. In the First World War period, volatility of inflation and output were higher in the short run. So, First World War had little negative impact to influence world inflation in the war period. However, in the First World War period, the supply of money was determined not by the rates of economic growth only, but by the amount of available gold and could not be adjusted in response to economic needs. So, new sources of gold would increase money supply and inflation and decrease interest rates , the opposite of what modern central banks would do to provide stable economic growth in First World War. So, it explained that the First World War occurrence caused the change from non-inflationary to inflationary long term development. Thus, it seems First World War brings more money supply and gold supply to stable economic growth in the future long term period.

On the labor productivity influence hand, leaving monetary issues aside, the First World War created the working time intellectual mood to change labor productivity, it would be a 15-18 hours working week for more enlightened leisure to Europe labors. Some prominent modern economists on the accuracy of the predictions on GDP growth per capital was remarkably accurate given to be fallen down that it was made at the time when economy growth theory did not even exist in the First World War period. Thus, it seems First World War also causes working time to be raised to the developing countries during the industrialization period. Then, the long time working time brought to the developing countries' workers to it is poor for labor health. Hence, although employers can raise productivity, but they need many workers to work long time to cause unhealthy. The majority found that the prediction on leisure is of the variations between world regions , due to income level exist, making European variety of capitalism. So, the First World War caused income inequality within countries and between nation states, trends in working hours , world poverty and ever growing needs (consumerism) and the like. Thus, the developed western countries' workers can work lesser time to compare to the developing Asia countries' workers. Consequently, First World War brought negative impact to influence the developing Asia countries' worker unhealthy and physical and mental illnesses number had been increasing as well as it brought positive impact to influence the labor productivity had been increasing to the Asia countries' employers, due to their workers need to work long time every day.

It seems on the positive impact hand, that the First World War caused the inflation occurrence to bring more money supply and gold supply to be raised to influence global economic growth. But, on the negative impact hand, it also brought low working hours in European developed countries and high working hours to the Asia developing countries which are needed to do different occupations in developing countries as well as the income inequality caused unfair social challenge had also occurred in developed countries, such as Europe, UK, US etc. and developing countries, such as China, Japan, Korea etc . Thus, First World War had brought developed countries better economy development and better salary and less working hours to labors because Europe had reached the mature stage of industrialization to avoid labors who needed to work overtime. Otherwise, it had brought developing countries poor economy development and poor salary and labors need work long time to raise productivities.

In conclusion, it implied that the First World War had bought some bad influences to developing countries' economic system, e.g. social income inequality, working hours inequality, inflation and GDP per capita going down in the past Europe economic history development, but it also bought welfares to developed countries' European labor working time intellectual mood to change labor productivity, it would be a 15-18 hours working week for more enlightened leisure to Europe labors. So, it seemed to cause negative economic influence to developing countries, but it cause positive economic influence to developed counties during the First World War time.

● Can US poor economic consequences of war influence tourism industry growth?

What are the macroeconomic effects of US government spending on the war? I believe modern times are that the human cost military spending has created positive economic outcomes for the US economy. I shall indicate how the human costs of war influences positive economic outcomes for the US on these aspects which include: GDP, consumption , investment , inflation and income distribution aspects.

In fact, US heightened military spending can create employment additional economic activity and contributes to the military weapon development of new technologies, which can bring advantages into other industries in US. For long term economic influence, US military weapon research and development on creating employment would potentially have the same low cost economic benefit in US. For example, US economy had higher GDP growth in the Afghanistan and Iraq war period. Another benefit is that US had appropriate conditions for future growth after the Second World War great depression period. It was a sharp decline in income inequality and the trend in declining inequality standard after the Second World War great depression period. Thus, America's human cost military spending could bring indirect military weapon research and development on creating employment benefit and it would potentially have the same low cost economic benefit in US. However, in the war period, the higher levels of government military weapon spending with war tends to generate some positive economic benefits in the short-term period, specifically through increases in economic growth during spending booms after war period.

Why it can bring GDP growth in the US war period. In general, by the end of World Ward II, US GDP was over 120 % and tax revenue increased more than three times to over 20% of GDP. However, GDP growth there was are increase in the trend lines after the war had finished when unemployment was eliminated, recovery was well underway prior to the war, are the key counterfactual is whether similar spending on US public works would have generated even more growth. However, US macroeconomic history over the past seventy years, that there are a number of negative economic effects from conducting any wars. But, there have also positive benefits of increases US government spending on military industry. Moreover, when an economy has excess capacity and unemployment , it is possible that increasing military spending can provide an important stimulus. When military and defense spending is important in providing security for the US nation as well as helping to support and protect US's national affect.

So, in war economic view point, it will bring this question: Is efficiency or justification for any particular macroeconomic effects of war spending for US? To answer this question, I shall suppose security is not only dependent on an adequate military capability , but security can also keep on economic stability. For example, price controls strategy and rationing strategy had a significant role to play to influence consumption in US, during war period. For example, it was difficult for household to purchase products , such as washing machines, irons or water heaters because the raw resources, e.g. steel and production capabilities are needed to be used to produce military weapons instead of these products effort to prepare to fight the enemy in the Second World War. So, the raw resources, e.g. steel price will be rasied, due to shortage to supply to produce the home consumer products , Then, it will bring the home consumer products price to be raised. So, war will bring negative impact to influence home consumer product prices to be raised, due to shortage of steel resources supply when they are supplied to produce weapon to win enemy in war period. Consequently, In war period negative resource shortge hand, as the same time, the war production board was able to assign priorities to scare materials, such as rubber, steel and aluminum to ensure which went to production of the military, rather than to civilian products. In addition, wages were controlled and personal savings were encouraged through the purchase of war bonds which further limited the size of individual's disposable income during the Second World War period.

Moreover, in the war period, it also bring food price raising, due to food supply shortage and poor living standrd to poor people, even rich people. Due to people were also encouraged to conserve food and produce as much of that own food as possible because food items were generally scare. Freezes were also stayed for wages. Combined with a general reduction in consumption, it can be said living standards for whose already employed, at least in material terms did not improved , even to rich people. It means that war will influence people quality of life to be fallen down. Even, in terms of total GDP. Such as World War II (WWII) did not create a permanent increase or change in the growth the trend after the war had ended. However, the positive lasting effort for WWII was a more even distribution of wealth. This reallocation of income created the ideal conditions for the formation of an advancement consumer economy till to nowadays.

However, on war long time influence hand, the WWII influenced US economy to be changed to be better, such as material well being was affected by tax increases, new price and wage controls which constrained private sector consumption and investment is encouraged, due to World War II had destroyed the traditional material development, so it also encouraged new investors to invest to any Asia or Europea new businesses.

● Can war economy policy influence peace and security?

I believe war economics policy may contribute to international peace and security as positive impact more than negative impact. The reasons are as below:

A first positive attitude behavioral possibility , any war economic policy can increase international interdependence through trade and finance raises the potential costs of war to a degree that makes welfare an irrational option of foreign policy can raise economic growth and builds good trading relationship between countries. Moreover, the use of superior economic and military power to harm an actual or potential aggressor's economy and make it stops preparing of waging war, e.g. US restricted Mexico imported to itself country, US invented military weapons to threaten to Korea to avoid nuclear war occurrence. In the past, US spent to military expenditure which could rise to employ soldier numbers to reduce unemployment as well as assisted military weapon manufacturers needed to employ many manufacturing workers to manufacture many military weapons for US government military fighting need.

Hence, the relationship between war and economy will bring this basic question: Whether either can economics provide a growing tool for avoiding war or whether may consumption for resources and markets result in an increased likelihood of war? Following the increase of international trade and financial transfers in modern times. However, there has been a growing to concern the economic wisdom of war.

Liberal economists oppose the idea that war might be a good business and advocated the promotion of peace and advocated the promotion of peace by international economic links among the different countries. Although, history has shown that enlightened economic self-interest was not always alike to contribute to the ultimate avoidance of war. But, a short overview of the liberal peace theory indicates, it takes a look at the amount ability of economic instruments as a means to enforce peace by an economically superior country or group of countries, e.g. within the framework of the United Nations or of regional organization for security and cooperation in Europe, the African Union or the organization of American States.

1.1.4 How civil wars influence positive or negative impact to traveler leisure needs?

On country itself civil war negative impact hand, what is the impact of civil wars on economic growth at domestic and in nearby countries? Some economists believe civil war can have a profound negative influence on the economic fortunes of a country or its neighbors, e.g. owing to a loss of human capital, a destruction of infrastructure and reductions in investment and trade and daily market activities. Within the period of measurement have economic consequences , the economists scale the civil war variable to be better identify their relative impacts. They indicate the distance between countries which is a factor provides the most accurate measure of the negative economic consequences of civil wars on other countries.

On country itself civil war positive impact hand, in economic view point, the country itself civil war indicates the income and capital input terms. Since, everything is in per capita terms. Due to civil war encourage technological development. Technology changes are in the investment in labor effectiveness. The capital includes physical and human capital . How civil war influences efficiency growth . The growth in labor's enhanced efficiency is from technology change and capital depreciation. So, anything that can raise labor growth or its improved efficiency, increases the denominator or capital per capita and so reduced its growth and that of incomer per capita. Depreciation or the gradual wearing down of capita; through use or age also limits capital growth. Some economists suggest that war migration is a good growth of labor to influence the immigration country's economic growth. For example, the inflow of refugees from a nearby civil war can lead to in-migration and adversely affect income per capita growth. Migration may , however, influences the in-migration country economic growth if the migrants bring in human capital, due to civil war.

Consequently, from a theoretical perspective, civil wars can adversely affect income per capita growth at home through a number of avenues. So civil war will cause bad influence to home country, the reasons are as below:

The reasons include:

First, a civil conflict can destroy physical and human capital. Second, by the international trade flows, and day-to-day marketing activities, civil wars can inhibit growth. Third, civil wars may divert the inflow of foreign direct investment (FDI) owing to heightened perceived risks of investors. Because (FDI) perceived is an imported source of savings that finances investment. So, a fill in FDI results in reduced growth. Heightened instability and risks will also limit investment at home and cause a flight of savings abroad. Fourth, civil wars cause indirect government defense expenditures from productive social overhead capital e.g. roads, public schools and bridges, gardens to less productive defense spending. Fifth, such wars may cause the internal displacement of people as their homes either come under serious control or are destroyed. So that income per capita is adversely influenced. Sixth, civil wars often result in the breakdown of the health lead to lack of medical care, less clean drinking water and reduced sanitation , all of which have negative consequences on economic activities and growth .

Thus, any country itelf civil war can bring negative impacts more than positive impacts. Due to economic impacts may even increase further from some conflicts as nearby countries reduce trade with others in the regions and potential investors brand , even non-neighboring countries have as poor investment risks. Thus, there are four potential channels , such as human capital, physical capital, labor growth and an intercept shift are influenced by civil wars as well as which can influence income per capita growth in other nearby countries. To conclude, neighboring countries need to concern how to avoid civil war is caused to occur among themselves because civil wars will have negative impact to influence their economic growth.

● How economic positive and negative impact of the war to higher military spending?

Most models show that military spending to divert resources from productive uses, such as consumption and investment , and ultimately slows economic growth and reduces employment. So, it seems war causes disadvantages more than advantages to influence economy growth to any countries in possible.

Some economists showed global insight produced a set of projections that compared a scenario with an increase in annual military spending equal to 1.0% of GDP current about $135billions relative to its baseline scenario . This is approximately equal to the increase in defense spending that has taken place compared with the pre-Sept. 11th terrorism Iraq war baseline to US government higher military spending. However, who also indicated military spending is not generally perceived to cost jobs.

In standard economic models, war its positive impact can be thought of in the same way as spending on the environment from war bad influence. When tax and emission restrictions are often used to achieve environment protection during and after war. It is also possible to reach environmental targets by paying people to do things that will reduce pollution. For example, it is possible to reduce greenhouse gas emissions by paying people to buy more fuel efficient cars and appliances, or paying than to install insulation and other energy saving devices. So, during the war period, more greenhouse gas fuel efficient cars will increase demand in car market. Thus, war can reduce air and water pollution cost and encourage greenhouse gas fuel consumption. In the case of both increased military spending and paying people to take steps to reduce greenhouse gas emissions, resources would be reduced to supply to these countries' domestic market directed uses.

In standard economic models, war it's negative impact to this redirection of other resources, due to the original resources are used to increase military spending to manufacturing any new weapons and it will cause this original resources are shortage to prepare for these countries' manufacturing countries. So, these resources shortage challenges will cause these military spending countries' economy to operate less efficiently and therefore lead to slower growth and fewer jobs supplies. Thus, war will bring resource shortage challenges and fewer jobs supplies bad influence. In policy debates, it is important to recognize the potential jobs losses are caused from military spending factor mainly. Also the potential economic costs are often a factor in debates over environment policy.

Due to war causes the military countries' air and water pollution challenges. So, the military countries' wars occurrence will raise the water and air pollution cost of chance. It is often believed environmental pollution challenge has relationship between wars and increases in military spending. So, in this way, any country is carrying on military spending is comparable in most models to any other form of any country's spending, such as spending on public products or improving the environment pollution expenditures. Thus, it seems war will bring environment pollution economic cost more than environment protection economic benefit to any military expending countries.

Country itself internal civil war influences

2.1 The relationship between country itself internal civil war and human welfare

2.1.1 How internal civil war influences human welfare?

Nowadays, a growing number of economists and political scientists often ask this simple question: Why there is so much civil wars in any country itself the world? Poverty is commonly held to be a leading cause of internal wars. Indeed, it has close relationship between low per capita incomes and higher propensities for internal war's countries. Such as developing country Africa, it has many times more internal wars. So, it brings poverty and low living standards and poor health and poor air and water pollution environment to let African to live. Then, hunger and disease will also be caused easily in Africa.

However, internal civil wars also bring negative influences to developed countries, such as Australia, US Canada, UK , Japan, Korea etc. countries. The reason is because the internal civil war counties which refugee flows will choose to immigrate to those developed countries. Such as developing countries, South Korea and Africa and India , there have many times more internal civil wars .So it brings poverty and low living standards and poor health and poor environment to let African , South Korean, Indian to choose to live to these developed countries. Then, hunger and disease will be caused easily in developing and developed both countries, due to developed countries permit these developing countries' refugee who immigrate to themselves countries to live from internal civil war counties refugee immigration easily.

Moreover, internal civil war can also influence developed countries, such as Australia, US, Canada , UK refugee flows will choose to immigrate to these developed countries lawlessness as well as the illicit trades in drugs , arms and minerals will appear into these developed countries neighboring conflict zones . The destructive consequences of internal civil welfare may be a great as to potentially be a factor in the growing gap between the world's richest and poorest nations.

2.1.2 Can internal civil wars influence the country's long run economic development to assist tourism industry experience growth cycle stage?

Has it relationship between long run economic growth and internal civil war? Some economists recommend that it focuses on impacts on capital and population, the basic of economic production and whether the internal civil war country is possible rapid recovery as well as the internal civil wars cause economic impacts which can also been found for human capital, including measures of education, nutrition, health and productivity to the internal civil war countries.

What are intenal civil war negative impacts? Some behavior economists had experimented one interesting research to indicate that any internal civil war country will reduce human resource productivity growth , will reduce overall GDP in possible. Their research indicated the internal war armed group leaders are most motivate citizens to be soldiers for their side. Participation becomes easier to motivate the lower is citizen's opportunity cost of fighting . So there models predict that the amount of citizens' time devoted to fighting increases as the returns to fighting rise relative to the returns to reduce human resources supply to society to assist enterprises to raise any productive activities.

Consequently, in economic view point, if the internal civil war countries citizen will be trained to be soldiers. Then, it will reduce citizen to do other occupations in the internal war period. Also, the internal civil war countries will reduce their citizen have time and effort to do other social occupations to assist countries' economy development in the internal civil war period. Moreover, the internal civil war countries citizen, such as human resource number will be shortage to supply to satisfy their countries' enterprises' needs in the internal civil war period. It will influence economic growth to be go down during the internal civil war period to the internal civil war countries for either short term or long term. Even, the natural resource supply, e.g. water, food, vehicle gas etc. will be concentrate on spending to satisfy the soldiers' needs. It will cause natural resource shortage to supply to satisfy to citizen's life needs daily in the natural civil war period. So, the internal civil war will bring disadvantage to influence economic growth to the internal civil war countries.

2.1.3 How can reduce the risks of the civil internal war to influence economy growth and cause traveler individual tourism need reduces?

How can reduce the risks when internal civil war occurs in the country? What factors explain variations in the duration of civil internal wars, and why should policymakers care? I shall suppose to the duration of civil internal wars , which should be implicated in their destructiveness to the civil internal war country as well as long time duration of civil internal wars should have long time poor economic influence to the civil internal war country.

At any given point in a civil internal war, the civil internal war country government (A) and the civil internal war country rebels(B) each must choose between stopping or continuing to flight.

This implies four possible outcomes from their joint decisions at any time.

The first outcome is that if (B) continues flight and (A) stops, (B) wins and the government (A) is overthrown.

The second outcome is that if government (A) flights and (B) stops, (A) wins and the revolt is defeated (B) .

The third outcome is that if both (A) and (B) choose to stop flight at the same time, the civil internal war ends to be a negotiated settlement.

The fourth outcome is that if neither decides to stop, the civil internal war continues (Stam 1996 , 34-37).

Stam (1996, 353) again indicated the four outcomes can be represented as an two person game. Continued flight is the dominant strategy for both sides.

Thus, it seems negotiated settlement is the best solution to solve any civil internal war because it won't have either win or loss outcome to either of party, it will have win outcome to both countries.

In economic welfare view point, they will discuss how to earn the much economic benefits to achieve the reasonable negotiation fairly. It is a two parties win-to-win method to both supported government and not supported government parties both. Because usually the cause of any internal civil war , due to the not supported (disagreed) government party feel whose government is unfair to give reasonable and fair much economic welfare to them in society. So, they (part of citizen) only choose to cause internal civil war to let their country to know that who feel dissatisfactory at the time.

In economic view point, unfair resource allocation challenge will cause any internal civil war easily in any country. Thus, it means that any country government ought to know when and how to allocate its limited resources to let its citizen to feel fair to use (spend) in society when resources are not shortage to supply to them to consume. Also, it means how to allocate (spend) limited resource to prepare any countries' citizen to enjoy to consume. So, it is one important question to any country government to concern if which wanted to reduce internal civil war occurrence chance on nowadays societies. Thus, it seems that any country itself internal civil war will bring disadvantages more than advantages to bring its tourism leisure industy experiences declines cycle stage easily in possible

Bibliography

Stam , A. C. 1996, Win, Lose or Draw: Domestic politics and the crucible of war . Ann Arbor: University of Michigan Press.

Economic recession or boom how influences consumer behavior when the business had been experiencing decline life cycle stage
● COVID -19 disease how influence businesses may experience either growing life cycle stage or decline life cycle stage.
Nowadays, we are facing global economic recession period, since COVID 19 human mouth disease effect can bring economic crisis. Can it influence businesses feel difficult to adapt how global economic recession change after their decline life cycle stage? However, the effects of COVID 19 spreading will have wider implication , not just on how economies function, but also on how consumers behave, across china, Asia-pacific and around the world. Another effect of China;s economic rise is its influence in the adoption and adaption to new technological invention to manufacture , e.g. manufacturing robotic products had sold to China factories to replace workers to manufacturer products. It also will influence many China manufacturing workers lose jobs, when many China factories apply manufacture robotics to replace them in nowadays economic recession period.
Considering the adoption of online-offline shopping and home online office tasks, they are influenced by COVID-19 human disease influence, it also influences on regional travel in China, even global travel income is also reducing, because many travelers feel afraid to catch air planes to avoid to get COVID 19 human disease when they are sitting in close window airplanes by air . HOwever, COVID 19 also influences global consumer behavior changes to online shopping, because many people are afraid to enter crowd shops to avoid get COVID 19 human disease easily. So global shops will lose many visiting shop consumers, if they do not decide to attempt to open online stores to let customers to apply internet to buy their products. So, COVID 19 human mouth disease induced changes in consumer behavior. Shop online will be one new trend to influence young and old consumers make shopping from online stores. They will enquire whether the kind of product is worth to choose to buy by social media, e.g. facebook, online post . Hence, COVID19 human mouth disease may influence global economic recession, but it also brings e-commerce boom chance, when many consumers are fear to enter any crowd shops , when they need to stay long time in any shops. Then, they get COVID 19 human mouth disease chance will increase. Hence, it will influence many customers reduce to visit shops times, but it also creates online-shopping new business model . For example, China families are renewing their joy in home cooking. Onlins cooking videos are helping with the discovery od new recipes, new

ways to create dishes , and new influences. So, opportunities are opening for more cleaning products, new ways to clean and new home hacks from online videos will bring global home consumers spend more time on their wellness or beauty routines ? So, COVID-19 disease also influences many families choose to cook dinner at homes at nght. Restaurants will lose many eating clients, because they are fear to enter restaurants to eat together to avoid to get COVID19 human mouth disease. But, it also creates home cooking products sale chance, e.g. rice cookers, dishes or any cooking tools because many families choose to cool at home. Hence, in some situation, economic recession will create new business chance , such as online store or rice cooker sale increases, they may be influenced in this COVID 19 human mouth disease occurrence environment.

Economic recession also influences business strategy changes. Many companies seem to be applying many aspects of a retrenchment approach , e.g. reduced fixed costs, narrower product offering, reduced staffs, but also there are some aspects of an investment approach which can be observed , because customers number will be influenced to reduce in economic recession environment. Companies have felt the robustness and quality of the approaches being applied had been allowed to decline. As a consequence of the challenges of a recession, urgent improvement have needed to be made because factories will reduce workers number to avoid salary expenditure spending more , but customers umber reduced in recession environment .

Hence, they will choose to buy manufacturing robotics to replace workers. If robotics can be improved to be proficient manufacture. Then, they won't need to buy many robotics to help them to replace to replace many workers to manufacture any products efficiently. So, manufacturing and improvement to robotics number demand may increase to any factories , e.g. vehicle manufacture, electronic products, e.g. computer hime cooking electronic products , e.g. rice cookers, heaters etc. products may be manufactured by manufacturing robotics. It creates the manufacturing robotic sale improvement quality chance in recession environment. It may impact on medium, or long term, it depends on how long time of recession. So, economic recession may bring robotic manufacture industry boom , when electronic products manufacturers need many improved robotics to replace workers in factries in order to reduce spending too much salaries expenditure in recession.

It is one external environmental factor to influence sudden manufacture robotic industry boom absolutely ,because electronic manufacturer's manufacturing robotic needs increases in recession environment. So, robotic manufacturers' strategy need to change , such as how to improve any manufacturers' needs in recession, e.g. manufacturing robotic product categories, market segments, geographic areas, core technologies, reliability , price, customisation, robotic manufacturing efficiency how to be improved of business.Change strategy to any manufacturing robotics manufacturers. So, recession may influence some kinds of manufacturing robotics' needs raise in robotic manufacturing market.

● How recession influences the role of advertising changes?

Advertising plays a key role in a dynamic economy. It may provide valuable information about products and services in an efficient manner, communicates client value, builds brand awareness and creates demand. However, when one country is experiencing recession, how it influences the country's businessmen spending on advertisement behaviors? Due to clients number reduces, a company usualy cuts come from the advertising budget than companies begin to cut back on advertiseing during an economic recession, they become less visible to the public because they predict clients number ought reduce next three months, even half year or one year. It depends on how long economt recession occurs. So, economic recession many impact any companies' advertising budget expenditure to be reduce . How much on the reduction on advertising budget expenditure, it depends on the company predicts how many clients number will reduce.However, due to advertising number reduces, it can influence consumer behavior changes indirectly.

In economic boom environment, consumers can watch to different kinds advertisement from television. Advertisement may bring positive alternative evaluation phase of biying decision-making process is bring exposed to buy several communication messages. In such an economic boom environment, any organizations may be clearly heard by the consumers, after any advertisement programs are broadcasted on television. Therefore, advertisemtn can persuade clients to choose to buy the kind of product after the kind of product advertisement is broadcasted from television absolutely.

However, when recession occurs, any companies; advertisement time is shortened , even number is reduced . Hence, they can not receive any client's positive or negative feedback immediately in short time afer advertisements are broadcasted from television . So, recession may influence advertisement time is shortened and number is rediced . On consequence, companies can not have any repsonse to know whether how market or customers' demand is changing to themselves products in shor time.

However, recession may bring worse advertisement effect to influence any businesses . On one hand, there is a negative economic recession environment because of the negative media reporting, these would be a decline in demand for the products and services and eventually companies would want to save more than they spend , But in the other hand, when the companies cut back advertiseing expenditures, they become less visible to public. Hence recession may influence many companies brand image will be lost, due to spending on advertisement expenditure wil reduce. Then, clients number may be influenced to reduce, because they can not watch the kind of product advertment from television home often.

When one country is encountering recession, how are the various components of household consumption affected ? How is the impact of the recesion distributed across socio-demographic group? How does the recession compare to previous recessions? When book will boom? In fact, any country's recession may impact consumer behavior changes, it depends on these factors: age, race, education and wealth groups resulted in a decline in consumption inequality. The rich group is the " wealth effect influence group" when recession comes, it may influence their wealth reduces, so their enjoyment dsires will be influenced to reduce, e.g. purchase expensive cars driving enjoyment desires, purchase expensive house living enjoyment desires. If one rich person loses jobs , it may influence him to spend less time to drive themselves cars, so consumption of gasline will be influenced to reduce.

Economic theory (e.g. consumer behavioral economic theory) predicts that when economic recession occurs, it will cause many businesses may experience decline cycle life stage rapidly, that link between income shocks and consumption has close relationship, such as rich person consumer group, if his income reduces, then he will buy less gas to drive himself car, even if he loses his job in recession environment, he will choose to sell his car to exchange cash. Hence, consumption may fall as a direct consequence of a fall in income induced by job loss, reduced hours or productivity and negative returns from assets, if there are long term changes to a household's econmic resource in recession environment. Hence, in recession environment, job loss or income reduction factors that may affect consumers and their shopping attitudes in the recession period. Otherwise, for low income group, recession may influence food consumption to low income consumer behavior changes to worse. Because low income person may reduce income ot lose job, then cheap food consumption will be influenced to worse to low income consumer group. In recession period, if the food price is raised , due to the cost increase of food, it will lead to change in the reductin on quantity and type of food being purchase to low income food buyers. This may lead to a reduction in the quantity of food consumed and/or the substitution of high-priced food for cheaper food, which is often less nutritous and of worse quality. Hence in recession perios, low income food consumers will consider whether the kind of food price has how much increase or decrease. They won't consider the quantity of food consumed for maintaining energy balance and the quality of food consumed for maintaining ample intakes of protains, fats and micronutrients, such as vitamins, minerals and trace elements on food issue. So, if the kind of food price reduced in recession period, it ought may attract many low income food consumers number, even its food nutritious is worse. Hence, if the kind of meat price can be reduced in recession , the cheap types of meat consumption to low income consumer may be increased, even its nutritious is worse to compare the recession occurs before period.

On conclusion, in either economic recession or boom period, in general, consumer behavior will be influenced to change. Some products may be influenced to have higher sale in recession period, e.g. home electronic rice cookers , due to COVID 19 human mouth disease influenced many households choose to cook dinner at home at ight. Otherwise, some products may be influenced to have lowr sale., e.g. expensive cars sale in recession period, many high income people may lose jobs or reduce salaries , then it will influence their car purchase desires to be reduced. But if COVID 19 human mouth disease has medicine to kill this kind of disease. Then, economy will boom, many households will choose to go to restaurants to eat dinner. The, the electronic rice cookers sale number may reduce, when they reduce time to cook at home at night. Hence, it explains why economic recession or boom period may have impact to influence consumer behavior in behavioral economic view.

CHAPTER VII

Tourism industry life cycle stage strategy

Our global tourism development had been developed from birth cycle stage to decline life cycle stage nowadays. From 1960 beginning, when airplanes were popular to be increased need to global travelers. Hence, from 1960 to 1970 is whole global tourism industry birth cycle stage. Till to 1971 beginning, many Asia, e.g. Singapore, Japan, China and Western, e.g. UK, UK etc. countries people, they have jobs to do ,and they have more extra money to prepare to choose any leisure activities. From 1971 to 1980, it is growth life cycle stage to global tourism industry. Many airplane manufacturers had been beginning to manufacturer many airplanes because they felt global traveler number would increase. In fact, in this ten years, global traveler number had been increasing every year. Then, from 1981 to 2019 this fourty years, it is global tourism industry nature life cycle stage. It means that every year travel number had been increasing more significantly to compare past. Also, many travelers feel need to travel every year. So, global travel tourism industry may reach the most top travel clients level in this fourty years. However, till to 2020 , due to COVD19 human mouth and disease occurrence, it influences global travelers feel fear to catch air planes to travel because this kind COVD 19 human mouth disease may cause lung disease from air. When many travelers are sitting in the close window air plane, if one person has ths kind COVD19 human mouth disease. The sick person may contact air to let the persons to breath to cause lung disease in possible in airplane. So, global travelers number is decreasing after 2019 . Also, it implies that tourism industry is facing decline life cysle stage.

It brings these questions: IS it right time to develop space tourism? Can space tourism help future tourism industry to re-grow its life cycle stage from nowadays decline life cycle stage? Can space tourism develop to nature stage from birth life cycle stage ? I shall attempt to give evidence to explain whether space tourism may be developed to let human has more one kind tourism . It may be future leisure new trend for travelers, instead of earth travel. Because one day earth tourism destination may not bring leisure interesting to global traveler, then space tourism may be attempted to replace this kind of travelling activity . So, space tourism is birth life cycle stage. However, our earth tourism may define moral tourism, nature tourism, green tourism, responsible tourism in future new travelling leisure trend.

It bring these questions: Can our future tourism industry meet the expectations with the terms " ecological tourist"? Which factors affect the product life cycle of eco tourism? Nature and green tourism may be our earth new kind of travel activities, when many young and old age travelers like to climb mountains, they feel life nature scene more than non-man made) nature scene in their journeys, they do not like to visit cities to travel. It is possible that they often work in offices, this office working factor may influence many travelers like green tourism in the future. So, green or nature tourism will be our future popular tourism leisure activities. It may influence nowadays our tourism decline life stage to re-grown to nature life cycle stage in possible in this COVD19 people mouth disease influential environment.

New economic development in Tourism and oil industries

● How to develop new economic tourism industry

How to develop tourism industry in new economic environment? Any examination of the new economic development of travel and tourism requires definitions of the subject and its components, which are suitable for economic analysis. However, in new economic development to tourism industry, it is also important to look at tourism conceptually, in order to set the scene for a deeper understanding of the future new tourism industry development.

Tourism is neither a phenomenon nor a simple set if industries, however, in new or old economic development environment. It is a human activity which encompasses human behavior, use of resources, and interaction with other people, economies and leisure enjoyment environment. It is also involved physical movement of tourists to locales other than their normal living places.

In future new economic environment, traditional travel needs to include these element in order to satisfy traveler enjoyment and leisure feeling: They may include: Tourist needs and motivations, tourism selection and behavior and constraints , travel away from home , market interactions between tourists and those supplying products to satisfy tourist needs and impacts on tourists , hosts, economies and environments.

In new economic environment, the tourism products may include: carriers, in any forms of transport for tourist travel accommodation, man-made attractions, which could also include the managed areas of natural attractions, private sector and public sector support services, middlemen, such as tour wholesalers and travel agents.

The tourism resources may also include: Natural resources, lands , minerals, water and biological; labor resources, human work, and enterprise; capital resources, manmade enhancement and other resources. The travel and tourism resources problems may include: As there is frequently a mismatch between producer and consumer perception of what constitutes the tourism product , there may be conflict in ideas of which resources are properly involved as well as many of the resources likely to be in demand for tourism are public goods , or even free resources.

In new economic development to tourism industry view, we need to consider that tourism and travel has the reputation of being a relatively clean and pleasant industry in which to work or invest in order to attract a greater number of resource suppliers than as less well-perceived industry, which therefore keeps rewards prices down by competition, how to attract those retiring from or travel business for example, if their finances are already sound, income from travel is not expected to be optimal , travel and tourism is frequently highly seasonal , offering rewards that are competitive with other industries only some of the time, destination products are often in locations which are of little use to other industries, so that competition for resource use if minimal and hence rewards are low.

In general, tourist purpose may include: recreational purpose : holiday, health and sport and religion as well as business purpose: company business , e.g. conventions and sales trips. So, in new economic tourism development aim, tourism industry need consider hoe to achieve incentive trips to let these both tourists to feel. For example, the overall type of tourism required, destination arrangement, travel mode, accommodation and attraction visiting and purchasing method or distribution channel. The purchasing method choices may include: whether to buy an inclusive package or separate service, whether to buy direct from suppliers, such as airlines or hotels or use an agent , which tour wholesaler or operate or agent to use.

I predict the tourism development in new economic view, it may have these characteristics: Few enterprises in travel and tourism are large, highly cashed-up and have a large asset base, enterprises within travel and tourism that are not in a financial position to diversify, and those do well success to the above –average growth obtainable in travel and tourism compared with many other industries, they would therefore tend to expand within the sector. The result of individual enterprise growth and integration within travel and tourism is an increase in the concentration of that industry. The degree to which output is produced of fewer and fewer enterprises. This can be only be accounted for realistically with the context of an individual economy, Levels of concentration in any part of travel and tourism in the future are likely to depend on two opposing factors: The constant demand by many tourist market segments for new experiences and products, which encourages the development and survival of more and diverse enterprises, and therefore leads to the reduction of concentration as well as technology, which in travel and tourism frequently calls for large capital outlays and requires mass markets for efficient use, promotes integrations and large scale enterprise, especially in air travel and non-personal services (marketing and information communication, travel insurance , tourism payment methods). IN these areas, concentration will undoubtedly increase in future new economic development environment.

HOW TO PROLONG TOURISM LEISURE MATURE LIFE CYCLE STAGE AS WELL AS AVOID DECLINE AND DEATH LIFE CYCLE STAGE OCCURENCE FROM COVID 19 HUMAN DISEASE

Any businesses expect to reach the mature life service cycle stage and they also hope to prolong to stay in this stage and avoid to have chance experience decline life service cycle stage, even death stage in future whole business life cycle stages. However, in fact, there are many businesses need to spend long time to have effort to reach mature life cycle stage from birth and growth both stages, even when they have effort to experience this the topest level stage, many can not stay to prolong time in this stage, then they will reach next stage, such as decline life cycle stage, even final death life cycle stage possibly. Hence , research whether how can reach the mature life cycle stage in short time and prolong to say in this stage. It is one common researching value question to any businesses. Such as COVID 19 human disease had been occurrence in 2019 end , it bring global tourism industry traveller number began to reduce. I shall attempt to explain how airline organizations implement strategies to avoid to enter decline service life cycle stage as below:

● How to avoid to reach the decline service life stage rapidly to global airlines tourism service industry due to COVID 19 human disease occurred

Strategies for growing and maturity a product or raise service performance, and increasing profit margins and prolonging to stay on the mature service life stage. I believe that it is any service businesses final aim. However, in any service life cycle stages, when the service , e.g. airline tourism leisure service industry will experience the decline service life stage , due to the COVID19 human disease influences to global travelers began to feel fear to catch airplanes to avoid air contact to give this kind of disease from 2020. So, nowadays, airlines ought have the suitable or right strategies to help them to solve travelers reducing number to influence their profit growth to encounter decline life service cycle stage later.

Life cycle strategy is based on product or service life cycle thinking from marketing, the factors may influence when the business can reach the mature life cycle stage, but some unpredicted factors may influence their clients number reduce, such as this airlines organizations traveler number reduces is due to COVID 19 human disease influences they feel fear to catch airplanes to travel case, their strategies may include: market growth rate, market growth potential, breach of service lines, number of competitor, distribution of market, share among competitors, customer loyalty , barriers to entry and technology improvement etc. factors to influence the global airlines tourism service industry can continue develop or expand to future overseas tourism market, when COVID 19 human disease may be killed by new medicine later.

Such as this COVID 19 human disease influences travelers feel fear to catch airplanes to avoid get this kind of disease and it influences global travelers number is decreasing in 2020 case, when the airline organization reaches the growth life service cycle stage from the birth stage, if it expects to spend short time to reach the mature life service cycle stage. Before COVID 19 human disease had not been killed by new medicine, if they hope to attract many travelers to choose to catch their airplanes to fly , the extension strategies that any airline organization can attempt to achieve, they may include, rebranding, establishing airline service in order to differentiate the other airline competitors tourism service , ticket price discounting and seeking new marketers, rebranding is the creation od a new look and feel for an established airline tourism service from the airline's competitors.

The airline service life cycle extension strategies also may include these methods to help the airline organization to grow or grow up or develop its airline tourism market rapidly, e.g. repackaging and new sizes, the appearance of airline tourism service can be crucial gaining a passenger's attention and developing tourism interest , new formulas or additional airline tourism features to the tourism country, lower ticket prices to maintain interest or liquidate surplus stock new airline tourism service advertising campaign, altering the new airline channel of destination, such as online ticket purchase.

Hence, after COVID 19 human disease had been skilled by new medicine , any airline organizations need to consider how to choose the most suitable strategy from different kinds of key strategies to expand their airline new tourism channels throughout the different airline tourism service life stages, in these four distinct stages: introduction, growth, maturity and decline or possible death stage, when this COVID 19 human disease had occurred from 2019 end, it may influence global travelers number had significant been reducing to bring any airline organizations may enter the decline life service cycle stage rapidly, even death life service cycle stage comes consequently.

Any airline organizations can use various marketing strategies in each stage to try to prolong the life cycle or attempt to reach the mature life cycle stage in short time. Avoiding to experience decline life service cycle stage, such as the COVID 19 human disease occurrence causes global travelers number began to reduce. It is ensure that any airline organizations do not expect to experience or reach the decline service life stage due to this COVID 19 human disease influences. The question is that how the airline organizations can maintain a strategy in the decline stage , such as COVID19 human disease influences global travelers number reduced and it brings many airlines income began to reduce, for example, reducing the airline promotional expenditure in this COVID 19 human disease occurrence period, reducing the number of airline distribution outlets , e.g. Hong Kong to New York airline flight channel reduces implementing ticket price cuts to get passengers to but the maintaining the airline tourism service and waiting for airline competitors to withdraw from the global airline tourism market.

Thus, following the initial growth, in this COVID human disease occurrence period, when the new airline organization enterprise enters the expansion stage during which the routing operation succeeds. The new airline organization can either reach the mature life service cycle stage either it can prolong to stay in this stage or it can not prolong to stay and enters to decline service life cycle stage , even death service life cycle stage. So , how to avoid the decline service life cycle stage comes to the new airline organization in this COVID 19 human disease occurrence period. It is any airline organizations concerning question when they are experiencing in the mature life cycle stage, but when COVID 19 human disease occurs to influence global travelers number began to reduce. May the airline organization experience the decline service life cycle stage rapidly when the COVID 19 human disease occurs ? It depends on whether it's strategies implementation are effective , its' strategies are effective, it may avoid to reach the decline life service cycle stage in short time easily due to COVID 19 human disease influences.

For this COVID 19 human mouth disease case , since 2019 had occurred, it brought serious tourism industry economic loss to any countries, many people loss jobs, many people feel fear to enter any shops when they are in crowd shop environment, e.g. restaurants can not permit to allow many people to sit closely, because when one person has COVID 19 human mouth disease, he can bring this disease to another person from air. So, many restaurants lose many clients in morning, lunch and night busy eating time, even ships also can not permit many people to enter their ships, because they avoid many people may contact, if one or some people has/have COVID 19 mouth disease, when he/she talks to the salespeople in the shop. It has high chance to cause many people get COVID human disease by mouth. So, any shops can not allow crowd in themselves shops to avoid any people have COVID 19 human disease occurrence. So, this COVID 19 human mouth disease may influence many businesses are experiencing decline life cycle stage, because clients number is continue decreasing, unless drug invention succeeds to fill this kind human mouth disease. Otherwise, on the consequence, many businesses will face death life cycle stage in short time possible. So, it is good example to explain unpredicted external environmental factor to bring global businesses will face decline life cycle in 2020 or next year, even after two years latter. So, COVID -19 human mouth disease may also influence any businesses had been experiencing long time in the mature life cycle to change to decline life cycle stage in possible.

Instead of the businesses are experiencing in either birth or growth life cycle stage. for example, UK Cathay airline had been experiencing long time in the mature life cycle stage from 2000, when its clients number had been increasing, but when the end of 2019, COVID-19 human mouth and air contact disease had occurred in global to influence any people feel fear to catch airplanes to travel or business travel frequently, due to airplanes have none windows, its none window environment will bring COVID-19 disease to any passengers when the airplane has many passengers are sitting together closely, if anyone has COVID-19 disease, he will cause any one airplane service waiter, passenger , even pilot to have COVID-19 disease easily.

So, global airline industry is experiencing decline life cycle stage. even Cathay airline is one big UK developed airline , it's passengers number is large in the past, but when COVID-19 disease occurs to cause travelers number had been decreasing. Hence, Cathay airline is experiencing decline life cycle stage from mature life cycle stage. It needs to implement dismissing staffs to keep salaries expenditure reducing strategy in global, e.g. HK will have 4,000 front line airline service staffs or airport check in service staffs , they will be dismisses in HK Cathay airline market. Although, HK government had given money to support it to continue to alive in order to avoid dismissing employees decision . But, Cathay airline had made decision that it will dismiss many airline service staffs in different countries. In fact, if Cathay airline expects it would not reach to the decline life cycle stage later, this dismissing employees strategy aims to avoid spending much salaries expenditure , it may be one good method to avoid decline , even death life cycle stage occurs in this year or latter.

On conclusion, it is difficult to predict what factors may cause the business itself will face decline life cycle stage occurrence in any time. Hence, any businesses ought to spend time to research whether which methods or strategies can help them to continue to expand their market or fight any kinds of threats in those four identified business life cycle stages. To avoid business can not continue develop or die, when the business is experiencing in the decline life cycle stage, the strategy is that , the organization needs to spend time to observe or learn how and why its market environment is changing in order to make the most accurate or effective strategies decisions to solve any challenges in any one of these four life cycle stages successfully.

● How new economic development in oil industry

The future global economic growth, it will influence personal incomes and GDP rise. They would carry different weight in different countries at different times. Starting from low levels of incomer and economic development. Household consumption will change from being dominated by basic heat to rapidly rising energy use for higher levels of comfort in space heating and cooling (and large dwellings), and greater use of electrical appliances, finally to a degree of saturation influenced by the income distribution patterns of the country concerned. Income distribution typically changes very slowly, so that the technical market for heart will never be saturated because there will always be a proportion of poor people living in small spaces less comfortably than the average. Industrial energy consumption will be influenced by technical efficiency within each sector, and by changes in the structures of the economy, e.g. changing proportions of agriculture, heavy and light industry, and services. One may eventually see evidence of diminishing marginal returns to additional energy inputs compared to other inputs. Energy consumption in the energy transformation sector may be influenced by income, which drives the demand for electricity to influenced by income, which drives the demand for electricity to grow faster than the demand for heat, but is also subject to the chosen technology of transformation, which is influenced by the cost and availability of primary energy inputs (fuels) in new economic development environment.

IN new economic development environment, it will influences that fuels do not compete in all sectors; for example, the transport sector is dominated by oil. Nuclear and hydroelectric power (and most renewables) reach the user through electricity; electricity itself competes with the direct burning of fossil fuels. Electricity provides the means by which other fuels can compete with oil and gas in sectors, such as space heating and process heat. It also is the only means of powering applications such as motors, computers and lighting: these subsectors are difficult to analyze. However, there is strong evidence that higher incomes do not weaken the demand for electricity so much as the demand for energy in total (in contrast to the effect on the demand for non-electric energy forms).

Econometricians look at the historical record of change in fuel prices and quantities to distinguish several factors between the new economic development and old economic development to oil industry in the future. An income effect. Increasing (reducing) fuel prices reduces (increases) the purchasing power of consumers' income: higher incomes caused by lower prices will increase energy consumption; the consumers' allocation of the increased income to energy purchases may reduce as income rises. Thus income may be heading in a different direction from fuel prices that the effect of fuel price changes when incomes are rising means simply that rising incomes have increased demand. Reducing the cost of using energy through win-win efficiency measures causes a similar problem . On the consequence, in future new economic development environment, it may influence in both cases demand will be less than if the future oil price or efficiency has not changed. The other effect is that an efficiency or substitution effect. An increase in fuel prices may cause consumers to spend more on new equipment, building materials and management operations, which will reduce the amount of fuel required to give the same energy result to the user. The extent of the efficiency effect depends on what happens to the price of the new equipment or building: if those price s rise in line with the fuel price, changes in the balances between fuel and capital or management will not occur. A new user technology , such as the development of the combined cycle gas turbine generator may increase efficiency and thus greatly reduce the quantity of primary fuel needed to produce the required output in this case electricity. If electricity prices had remained sticky, and the electricity and gas markets were not competitive, some of this advantages could have accrued to the gas suppliers in the form of an increase in price, because th4 unit of gas produces more output of electricity, it would have a higher value. In reality, the development of new economic competitive environment in both gas and electricity has tended to ensure that the benefits of such technical advanced accrue to the consumer through lower final prices. The same many apply in the case of improved efficiency in future non-manual driving auto vehicle development: the consumer's cost of motoring is reduced in new economic non-manual driven auto vehicle (Artificial intelligent vehicle) can replace manual driven vehicle , even electricity battery can replace oil energy to be used in vehicles. So, oil price may be influenced to reduce in future new economic development environment.

New and old economic theories explain oil is not main factor to influence tourism income

- Can economic theory explain old price change to influence tourism income?

I shall attempt to apply old and new economic theory to explain whether oil changing price has direct relationship to influence global tourism indusry development or tourism income as below:

Is oil changing price the main to influence tourism income or tourism development or economic growth ? If oil price rises ar falls, it will or won't cause tourism income decreases or increases? If they have cause and effect relationship, what are the main factors to influence tourism income changes by oil price rises or falls ?

I aim to investigate how any why among oil price shocks will influence tourism income variables. We may distinguish between these oil price shocks: Supply-side , aggregate demand and oil specific demand shocks. I assume that oil specific demand shocks affect inflation and the tourism sector equity index. By constrast, I also believe that aggregate demand oil price shock exercisr an effect, either directly and indirectly tourism generated income and economic growth. So, in old economic theory, supply-side , aggregate demand view to oil specific demand shocks will influence tourism income varies. So, governments ought implement strategies against future oil price movements or plan for economic policy development.

In fact, instead of oil price changes will influence tourism income, it could also harm economic growth and tourism activities, due to the effect they expert on transporation, production cost, economic uncertainty.Because tourism activities is one important sector to influence any country's leisure consumption GDP income source. So, sudden fluctuations in oil prices may also influence economic growth. It is based a hyphthesis known as the tourism led economic growth. So, it seems that they have direct or indirect relationship to case effect between oil price and tourism activities and development. So, increase on tourism income, the called " economic-driven tourism growth". In addition, high oil prices are affecting certain tourism industry segments , e.g. airlines, cruises lines, hotel, rent travelling car services etc. for oil, importing countries example, with reference to macro economic effects, higher oil prices generally lead to higher inflation, when they negatively influence to country's income.

Hence, from a micro-economic perspective, positive oil price shocks lead to a decline in disposable income. for low income people, it will bring an immediate and negative impact on tourism, mainly due to they feel tourism leisure is regarded as a luxury good, when oil price shocks to rise suddenly . It influences any airline or cruise entertainment service providers' costs are influenced to raise. Then, they need to increase air ticket or cruise ticket price. It will bring on negative tourism leisure demands-side the oil price increases low income group, potential tourism leisure consumers. Hence, it seems that oil price may have indirect relationship to influence tourism leisure consumers' needs.

● How the price of oil changes influences global tourism industry growth or recession?

In macro-economic view, sudden mid and long term oil price shock can influence global torusim industry growth or recession. For example, a oil price of US$180 per barrel was considered only a few years ago, now this has a realistic scenario to which all plaers in the T&T sector have to adapt. At such a high level, the price of oil will become even more critical to almost every part of the tourism value chain. Although, weak global demand, caused by global economic recesson, resulted in a steep oil price decline to US$45 per barrel by the fourth quarter of 2008 in the past low oil price occurrence history, this won't change the mid to long -term oil forecast.

In fact, the past oil price occurrence history of the dramatic structural had changed a high price imposed on airlines, travelers, and destination countries, all of which will have to navigate through times of shifting or even declining travel demand. I assume that a high oil price scenario is assumed in the long term in order to highlight the changes , such a senario would mean for consumer behavior and the competitiveness of several destinations.

Low oil price in the 1970 and early 1980 did not bring significant growth of international air travel, but its growth has been strongest between 1980 and 2004, a period with stable and relatively moderate oil prices. Also, the rapid development of the low-cost carrier business model in the 1990s further fueled air travel growth by capturing tourism leisure demand , such as weekend leisure travel to cities using mostly secondary airports in any big area countries, such as UK, US . However, the tourism growth is whole influenced by high oil prices, due to oil price had been continue rising in possible.

Basis of oil is shortage supply product, oil is assumed to be the main energy source for the aviation sector for the nest 30 years. Although, second-generation biofuels seem to be on the horizon, the economics as well as the production scalability and aviation biofuel shortage will be a main challenge to airline industry. So, I assume that oil price will continue rise up, if there have none any aviation biofuel can be reflected to oil to use for air plane energy.

Until 2004, the only factors to have affected air travel growth, negatively were in external shocks , such as 9/ 11, causes catching air plane crisis or US regional geopolitical conflicts. It brings some travelers feel fear to go to US travel, as well as until recently 2019, human mouth disease can influence air to have disease to anyone from mouth. So, global travelers number had been continue decreasing, because they are fear to get disease by air when many themselves every stranger travelers are sitting on the without windows air planes. Although, mouth human and air disease and US 9/11 air attack both matters may influence oil price falls effect, because air planes flying times will reduce. They won't need frequent to fly, to cause aviation oil energy need reduce. Consequently, oil price will decrease, due to travelers number reduces and air planes flying times are also influenced to reduce. (oil demand decreases cause oil price decrease). Although, air lines ' cost will also be influenced reduce, but oil price decrease can not bring travelers number increase , when air ticket price reduce because global many leisure and business trip travelers feel fear to catch air planes frequently when human mouth air disease occured in 2019. So, oil price decreases can not grow up tourism industry growth or rise tourism income.

However, the obvious impact of a high oil price is an increase in the operating costs of airline. Moreover, fuel cost as a percentage of airline operating costs vary significantly based on the length of the flight. The longer the flight, the higher the fuel costs as a percentage of the airline operating cost. So, from an online's perspective, long -hauel flights represent the most criticial challenge to profitable operation because the share of fuel on these flights, compared with other cost items, is largest, because of the unfacorable fuel economics, due to fuel costs even at high-load factors. For example, Thai airways dropped its non-stop Bongkok to US flights in the summer of 2008 for commercial reasons, because fuel reached operating cost levels of 55 percent on this route, a cost burden that could not be passed on to their customers. So, the estimated price elacticity of passengers demand at this Bongkok to US flights route is high, if Thai Airways rises less air ticket price, it will influence many travelers to choose other airlines to catch air plan to fly. Hence, due to Thai Airways can not make decision to rise air ticket price, because it believes that it will lose many travelers, so it only chooses to drop this non-stop Bongkok to US flights to avoid fuel cost rising economic loss.

However, although micro and macro economic theories may also that oil price variable or change, it may influence global tourism income. But, recently, on 2019, human mouth and air diseases, it can influence global individual leisure and business trip travelers feel fear to catch air plans to avoid their bodies get this kind of death sickness when they sit in the no fresh air supplying air planes. They feel that they reduce leisure travelling flying times or business trip flying times with strange travelers to sit in crowd air planes together. Then, they must many avoid human moth and air disease to avoid death crisis. Hence, in this global human mouth and air diseases threat environment occurrence, even oil price sudden reduces to low price, it brings airline's cost reduces and air ticke price reduces. However, when air ticket price reduce to be very cheaper, it can not still attract global many leisure or business trip travelers to buy air tickets to fly frequently. Why does air ticket reduction, it can not attract many leisure or businee trip travelers to buy air ticket to fly ? The main reason is because human mouth and air disease influences global many travelers feel fear to catch air planes frequently. In psychological view, this kind of human mouth and air sickness will bring long time negative influence to global traveles do not want to catch air planes for business trips or travelling leisure frequently. So, it implies that oil price changing to influence air ticket price reduction factor ought not main factor to influence tourism income. It may include traveler individual negative emotion psychological factor, such as human mouth and air disease or 2019 9/11 attack both cases, they can influence global travelers feel fear to catch air planes to fly to avoid death threat. So, oil changing price ought not be only one absolute main factor to influence global tourism income significantly.

On conclusion, in economic view, it seems that oil chang price may have indirect or direct relationship to influence tourism income, instead of some unpredicted external environment factors influence, such as US 9/11 attack crisis and human mouth and air disease factors, they may be main factors to influence travellers number to reduce in non-economic external unpredicted environment view.

How can artificial intelligent tools predict travelling consumer behavior in airline and air agent travelling market

I believe that applying (AI) big data tool to predict vehicle buyer consumption choice behavior, it is similar to predict traveler consumption choice behavior. In this chapter, I shall indicate how to apply (AI) big data gathering tool to predict vehicle buyer consumption choice behavior. Then, I shall its what its similar points to be applied to predict traveler consumption choice behavior.

Nowadays, many vehicle manufacturers hope their vehicles can attract to vehicle buyers to choose to buy their vehicles. However, there are many different brands of vehicles to provide to them to choose, so the vehicle market competition is very serious.

How to judge their different kinds of vehicle price which is reasonable acceptance to attract vehicle buyers to choose to buy the brand of vehicle manufacturers' any kinds of vehicles, e.g. fast speed sport style vehicles, comfortable and slow speed common cars, for four passengers common small size or more than four passengers common large car size?

How to evaluate the vehicle prices issue is important factor to influence vehicle buyers' choices. Either if the brand of vehicle price is too high to compare other brands of similar vehicle price, it will influence many vehicle buyers choose to buy other brands' vehicles or if the brand of vehicle price is too low, it will influence vehicle buyers feel this brand's vehicle machine quality or safe driving level or manufacturing steel material or speed or not comfortable sitting etc. different factors is worse to compare to other vehicle brands' similar vehicle products.

Thus, if the brand of vehicle manufacturers can predict how to design vehicles which can attract many vehicle buyers to choose to buy whose any vehicle products. What are future vehicle buyers' favorable vehicle styles? Then, the vehicle manufacturer can concentrate on manufacturing the kind style of vehicle products to sell already. It will reduce its vehicle manufacturing investment risk.

How to apply (AI) tools to predict vehicle buyers' behavioral consumption model? Whether artificial intelligent tools can predict automotive buyers' behavioral consumption model and predict future vehicle design trend. In fact, automotive brands and dealerships are facing an increasingly competition when attempting to manually gathering the vast quantities of data required to create customer focused programs that increase retention, ultimately new sales and service automotive business.

Building a based on that client's intrinsic needs and interests to any kinds of automotive vehicles at any given time. This is especially true in the automotive industry where the time span between purchases is measured in years. Because vehicle buyers would not like often to change their old vehicle to another new one. So, their decisions to buying another new vehicle, the time is usually after one year, even longer time. Hence, it seems any vehicles won't be frequent consumption products to the owned at least one vehicle family consumers (vehicle buyers). It implies that why vehicle manufacturers ought need to spend time to predict future vehicle buyer design choice for whole year vehicle buyer number growth because they won't often change preferable vehicle design to change another new vehicle more easily.

Hence, how to predict vehicle consumers' taste or preferable which styles of vehicle choices issues is very important. If the vehicle manufacturers can not manufacture any attractive vehicles to sell easily in this year. Then, it will lose time, money in this year because it won't know when the owned least one vehicle users or non-owned any vehicle users who will decide to buy one new vehicle or change another new vehicle ensure. The different brand vehicle dealers will possible wait more than one year to attract them to buy their vehicles if their styles are not attractive to compare other brands of vehicle competitors.

However, artificial intelligence and machine learning can help any vehicle manufacturers to find solution to solve patterns in highly to solve patterns in highly complex data-sets that are beyond the capability of a human brain, and then building and automatically acting on the customer insights it generates.

Given the automotive customer need for individualized communications, this technology is positioned to become a critical component of any successful vehicle retailer's domestic or/and overseas vehicle markets. How can vehicle manufacturers and retailers use (AI) to enhance their vehicle marketing campaigns? How will (AI) affect their vehicle sale marketing strategy? What criteria would they use when selecting on (AI) solution?

Vehicle consumers today are able to quickly access different brands of vehicle information, research vehicle products and reviews, negotiate prices and compare one vehicle brand or retailer to another resulting of the brands of vehicle customers. At the same time, the rise of " big -data mining", wearable devices that track user's every move and preference and greater contextualization in advertising and social media has resulted in consumer expectations of individualized. Thus, it seems that (AI) tools can be used to gather " big-data" and then they can make human's mind to analyze how to design kinds of vehicles to satisfy vehicle buyers' needs.

As automotive vehicle marketers can apply (AI) tools to achieve messaging strategies to meet the needs of this new generation of informed vehicle consumers, using data from a variety of sources to move from a variety of sources to move from mass- messaging to more personalized messages aimed at particular vehicle buyer segments, e.g. fast speed sport vehicle buyer segment, slow speed comfortable small size or large size of buyer segment. However, when 90% of vehicle marketers believe having a single vehicle buyer view is important, only 6% have achieved it.

However, one of the main issues vehicle marketers are facing the lack of capacity to efficiently sift through and analyze the massive vehicle buyer amounts of data required to create vehicle buyer individualized vehicle customer experiences easily. This is especially difficult for automotive dealers, the long periods between purchase cycles, and the highly considered nature of the vehicle purchase means that each vehicle dealer needs to not only track a large number of potential vehicle customers for an extremely long period of time, but each of those vehicle customers will generate a huge amount of different kinds of vehicle behavioral consumption data as they research their next vehicle purchase. However, by choosing the right (AI) technological tools and programs , vehicle dealers can solve this big data gathering challenge into a major advantage.

For Forrester vehicle brand example, vehicle consumers have more power over the Forrester vehicle brand's reputation than ever before. Mayne, L. (2014) indicated that Forrester calls this new (AI) tools is the " age of the vehicle customer", a 20 year business cycle in which the most successful vehicle enterprises will reinvent themselves to systematically understand and serve increasingly powerful vehicle consumers. To win in this new age, Forrester declares companies must become vehicle customer obsessed and the only sustainable competitive advantage is knowledge and engagement with customers, such as (AI) gathering data knowledge.

Thus, the biggest challenge vehicle businesses currently face is not the collection of a large quantity of vehicle consumer data, but what to do with that data once they have it. Even at a large vehicle data research firm, the data sets are often too big for a single analyze, or even a team of analysts to sort through and draw conclusion from. However, enter artificial intelligence and machine learning , an efficient technology solution that can continuously find patterns in highly complex data sets that are way beyond the capacity of a human brain and then automatic drive action based on the customer insights is generated.

What is (AI) machine learning tool? Machine learning is a type of (AI) that learns from data and is not explicitly program. Think Amazon, face book. Machine learning serves up relevant content based on an individual vehicle purchase behavior and experiences. More simply, machine learning is a computer program that can learn relationships between data, subject those learnings to errors functions, and then learn from its errors. The program in effect, trains itself.

Lee, T. (2016) explained that "Thus, (AI) tools can learn deep a more advanced branch of machine learning inspired by how our brain's nervous function, has also been found to be especial effective in identifying patterns from data."

When this way sound is complicated from a vehicle dealer perspective, the implementation of a marketing program driven by artificial intelligence can take care of these tasks in an automatic vehicle fashion with little to no manual intervention required from the staff at time vehicle stores.

In practice at a vehicle dealership, the program will continue track vehicle customer behavior online, merging that data with any offline source (like CRM or DMS data) and then analyze this aggregated vehicle buyer data set to predict what vehicle customer may be shopping for and what information they might like to relevance from different kinds style of vehicle design photos.

Why does travelling market seem to similar to vehicle market which can apply (AI) learning tool to predict travellingconsumer behaviors?

Artificial intelligence refers to complex in vehicle market and travelling entertainment market which is very seem to be applied to predict consumer behaviors.

(AI) machine learning that posses the same characteristics of human intelligence and that have all our sense, all our reason and think just like human vehicle buyer who prefer vehicle purchase choice or travelling consumer who prefer travelling package or travelling destination and airline choice. Besides, machine learning is the practice of using algorithms to collect and examine data, learn from it, and then make a determination or prediction about something in the world.

So, it can be attempted to gather data concerns that travelling consumer past travelling destination choice and air ticket price choice and different travelling package, e.g. high, middle, or low class hotel and foods supply and entertainment places choice in their past travelling journeys.

The machine is " trained" using large amounts of data and algorithms that give it the ability to learn how to automatically perform a task with increasing accuracy. Otherwise, deep learning is primarily based on artificial neural networks inspired by our understanding of the biology of human's brains.

Thus, (AI) big data can gather all these past traveler consumption behavioral choice data to make reference to analyze whether how many travelers will choose to go to the specific travelling destination in any time by the past traveler number record to different travelling destinations, then it can gather the past air ticket sale price to different destinations and past travelling package design to different destinations in order to analyze whether it is the cheap airline ticket price factor or attractive travelling package factor or attractive travelling entertainment etc. in order to predict which factor is the most potential influential factor to they choose to go to the destination to travel in different time within one year. Then, traveler agent or airline can collect these big data to judge how to design their package to attract travelers to go to anywhere to travel or what the main factor influence most of them to choose to visit the destination to travel.

For example, travel agents or airlines can apply "Deep learning" breaks down tasks in ways that enables machines to assist them to predict when travelling consumer choice will be changed and why their travelling choice will change and how their travelling choice will change with increasingly complex tasks.

So, such as why (AI) technology can be applied to predict how travelling consumer behavior changes to bring to judge whether anywhere will be many travelling consumers who will prefer to choose travelling hot destinations next year or next month.

Then, travel agents and airlines can gather overall past travelling consumer data to analyze and conclude the more accurate prediction of different travelling destinations to the number of traveler. Then, they can choose how much air ticket price is more reasonable to charge to the travelling destination or how to design the travelling package which can bring more attractive to the prediction number of different travelling destination travelers in order to achieve to raise the different travelling destination number next year.

Thus, (AI) big data machine learning can help airlines or travel agents to solve how to design any attractive travelling package challenge. A travelling package is both one of the most important and carefully considered travelling entertainment consumption the majority of travelling people will ever make in their lifetime at least one travelling time.

It is also a prediction how travelling package will be designed that tends to be fundamentally tied to a travelling person's travelling destination choice identify and travelling package view of themselves. As the same time, travelling consumers' travelling choice changing lifestyles result in changing travelling destination needs, e.g. the country's young travelers can choose to change non-extreme exciting travelling entertainment package from past extreme exciting travelling entertainment package. Due to personal feeling factor in general. However, I believe that (AI) big data can also be attempted to predict when the country's young travelers will choose to change non-extreme exciting travelling behavior.

It is similar to automotive dealers need to remember that vehicle customers and prospects are individual human beings with risk, complex and ever-changing lives factors, these factors will influence every vehicle consumer why who feels has vehicle purchase need, and how who choose to buy the first vehicle if who decided to buy the first vehicle.

It seems that travelling agents or airlines need to remember that travelling consumers and different features or designs are very traveler beings with risk, complex and ever-travelling package attitude personal changing factors in different travel season, these factor will influence every individual traveler why who feels has travel entertainment need, and how who choose to buy different feature or design travelling package if who decide to travel.

The (AI) big data technological travelling customer behavioral prediction tool seems to be the best travelling behavioral prediction tool in the world are those that know every one of different country's traveler need. Their likes and dislikes which style of travelling package, preferences and travel destination changing tastes to travelling destination choices.

The capacity of the human brain, however, limits us from achieving these different type of travel package sales. In this competitive travelling destination choice entertainment environment, (AI) big data machine learning enables platforms to assist the air ticket and travel package sales team by tracking the travelling consumer behaviors of each travelling customer, learning and memorizing their preferences and predicting their future travelling destination choice and travelling package design needs.

Finally, I recommend that for a travel agent or airline travelling marketing platform to make their travelling customer engagement efficient and fully-functional, I should be able to: applying (AI) tools to track every travelling customer behavior across the web, connecting to a society of data sources, CRM, DMS, third-party, web travelling brands, social traveler email, click etc., aggregating and accurately cross-reference data from a variety of sources, leveraging this data to drive insights on a mass scale, as well as on an individualized basis, driving actions and automatically direct travelling customer engagement via multiple channels based on where each customer is in their travelling individual lifecycle.

Why is (AI) big data gathering tool better than psychological and survey methods to predict traveler individual travel choice behavior?

Prediction travel behavioral consumption from psychology and survey methods.

How to predict travel consumption? It is one question to any travel agents concern to use what methods which can predict how many numbers of travelers where who will choose to go to travel more accurately. I think that who can consider how to predict travel behavioral consumption from psychology and survey travel choice prediction method, but it is better to apply (AI) big data gathering method to predict travel consumer's destination choice more accurate. The reason is as below:

The first reason is that traveller individual travel psychological desire is difficult to predict accurate more than (AI) big data gathering method, it is due that the data is past traveler's destination choice and travel package and ticket price actual data from (AI) big data gathering method. Otherwise, survey investigation is only traveler psychological thinking method. It lacks enough past actual traveler data gathering.

The second reason is that on the weakness of traveler individual psychological thinking view of survey investigation. It has evidence to support the relationship between self-identify threat and resistance to change travel behavior to any travelers, controlling for whose past travelling behavior, resistance to change if a psychological phenomenon of long standing interest in many applied branches of psychology.

Past travelling behavior has been acknowledged as a predictor of future action. Such as travelling behavior that is experienced as successful is likely to be repeated and may lead to habitual patterns. Some psychologists differentiate habit between two concepts, such as goal oriented and automatic oriented both. Although repeated past travelling behavior is addition goal oriented and automatic oriented. Further non-deliberative nature of habit may make appeals to judge and to predict future individual traveler's behavior accurately.

However, repeated one traveler will choose the destination to repeat to travel without a necessary constraint of goal orientation and automatic oriented both. So, it seems that psychological factor can influence any individual traveler why and how who choose to decide to repeat to choose the destination to travel.

So, survey investigation is only the traveler's thinking to answer the travel firm. It is not sure that the traveler's past travel experience is real answer. Otherwise, (AI) big data gathering method is computer gathering method which gather past traveler consumption actual data to analyze and conclude future traveler possible repeated travel destination choice and travel package choice more accurate.

The third reason is that on the strength of (AI) big data gathering method computer statistic view to predict future traveller consumer's destination and travel package choice. It is structural equation modeling is an extremely flexible linear-in-parameters multivariate statistical modeling technique. It has been used in modeling travel behavior and values since about 1980 year. It is a software method to handle a large number of variables, as well as unobserved variables specified as linear combinations (weighted averages) of the observed variable.

Can (AI) big data gather data to predict when climate will change to influence poor travelling behaviours?

(AI) big data tool can predict the flexibility of human travelling behavioral change is at least the result of one such mechanism, our ability to travel mentally in time and entertain potential future. Understanding of the impacts is holidays, particularly those involving travel.

Using focus groups research to explores tourists' awareness of the impacts of travel own climate change, examines the extent to which climate change features in holiday travel decisions and identifies some of the barriers to the adoption of less carbon intensive tourism practices.

The findings suggest many tourists don't consider climate change when planning their holidays. The failure of tourists to engage with the climate change to impact of holidays, combined with significant barriers to behavioral change, presents a considerable challenge in the tourism industry. In the future, computer (AI) big data tool can attempt to predict when the country's climate change to influence travelers to choose to go to the country to travel, e.g. next month or next half year or next year hot travelling destinations.

Tourism is a highly energy intensive industry and has only recently attracted attention as an important contributions to climate change through greenhouse gas emissions. It has been estimated that tourism contributes 5% of global carbon dioxide emissions. There have been a number of potential changes proposed for reducing the impact of air travel on climate change. These include technological changes, market based changes and behavioral changes.

However, the role that climate change plays in the holiday and travel decisions of global tourists. How the global tourists of the impacts travel has on climate change to establish the extent to which climate change, considerations features in holiday travel decision making processes and to investigate the major barriers to global tourists adopting less carbon intensive travel practices.

It will bring this question: Will tourists aware the impacts that their holidays and travel have on climate changes to influence their travelling decision?

When, it comes to understand individual traveler's behavioral change, wide range of conceptual theories have been developed, utilizing various social, psychological, subjective and objective variables in order to model travel consumption behavior. These theories of travel behavioral change operate at a number of different levels, including the individual level, the interpersonal level and community level. Whether pro-environmental behavior can be used to predict travel consumption behavior in a climate change. However, the question of what determines pro-environmental behavior in such a complex one that it can not be visualized through one single framework or diagram.

Despite the potentially high risk scenario for the tourism industry and the global environment, the tourism and climate change ought have close relationship.

However, (AI) big data tool can be applied to find what factors to influence the time of travelers' travelling choices. What are the important factors and variables which can limit tourism? e.g. money, time, family problem, extreme hot or cold weather change, air ticket price, journey attraction etc. variable factors.

Mention of holidays and travel were deliberately avoided in the recruitment process, so as not to create a connection factor to influence traveler's individual mind. However, the dismissal of alternative transportation modes can be conceived as either a structural barrier, in the sense that flying is perhaps the only realistic option to reach long-haul holiday destination, or a perceived behavioral control barriers in that an individual perceives flying as the only option open to whom.

The transportation tool factor will be depend to extent on the distance to the destination. This can also be interpreted in a social perspective as an intention with the resources available where much international tourism is structured around flying. To increase the availability of different transportation modes, tourists could choose holiday destination closer to home.

Finally, also how to predict future travel behavioral consumption. I feel that travel agents need to predict whether any country's random daily variation of weather factor is also important to influence travel behavior. e.g. in weather, temperature, rainfall and snowfall with traffic accidents factors will have relationship to cause travel demand.

Some scientists estimate suggest that when warmed temperatures and reduced snowfall are associated with a moderate decline in non-fatal accidents, they are also associated with a significant increase in fatal accidents. Thus increase in fatalities and temperature. Half of the estimated effect of temperature on fatalities is due to changes in the exposure to pedestrians, bicyclists and motorcyclists as temperature increase.

So, if any countries have rainfall, snowfall and low temperature to cause traffic accidents, whether this accident occurrence will influence the travelers who liking climb snow hills, riding bicycle, running sports who will avoid to travel to these countries' bad weather after occurs. So, why I feel that this natural climate factor will also be one serious factor to influence travel behavioral consumption. However, (AI) big data tool can predict more accurate than survey method when climate change to influence the country's climate to be poor, then it can predict when which countries are not popular acceptable to global country consumers' travel choice next month.

How can apply (AI) to provide travelling businesses with better-informed decisions ?

I shall explain how (AI) big data gathering technology can provide travelling businesses with better-informed decisions to drive top-line growth, deliver meaningful experience for travelling customers and smooth their path along the travelling consumer journey. The widely understood definition of (AI) involves the ability of machines or computers to learn human thinking, reasoning and decision-making abilities.

So, such as (AI) learning machine system can attempt to learn travelling consumer's travel destination or travel package thinking, judgement of their reasons why they choose to go to the destination to travel or why they choose to buy the travel package and learn how and why they make their past travelling decisions from their past travel big data gathering.

A Narrative science study in 2015 year identified that (AI) was being used primarily in voice recognition, machine learning virtual assistants and decision support. This study also highlighted the many branches of (AI) and that techniques and their definition are used interchangeably. It is possible that (AI) can be used to gather big data , then to analyze to help travel businesses to predict travelling consumer travel destination and travel package choice behaviors. For example, one of the most common techniques is traveler machine learning, where algorithms are used to perform tasks by learning from the airline or travel agent whose past all travelers' travelling destination choice and travel package choice historical data.

However, during 2017 year, search engines will begin to find what additional factors can influence past traveler personal travelling destination and travelling package travelling behavioral data into prediction of future travelling customer behavioral results, such as the online traveler (user's) history of travelling data searches, such as anywhere are the most popular travelling locations or travelling destinations and previously captures conservations.

Artificial intelligence will use this past travelling destinations and travelling package information to power predictive search results, e.g. predictive future travelling consumer's choice behavioral processing for where will be their preferable travelling destination choice and how to design travelling package to satisfy future travelling clients' needs. Predictive search will improve the quality of online travelling search results, and provide new insights into travelling consumers' travelling destination and package behavior and the moments which matter to them. Search will give recommendation into tailored how travelling consumer individual travelling destination choice in travelling decision making process. Several of the largest online platforms already use (AI) travelling machine learning to improve predictive travelling consumer behavioral search results.

For example, Google's rank brain technology adds research by understanding the context in which the travelling consumer has entered it. Over time, rank brain will learn further from user behaviors Amazon's DSSTNE (pronouned destiny) learns from shoppers' purchasing habits and consumption behavior to offer better product recommend actions, which Amazon can offer before a consumer has entered anything into the search bar.

Such as (AI) big data can gather past online travelers' e-ticket purchase transactions to conclude that online traveler's travelling choice habits and online traveler consumption behavior to offer better travelling destinations and travelling package opinions to travel agents or airlines. However, this technology is not independent of human input. For example, Google engineers will periodically retain the rank brain system to improve the models it uses.

For another example, in 2016 year , Apple computer revamped its travelling scene photos app to allow travelling consumers to search for specific travelling destinations in the travelling scene phots, they want to find anywhere travelling destination photos, not just dates and locations. Each travelling photo that an intelligent phone or intelligent pad user takes goes through 11 billion computations, so that travelling scene photos can understand exactly where is the travelling destination photography to let online travelling consumer to feel anywhere they plan to go to the location to travel. So, (AI) learning machine can make online travelling photos more attractive to influence potential travelers choose to the destination to travel after they see the travelling destination scene photos from internet.

It seems that in future, (AI) machine learning will allow online travelling search to evolve even further. Search engineers will deliver refined recommendations to airlines' online traveler e-ticket search users and use less human input to predict travelling consumers' needs from internet channel. For IBM computer example, it indicated 90% of the data that exists today has been created in the last two years.

This huge explosion of past traveler's e-ticket consumption data gives the opportunity to quickly spot and react to the latest trends, fashion and fads among its travelling clients and potential clients. This will allow airline or travel agent companies to better engage with younger travelling consumers, who gain influence access to the latest travelling destination and package trends.

They associate with to help define who they are as individuals. Thus, travelling company brands have to identify and make use of them before travelling consumers move on, but the vast quantity of past e-ticket purchase data available makes from internet channel. This a resource-intensive task. For next example, Lesara, a based online clothes store, uses this machine learning to inform its product decision often gathering information from internal and external sources.

When its trends -spotting shoes. Lesara has a range of over 20 styles and sells hundreds of pairs a day. It focus on giving consumers, the very latest trends allow Lesara to develop on average of 50,000 new items each year. It compared to 11,000 old items each year. Thus, travelling agents or airlines can attempt to apply (AI) big data gathering method to gather all past e-ticket purchase data, concerns where they prefer to choose to go to the destinations to travel and what travelling packages are the most attractive to the travelers to choose to buy. It aims to help them to predict where future travelers will prefer to choose to go to travel or what travelling package they will prefer to choose to buy next year.

For another (AI) big data prediction example, Lesara is one online clothes store, uses machine learning decisions after gathering information from internal and external sources. One of its most popular products, shoes with LED started life when its trend spotting software flagged up a blogger wearing similar shoes. Now Lesara has a range of over 20 styles and sells hundreds of pairs a day. Its focus on giving consumers the very latest trends allows Lesara to develop an average of 50,000 new items each year, compared to 11,000 for its competitor Lara.

It seems (AI) big data gathering machine learning can help Lesara business to predict what kinds of shoes design or style that shoe consumers will prefer choose to buy in future shoe market trend. Thus, Lesara can predict shoe consumers' taste successfully and it can manufacture many attractive style of shoes.

(AI) machine learning can gather global past shoe consumer's shoe shopping experiences, then analyzes to make conclusion to give lesara recommendation successfully. This will make the experience more enjoyable for shoe consumers and allow Lesara to advert whose different new style or design of shoes to deliver them move relevant messages by understanding the context of the experience.

So, online travel agents or online airline can also attempt to apply (AI) big data gathering method to predict where travelers will prefer to go to travel and how they ought design travelling packages to attract them to choose to buy next year. Hence, (AI) big data gathering technology can conclude how to design traveler agents' travelling package products to be the most attractive to excite many travelers choose to buy their travelling package, due to it has more accurate to predict travelling consumer destination and travelling package choice behaviors to compare human themselves prediction judgement effort, e.g. travelling survey or marketing research, or telephone enquire. It seems that (AI) machine judgement effort is more accurate to compare to human judgment effort in travelling industry.

Future travel consumption behavior

Can (AI) big data gathering tool predict traveler individual habitual behavior , e.g. renting travel transportation tools ?

Can (AI) big data gathering tool can predict past traveler destination and travelling package choice habit and it can be intended to predict of future traveler behavior to people are creatures of habits judgement of future anywhere travelling destination choice next year or next month or next half year destination prediction ?

Many of human's everyday goal-directed behaviors are performed in a habitual fashion, the transportation made and route one takes to work, one's choice of breakfast. Habits are formed when using the some behavior frequently and a similar consistency in a similar context for the some purpose whether the individual past travel consumption model will be caused a habit to whom. e.g. choosing whom travel agent to buy air ticket or traveling package; choosing the same or similar countries' destinations to go to travel ; choosing the business class or normal (general) class of quality airlines to catch planes.

Does habitual rent traveling car tools use not lead to more resistance to change of travel mode? It has been argued that past behavior is the best predictor of future behavior to travel consumption. If individual traveler's past consumption behavior was always reasoned, then frequency of prior travel consumption behavior should only have an indirect link to the individual traveler's behavior. It seems that renting travel car tools to use is a habit example. So, a strong rent traveling car tools useful habit makes traveling mode choice. People with a strong renting of traveling car tools of habit should have low motivation to attend to gather any information about public transportation in their choice of travelling country for individual or family or friends members during their traveling journeys.

Even when persuasive communication changes the traveler whose attitudes and intention, in the case of individual traveler or family travelers with a strong renting travel car tools habit. It is difficult to change whose travel behaviors to choose to catch public transportation in whose any trips in any countries. However, understanding of travel behavior and the reasons for choosing one mode of transportation over another. The arguments for rent traveling car tools to use, including convenience, speed, comfort and individual freedom and well known.
Increasingly, psychological factors include such as, perceptions, identity, social norms and habit are being used to understand travel mode choice. Whether how many travel consumers will choose to rent traveling car tools during their trips in any countries. It is difficult to estimate the numbers. As the average level of renting travel car tools of dependence or attitudes to certain travel package policies from travel agents. Instead different people must be treated in different ways because who are motivated in different ways and who are motivated by different travel package policies ways from travel agents.

In conclusion, the factors influence whose traveler's individual traveler destination choice behavior The factors include either who chooses to rent traveling car tools or who chooses to catch public transportation when who individual goes to travel in alone trip or family trip. It include influence mode choice factors, such as social psychology factor and marketing on segmentation factor both to influence whose transportation choice of behavior in whose trip. So, (AI) big data can be attempted to gather past traveler transportation tool choice, rent travelling car tools choice or catching public transportation tools choice to predict where destination can provide what kind of transportation tool to attract many travelers to choose to go to the place to travel.

How (AI) big data determine future travel behavior from past travel experience and perceptions of risk and safety for the benefits to travel consumers?

How (AI) big data determine future travel behavior from past travel experience and perceptions of risk and safety for the benefits to travel consumers? Why does individual traveler avoid certain destination(s) is(are) as relevant to tourist decision making as why who chooses to travel to others?
Perceptions of risk and safety and travel experience are likely to influence travel decisions. If travel agents had efforts to predict future travel behavior to guess whether travelers will feel where is(are) risk and unsafe to cause who does not choose to go to the country to travel. Then, the travel agents will avoid to choose to spend much time to design the different traveling package to attract their potential travel consumers to choose to travel. The reason is because in the case of individual traveler's tourism experience, the traveler whose past disappointment travel experience (psychological risk) will be a serious threat to the traveler's health or life (health, physical or terrorism risk). The past safety or unhealthy risk to the country(countries) will influence the traveler decides to choose not to go to the

countries(country) to travel again in the future.

What is push and pull factors to influence any traveler who chooses where is whose preferable travelling destination ?

How to apply (AI) big data to predict individual traveler's behavioral intention of choosing a travel destination? Understanding why people travel and what factors influence their behavioral intention of choosing a travel destination is beneficial to tourism planning and marketing. In general, an individual's choice of a travel destination into two forces.

The first force is the push factor that pushes an individual away from home and attempt to develop a general desire to go somewhere, without specifying where that may be.

The other force is the pull factor that pull an individual toward in destination, due to a region-specific or perceived attractiveness of a destination. The respective push and pull factors illustrate that people travel because who are pushed by whose internal motives and pulled by external forced of a destination. However, the decision making process leading to the choice of a travel destination is a very complex process.

For example, a Taiwanese traveler who might either choose new travel destination of Hong Kong or another old travel Asia destinations again or who also might choose any one of Western country, as a new travel destination. The travel agents can predict where who will have intention to choose to travel from whose past behavior and attitude, subjective and perceived behavioral control model. When (AI) big data gather past every country traveler number who chose to go to which countries to travel in order to judge where destinations will be the country travelers' travelling choice destinations in the future.

The factors influence where is the traveler choice, include personal safety, scenic beauty, cultural interest, climate changing, transportation tools, friendliness of local people, price of trip, trip package service in hotels and restaurants, quality and variety of food and shopping facilities and services etc. needs. So, whose factors will influence where is the individual travel's choice. It seems every traveler whose choice of travel process, will include past behavior. e.g. travelling experience, travelling habit, then to choose the best seasoned travelling action to satisfy whose travel needs. This process is the individual traveler's psychological choice process, who must need time to gather information to compare concerning of different travel packages, destination scene, climate change, transportation tools available to the destination, air ticket price etc. these factors, then to judge where is the best right destination to travel in the right time.

Hence, (AI) big data can gather past different countries' climate changing data, transportation tool changing data, destination scene environment changing etc. different data to give opinions to travelling businesses whether any country's these above factors will influence about how many traveler number will be increase or decrease in the future.

Why can expectation, motivation and attitude factor influence travelling behavior?

Social psychology is concerned with gaining insight into the psychological of socially relevant behaviors and the processes. For instance, on a global level bad influence to global warming, it influences some countries extreme cold or hot bad climate changing occurrence, then it ought influence some travelers' behavioral decision to change their mind to choose some countries to go to travel at the moment which do not occur extreme hot or cold climate (temperature). e.g. above than 40 degree in summer or below than 0 degree in winter. Due to the extreme climate changing environment in the countries, it will cause them to feel uncomfortable to play during their trips. So, the global warming causes to climate changing factor will influence the numbers of travel consumption to be reduced possibly. This is global climate changing environment factor influences to bad or uncomfortable social psychological feeling to global travelers' mind of traveling decision. What is individual traveler expectation, motivation and attitude? Tourism sector includes inbound (domestic) tourism and outbound (overseas) tourism both incomes to any countries. According to recent article, a tourist behavior model has been developed, called the expectation, motivation and attitude (EMA) model (Hsu et al., 2010).

This model focuses on the pre-visit stage of tourists by modeling the behavioral process by incorporating expectation, motivation and attitude. Travel motivation is considered as an essential component of the behavioral process, which has been increasing attention from the travel; industry. The economic approach defines "tourism" is an identifiable nationally important industry. It includes the component activities of transportation, accommodation, recreation, food and related service. So, tourism behavioral consumption is concerned the individual tourist's usual habituate of the industry which responds to whose needs, and of the impacts that both the tourist and the tourism industry have on the socio-cultural, economic and physical environment.

However, travel motivation means how to understand and predict factors that influence travel decision making. According to Backman and others (1995, p.15), motivation is conceptually viewed as " a state of need, a condition that services as a driving force to display different kind of behavior toward certain types of activities, developing preferences, arriving at some expected satisfactory outcome." So, motivation and expectancy which has close relationship to any tourist before who decided to do any tourism of behavior.

Some economists confirmed motivation and expectancy which has relations, such as expectation of visiting an outbound destination has a direct effect on motivation to visit the destination; motivation has a direct effect on attitude toward visiting the destination; expectation of visiting the outbound destination has a direct affection on attitude toward visiting the destination and motivation has a mediating effect on the relationship in between expectation and attitude.

Hence, (AI) big data can gather all the country's climate environment change, transportation tool change, entertainment scene change, hotel price and restaurant price change etc. data to give opinions whether the country will attract how many traveler to choose to go to travel in the year.

Reference

Backman and others "motivation is conceptually viewed as " a state of need, a condition that services as a driving force to display different kind of behavior toward certain types of activities, developing preferences, arriving at some expected satisfactory outcome.", 1995, p.15.

Fishbein & Ajzen, "The model based on the three constructs of attitude, subjective norm, and perceived behavioral control". 1975.

Hsu et al. "A tourist behavior model has been developed, called the expectation, motivation and attitude " (EMA) model ,2010.

ICT,WWW . "Switzerland has one of the highest population-to-computer ratio in Europe." Switzerland, 2005.

Jorea Ministry of Environment, " For South Korea environmental attitude is a major factor in decision making vis-a-vis the consumption of " green" food and services", Korea, 2015.

Korea Ministry Of Environment. Public Organizations spend 2.2 Trillon Korean Won To
Purchase green Products in 2014; Ministry Of Environment: Sejoung, Korea, 2015.

Lind , Lohmann & Danielsson , United Nations Population Division, "Demographic change is said to be one of the important drivers for new trends in consumer traveling change behavior in most European countries". 2001.

Mayne, Lonnie. " Evolve of die in the age of the consumer". Entrepreneur, N.P. , 16 Apr. 2014. web of Oct. 2016.

Lee, D.; Kim, M. ; Lee, J. adoption of green electricity policies: Investigating the role of environmental attitudes via big data-driven search-queries. Energy policy 2016. 90, 187-201.

Lee, Terrence, " Tech in Asia-connecting Asia's startup system " Tech. in Asia- connecting Asia's startup ecosystem, N.p.,4 July 2016.

Weber & Bottorn "risky decision is as choices among alternatives that can be described by probability distributions over possible outcomes" , 1989, p.114.

What factors can influence travel behavioural consumption

Prediction travel behavioral consumption from traditional human's mind of tourism market research method

How to predict travel consumption? It is one question to any travel agents concern to use what methods which can predict how many numbers of travelers where who will choose to go to travel more accurately. I think that who can consider how to predict travel behavioral consumption from psychology view and computer science view both.

On the psychology view, It has evidence to support the relationship between self-identify threat and resistance to change travel behavior to any travelers, controlling for whose past travelling behavior, resistance to change if a psychological phenomenon of long standing interest in many applied branches of psychology. Past travelling behavior has been acknowledged as a predictor of future action. Such as travelling behavior that is experienced as successful is likely to be repeated and may lead to habitual patterns. Some psychologists differentiate habit between two concepts, such as goal oriented and automatic oriented both. Although repeated past travelling behavior is addition goal oriented and automatic oriented. Further non-deliberative nature of habit may make appeals to judge and to predict future individual traveler's behaviour accrately. However, repeated travelling behavior without a necessary constraint of goal orientation and automatic oriented both. So, it seems that psychological factor can influence any individual traveler why and how who choose to decide whose travelling behaviour.

On the computer statistic view, structural equation modeling is an extremely flexible linear-in-parameters multivariate statistical modeling technique. It has been used in modeling travel behavior and values since about 1980 year. It is a software method to handle a large number of variables, as well as unobserved variables specified as linear combinations (weighted averages) of the observed variable.

Whether climate change can influence travelling behaviours.

The flexibility of human travelling behavior is at least the result of one such mechanism, our ability to travel mentally in time and entertain potential future. Understanding of the impacts is holidays, particularly those involving travel. Using focus groups research to explores tourists' awareness of the impacts of travel own climate change, examines the extent to which climate change features in holiday travel decisions and identifies some of the barriers to the adoption of less carbon intensive tourism practices. The findings suggest many tourists don't consider climate change when planning their holidays. The failure of tourists to engage with the climate change to impact of holidays, combined with significant barriers to behavioral change, presents a considerable challenge in the tourism industry.

Tourism is a highly energy intensive industry and has only recently attracted attention as an important contributions to climate change through greenhouse gas emissions. It has been estimated that tourism contributes 5% of global carbon dioxide emissions. There have been a number of potential changes proposed for reducing the impact of air travel on climate change. These include technological changes, market based changes and behavioral changes. However, the role that climate change plays in the holiday and travel decisions of global tourists. How the global tourists of the impacts travel has on climate change to establish the extent to which climate change, considerations features in holiday travel decision making processes and to investigate the major barriers to global tourists adopting less carbon intensive travel practices. Whether tourists will aware the impacts that their holidays and travel have on climate changes.

When, it comes to understand indvidual traveler's behavioral change, wide range of conceptual theories have been developed, utilizing various social, psychological, subjective and objective variables in order to model travel consumption behavior. These theories of travel behavioral change operate at a number of different levels, including the individual level, the interpersonal level and community level. Whether pro-environmental behavior can be used to predict travel consumption behavior in a climate change. However, the question of what determines pro-environmental behavior in such a complex one that it can not be visualized through one single framework or diagram.

Despite the potentially high risk scenario for the tourism industry and the global environment, the tourism and climate change ought have close relationship. Whether what are the important factors and variables which can limit tourism? e.g. money, time, family problem, extreme hot or cold weather change, air ticket price, journey attraction etc. variable factors. Mention of holidays and travel were deliberately avoided in the recruitment process, so as not to create a connection factor to influence traveler's individual mind. However, the dismissal of alternative transportation modes can be conceived as either a structural barrier, in the sense that flying is perhaps the only realistic option to reach long-haul holiday destination, or a perceived behavioral control barriers in that an individual perceives flying as the only option open to whom. The transportation tool factor will be depend to extent on the distance to the destination. This can also be interpreted in a social perspective as an intention with the resources available where much international tourism is structured around flying. To increase the availability of different transportation modes, tourists could choose holiday destination closer to home.

Finally, also how to predict future travel behavioural consumption. I feel that travel agents need to predict whether any country's random daily variation of weather factor is also important to influence travel behaviour. e.g. in weather, temperature, rainfall adn snowfall with traffic accidents factors will have relationship to cause travel demand. Some scientists estimate suggest that when warmed temperatures and reduced snowfall are associated with a moderate decline in non-fatal accidents, they are also associated with a significant increase in fatal accidents. Thus increase in fatalities and temperature. Half of the estimated effect of temperature on fatalities is due to changes in the exposure to pedestrians, bicyclists and motorcyclists as temperature increase. So, if any countries have rainfall, snowfall and low temperature to cause traffic accidents, whether this accident occurrence will influence the travelers who liking climb snow hills, riding bicycle, running sports who will avoid to travel to these countries' bad weather after occurs. So, why I feel that this natural climate factor will also be one serious factor to influence travel behavioral consumption.

Market method predicts future travel consumption behavior

Whether individual habitual behaviour can influence travelling behaviour : e.g. renting travel transportation tools

Whether habit can be intended to predict of future travel behavior to people are creatures of habits. Many of human's everyday goal-directed behaviors are performed in a habitual fashion, the transportation made and route one takes to work, one's choice of breakfast. Habits are formed when using the some behavior frequently and a similar consistency in a similar context for the some purpose whether the individual past travel consumption model will be caused a habit to whom. e.g. choosing whom travel agent to buy air ticket or traveling package; choosing the same or similar countries' destinations to go to travel ; choosing the business class or normal (general) class of quality airlines to catch planes. Does habitual rent traveling car tools use not lead to more resistance to change of travel mode? It has been argued that past behavior is the best predictor of future behavior to travel consumption. If individual traveler's past consumption behavior was always reasoned, then frequency of prior travel consumption behavior should only have an indirect link to the individual traveler's behavior. It seems that renting travel car tools to use is a habit example. So, a strong rent traveling car tools useful habit makes traveling mode choice. People with a strong renting of traveling car tools of habit should have low motivation to attend to gather any information about public transportation in their choice of travelling country for individual or family or friends members during their traveling journeys.

Even when persuasive communication changes the traveler whose attitudes and intention, in the case of individual traveler or family travelers with a strong renting travel car tools habit. It is difficult to change whose travel behaviors to choose to catch public transportation in whose any trips in any countries. However, understanding of travel behavior and the reasons for choosing one mode of transportation over another. The arguments for rent traveling car tools to use, including convenience, speed, comfort and individual freedom and well known. Increasingly, psychological factors include such as, perceptions, identity, social norms and habit are being used to understand travel mode choice. Whether how many travel consumers will choose to rent traveling car tools during their trips in any countries. It is difficult to estimate the numbers. As the average level of renting travel car tools of dependence or attitudes to certain travel package policies from travel agents. Instead different people must be treated in different ways because who are motivated in different ways and who are motivated by different travel package policies ways from travel agents.

In conclusion, the factors influence whose traveler's individual behavior either who chooses to rent traveling car tools or who chooses to catch public transportation when who individual goes to travel in alone trip or family trip. It include influence mode choice factors, such as social psychology factor and marketing on segmentation factor both to influence whose transportation choice of behavior in whose trip.

How to determine future travel behavior from past travel experience and perceptions of risk and safety for the benefits to travel consumers?

How to determine future travel behavior from past travel experience and perceptions of risk and safety for the benefits to travel consumers? Why does individual traveler avoid certain destination(s) is(are) as relevant to tourist decision making as why who chooses to travel to others. Perceptions of risk and safety and travel experience are likely to influence travel decisions. If travel agents had efforts to predict future travel behavior to guess whether travelers will feel where is(are) risk and unsafe to cause who does not choose to go to the country to travel. Then, the travel agents will avoid to choose to spend much time to design the different traveling package to attract their potential travel consumers to choose to travel. The reason is because in the case of individual traveler's tourism experience, the traveler whose past disappointment travel experience (psychological risk) will be a serious threat to the traveler's health or life (health, physical or terrorism risk). The past safety or unhealthy risk to the country(countries) will influence the traveler decides to choose not to go to the countries(country) to travel again in the future.

What is push and pull factors to influence any
traveler who chooses where is whose preferable travelling destination

How to predict individual traveler's behavioral intention of choosing a travel destination. Understanding why people travel and what factors influence their behavioral intention of choosing a travel destination is beneficial to tourism planning and marketing. In general, an individual's choice of a travel destination into two forces. The first force is the push factor that pushes an individual away from home and attempt to develop a general desire to go somewhere, without specifying where that may be. The other force is the pull factor that pull an individual toward in destination, due to a region-specific or perceived attractiveness of a destination. The respective push and pull factors illustrate that people travel because who are pushed by whose internal motives and pulled by external forced of a destination. However, the decision making process leading to the choice of a travel destination is a very complex process. For example, a Taiwanese traveler who might either choose new travel destination of Hong Kong or another old travel Asia destinations again or who also might choose any one of Western country, as a new travel destination. The travel agents can predict where who will have intention to choose to travel from whose past behavior and attitude, subjective and perceived behavioral control model.

The factors influence where is the traveler choice, include personal safety, scenic beauty, cultural interest, climate changing, transportation tools, friendliness of local people, price of trip, trip package service in hotels and restaurants, quality and variety of food and shopping facilities and services etc. needs. So, whose factors will influence where is the individual travel's choice. It seems every traveler whose choice of travel process, will include past behavior. e.g. travelling experience, travelling habit, then to choose the best seasoned travelling action to satisfy whose travel needs. This process is the individual traveler's psychological choice process, who must need time to gather information to compare concerning of different travel packages, destination scene, climate change, transportation tools available to the destination, air ticket price etc. these factors, then to judge where is the best right destination to travel in the right time.

Why expectation, motivation and attitude factor can influence travelling behaviour.

Social psychology is concerned with gaining insight into the psychological of socially relevant behaviors and the processes. For instance, on a global level bad influence to global warming, it influences some countries extreme cold or hot bad climate changing occurrence, then it ought influence some travelers' behavioral decision to change their mind to choose some countries to go to travel at the moment which do not occur extreme hot or cold climate (temperature). e.g. above than 40 degree in summer or below than 0 degree in winter. Due to the extreme climate changing environment in the countries, it will cause them to feel uncomfortable to play during their trips. So, the global warming causes to climate changing factor will influence the numbers of travel consumption to be reduced possibly. This is global climate changing environment factor influences to bad or uncomfortable social psychological feeling to global travelers' mind of traveling decision. What is individual traveler expectation, motivation and attitude? Tourism sector includes inbound (domestic) tourism and outbound (overseas) tourism both incomes to any countries. According to recent article, a tourist behavior model has been developed, called the expectation, motivation and attitude (EMA) model (Hsu et al., 2010).

This model focuses on the pre-visit stage of tourists by modeling the behavioral process by incorporating expectation, motivation and attitude. Travel motivation is considered as an essential component of the behavioral process, which has been increasing attention from the travel; industry. The economic approach defines "tourism" is an identifiable nationally important industry. It includes the component activities of transportation, accommodation, recreation, food and related service. So, tourism behavioral consumption is concerned the individual tourist's usual habituate of the industry which responds to whose needs, and of the impacts that both the tourist and the tourism industry have on the socio-cultural, economic and physical environment.

However, travel motivation means how to understand and predict factors that influence travel decision making. According to Backman and others (1995, p.15), motivation is conceptually viewed as " a state of need, a condition that services as a driving force to display different kind of behavior toward certain types of activities, developing preferences, arriving at some expected satisfactory outcome." So, motivation and expectancy which has close relationship to any tourist before who decided to do any tourism of behavior. Some economists confirmed motivation and expectancy which has relations, such as expectation of visiting an outbound destination has a direct effect on motivation to visit the destination; motivation has a direct effect on attitude toward visiting the destination; expectation of visiting the outbound destination has a direct affect on attitude toward visiting the destination and motivation has a mediating effect on the relationship in between expectation and attitude.

What methods can predict future travel behavioural consumption

How to use qualitative of travel behavioural method to predict future travel consumption?

I also suggest to use qualitative of travel behavioural method to predict future travel consumption. Methods such as focus groups interviews and participant observer techniques can be used with quantitative approaches on their own to fill the gaps left by quantitative techniques. These insights have contributed to the development of increasingly sophisticated models to forecast travel behavior and predict changes in behavior in response to change in the transportation system. First, survey methods restrict not only the question frame but the answer frame as well, anticipating the important issues and questions and the responses. However, these surveys methods are not well suited to exploratory areas of research where issues remain unidentified and the researched seek to answer the question "why?". Second, data collection methods using traditional travel diaries or telephone recruitment can under represent certain segments of the population, particularly the older persons with little education, minorities and the poor. Before the survey, focus group for example can be used to identify what socio-demographic variables to include in the survey, how best to structure the diary, even what incentives will be most effective in increasing the response rate. After the survey, focus, focus groups can be used to build explanations for the survey results to identify the "why" of the results as well as the implications. One Asia Pacific survey research result was made by tourism market investigation before. It indicated the travel in Asia Pacific market in the past, had often been undertaken in large groups through leisure package sold in bulk, or in large organized business groups, future travelers will be in smaller groups or alone, and for a much wider range of reasons. Significant new traveler segments, such as female business traveler. The small business traveler and the senior traveler, all of which have different aspirations and requirements from the travel experience.

Moreover, Asia tourism market will start to exist behaviors in the adoption of newer technologies, a giving the traveler new ways to manage the travel experience, creating new behaviors. This with provide new opportunities for travel providers. The use of mobile devices, smartphones, tablets etc. and social media are the obvious findings to become an integral part of the travel experience. Thus, quality method can attempt to predict Asia Pacific tourism market development in the future.

However, improving the predictive power of travel behavior models and to increase understanding travel behavior which lies in the use of panel data(repeated measures from the same individuals). Whereas, cross-sectional data only reveal inter-individual differences at one moment in time, panel data can reveal intra-individual changes over time. In effect, panel data are generally better suited to understand and predict (changes in) travel behavior. However, a substantial proportion was also observed to transition between very different activity/travel patterns over time, indicating that from one year to the next, many people renegotiated their activity/travel patterns.

How to apply advanced traveler information systems (ATIS) to predict future travelling behaviour?

Nowadays, information can impact on traveler behavior and network performance. For example, when steadily growing levels of vehicle ownership and vehicle miles traveled information has been identified as a potential strategy towards man aging travel demand, optimizing transportation networks and better utilizing available capacity. Toward, this goal to predict further tourist behavioral consumption. Many countries, government tourism development institutes has applied advanced traveler information systems (ATIS) which travel behavior models and high-fidelity network performance models made increasingly feasible through the rapid advances in computer power. Crucial components of this problem domain are the modeling of individual tourist drivers' response to travel information and the development accurate guidance of relevance to real would trip makers. So, this advanced traveler information systems (ATIS) can assist the tourist who like to rent travelling car tools to travel in any countries own free traveler information systems service conveniently. Also, this travel information system can be intended to assist travelers to make better travel choices. e.g. this system can improve the decision making of individual traveler rather than improvements of network performance overall. So, we need to understand how tourists make their travel plans. Also, understanding decision process that lead to booking of the trip is equally important, as it allows of a potential behavior.

How does online tourism sale channel can influence traveling consumption of behaviour?

Nowadays, internet is popular, it seems that booking air ticket behavior of using internet is predicted to influence overall tourism air tickets payment method. Tourism industry has grown in the previous several decades. Despite its global impact, questions related to better understanding of tourists and whose habits. Using online travel air ticket booking benefits include booking electronic air tickets can be made from entering any electronic travel agents websites in the short time and electronic travel ticket payers do not need leave home, who can pay visa card to pre booking any electronic travel ticket from online channel conveniently.

How to analyze activity based travel demand ? Nowadays, human are concerning the traffic congestion and air quality deterioration, the supply oriented focus of transportation planning has expanded to include how to manage travel demand within the available transportation supply. Consequently, there has been an increasing interest in travel demand management strategies, such as congestion pricing that attempts to change aggregate travel demand. The prediction aggregate level, long term travel demand to understanding disaggregate level (i.e. individual levels) behavioral responses to short term demand policies, such as ride sharing incentives, congestion pricing and employer based demand management schemes, alternate work schedules, telecommuting limitation of travel agent traditionally work nature shall influence oriented trip based travel modelling passenger travel demand indirectly.

Finally, online travel purchase will be popular to influence the number of travel behavioural consumption nowadays. Any travel package products can be sold from websites to attract travellers to choose to prebook air ticket for any trips conveniently. In the past ten years, the internet has become the predominant carrier of all types of information and transactions. Regarding travel decisions, internet has also become an important sales channels for the travel industry, because it is associated with comparably lower distribution and sales costs, but also because ir adapts to hign supply and demand dynamics in this industry. Consequently, the travel and tourism industry tries to increase the internet sale specific share of sales volumes. So, internet sale channel has changed travel consumption behavioural pattern and characteristics and travel experience. For example, Switzerland has one of the highest population-to-computer ratio in Europe. It is also one of the most highly internet penetrated countries in terms of use of the WWW on a day-to-day basis, with more than 75 percent of the population older than 14 years using the WWW daily (ICT, 2005).

The reason of booking online tourism may include: convenience, fast transaction, finding traveling package choice easily, more airline seats available. So, online booking tourism will influence the traditional tourism agents visiting of sales and air tickets and travelling package numbers to be decreased. Finally, the online booking tourism market shares will be expanded to more than traditional tourism agents visits sale market in the future one day. So, the travel agents who still use the traditional tourism visiting sale channel which ought raise whose features to compare to differ to online tourism sale channel if these traditional touriam agents want to keep competitive ability in tourism industry for long term.

Actively based patterns of urban population of travel behavioural prediction method.

Actively based patterns of urban population. It is a method of motivational framework means in which societal constraints and inherent individual motivations interact to shape activity participation patterns. It can be used to predict one city or urban the numbers of travel demand in the year. It has two elements: First, capability constraints refer to constraints are imposed by biological needs, such as eating and sleeping and/or resources, such as income, availability of cars etc. to undertake the urban or city's family activities in the year. Second, coupling constraints define where, when and the duration of planning activities that are to be pursued with other individuals. So, this method needs to gather information (data) to get the relationship between activities, travel and spending work time and space time to evaluate whether there are how many families who have real needs to spend time to go to travel in the year.

What is trip based versus activity based approaches?

What is trip based versus activity based approaches? The fundamental difference between the trip-based and activity based approaches is that the former approach directly focuses on trips without explicit recognition of the motivation or reason for the trips and travel. The activity based approach , on the other hand, views travel as a demand derived from the need to pursue travel activities. So, it is better understand the individual or family behavior basis for individual or family travelling decision regarding participation in travelling activities in certain places or cities or countries at given times and hence the resulting travel needs. This behavioral basis includes all the factors that influence the why, how, when and where of performed activities and resulting individuals and household, the cultural/social norms of the community and the travel surrounding environment.

Another difference between the two approaches is in the way travel is represented. The trip based approach represents travel as a collection of trips. Each trip is considered as independent of other trips, without considering the inter-relationship in the choice attributes , such as time, destination and mode of different trips. As tours are chains of trips beginning and ending at a same location , say home or work. The tour based representation helps maintain the consistency across and capture the interdependency and consistency of the modeled choice attributed among the trips of the same tour.

In addition to the tour based representation of travel, the activity based approach focuses on sequences or patterns of activity participation and travel behavior, using the whole day or longer periods of time is the unit of analysis. Such as approach can address travel demand management issues through an examination of how people modify their activity participation, for example, will individuals substitute more out-of-home activities for in home activities in the evening of who arrived early form work due-to a work schedule change?

The major difference between trip based and the activity based approaches is in the way, the time dimension of activities and travel is considered. In the trip based approach, time is reduced to being simply a cost making a trip and a day's viewed as a combination, defined peak and off peak time periods. On the other hand, activity based approach views individuals' activity travel patterns are a result of their time use decisions with a continuous time domain. As individuals have 24 hours in a day or multiples of 24 hours for longer periods of time and decide how to use that travel among or allocate that time to activities and travel and with who, subject to their socio-demographic, transportation system and other and scheduling of trips. So, determining the impact of travel demand management policies on time use behavior is an important step to assessing the impact of such policies on individual travel behavior. The final major difference between this two approaches relates to the level of aggregation. In the trip based approach, most aspect of travel, e.g. number of trips etc. are analyzed at an aggregate level.

Consequently, trip based methods accommodate the effect of socio-demographic attributes of households and individuals in a very limited fashion, which limits the activity of the method to evaluate travel impacts of long term socio-demographic characteristics of the individuals who actually make the activity travel choices and the travel service characteristics of the surrounding environment. So, the activity based models are better equipped to forecast the longer term changes in travel demand in response composition and the travel environment of urban areas. Also, using activity based models, the impact of policies can be assessed by predicting individual level behavioral responses instead of employing trip based statistical averages that are aggregated over defined demographic segments.

Why senior age will be main travelling target?

In the past, Germany government had established tourism survey analysis to analyze survey data in order to arrive at reliable conclusions on future trends in travel behavior. To aim to find how demographic change will influence the tourism market and how the industry can adapt to those changes. The travel analysis provided data on tourism consumer behavior, including attitudes, motives and intentions. Since, 1970 year, it is based on a random sample, representative for the population in private households aged 14 years or older. Then, a continuous high scientific standard combined with a national and international users makes the travel analysis a useful tool and reliable source for tourism industry and policy decisions. It aimed to gather statistical data. e.g. on the age structure and on demographic trends, quantitative and qualitative analysis with time series data from the travel analysis. It shows e.g. not only the future volume , quite different from today's seniors, or how who will travel of family holidays will change, e.g. single parents of low, but grandparents of growing significance for tourism.

Demographic change is said to be one of the important drivers for new trends in consumer traveling change behavior in most European countries (e.g. Lind 2001). Because the growing number of senior citizens in the European Union and other industralised countries, such as the USA and Japan, looks to become one of the major marketing challenges for the tourism industry. United Nations statistics predict that the share of people being 60 age or older will grow dramatically in the coming future, and is expected to rise from 10 percent of the world population in 2000 year to more than 20 percent in 2050 year (United Nations Population Division, 2001). From its statistic, some data showed that travel propensity increased throughout life until the age of about 50 years of age and was then kept stable until very late in life 75 age. The most important results is that the travel propensity when getting older is not going down between 65 and 75 age of course, the overall development of this variable is influenced by a lot of other factors which are rsponsible for quite a variation over time. It is now possible to suggest that the general pattern of travel propensity is one of the key indicators for holiday life cycle travel behaviour, includes three stages. The growth stage tends to increase from early aduithood until 45 age old or when reaching some 80%. The next stage is stabilisation from the ages of around 50 age,until 75 age old, starting with a lower increase. Finally, the decrease stage is a slight decrease occurs once people reach the more advanced age of 75 age to 85 age old (Lohmann & Danielsson 2001).

So, it seems Germany government tourism prediction to future travellers' behaviour indicated these findings, such as on how future senior generations will travel, who had used survey data to examine the patterns of travel behaviour of a generation getting older and applied the findings to draw conclusions on the future. Also, it predicted that on the future of family trips, family semgmentation will be the travel behaviour patterns in the future. These findings together with the statistical data on demographic change allowed for a better understanding of the coming tends in family holidays. It's aim developed in consumer behaviour related to demographic change and predicted what will happen future of tourism one had to consider other influences and drivers as well, for example, trends on the supply side. e.g. low cost airlines or in travelling consumption behaviour in general whether how the past may provide a key to predict travel patterns of senior sitizens to the future.

Given the projected growth of the senior citizens market, designing specific marketing strategies to meet the prospective needs of elderly tourists will become increasingly important. It has been an implict assumption that it will be a close relationship between the travel behaviour of today's senior citizens and the those of future ones. The growing number of senior citizens in the world. e.g. China, Hong Kong, Japan, USA etc. countries. Global senior citizen tourism market will be based solely on demographic predictions about the future of the population's age structure. However, many of these seniors won't only live longer but will be fitter and more active until later in life. Many of the will also have plenty in life. Many of them will also have plenty of time and money to spend on travel. So, will these new seniors behave like today's senior citizens? Will they adopt the same travel behaviour as the previous generation or become a new market of oldies for the leisure and tourism indudtry? However, to determine the actual number of senior citizens who will be travelling and to sought to evaluate and specify certain difficult to predict the actual numbers of senior citizen to any country. However, they can be based on the implicit assumption that there is a close relationship between the travel behaviour of past, present and future seniors. But is this a valid assumption? As the reiseanalyse travel analysis survey, which was conducted in Germany every year, offered some interesting data possibiltieis. It was designed to monitor the holiday travel behaviour, opinions and attitudes of Germans and has been carried out since 1970 year, questions in the questionnaire. Data are based on face to face interviews, with a representative sample of more than 7,500 repondents, the interviews being carried out in January each year. All results refer to the average for the defined generated, which ranges generally over ten years. The group of people then at the age of 60 to 69 age is described. This corresponds to the same generation ten years ago, when they had an age of 50 to 59 age. When this methodological approach is not necessarily very sophisticated, it does have the important advantages of being cost effective.

Psychological method to predict travel behavioural consumption.

On the psychological view point, I think individual traveler's character will have those kind of personal characteristics. First, simplicity searchers value above everything ease not transparency in their travel planning and holiday making, and are willing to avoid having to go through extensive research. Second, cultural purists use their travel as an opportunity to immerse themselves in an unfamiliar looking to break themselves entirely from their home lives and engage. Sincerely with a different way of living. Third, social capital seekers understand that to be well travelled is a personal quality, and their choices are shaped by their desire to take maximum of social reward from their travel. They will exploit the potential of digital media to enrich and inform their experiences, and structure their adventures always keeping in mind they are being watched by online audiences. Finally, reward hunters seek a return on the investment who make in their busy , high-achieving lives. Linked in part to the growing trend of wellness, including both physical and mental self improvement who seek truly extraordinary and often indulgent or luxurious' must have experiences.

Why needs to know the personal character of individual traveler's characteristics? Because if travel agents could feel which kinds of individual traveler's character, then who can predict which kind of travel package to design to them more easily. For example, how to determine future travel behaviour from past travel experience and perceptions of risk and safety? We need to concern that the influences of past international travel experience, types of risk associated with international travel and the overall degree of safety feeling during international travel on individual's travelling experiences likelihood of travelling to various geographic regions on their next international vacation trip or avoidance of those regions, due to perceived risk. Because individual traveler's experience of safety risk degree to the countries, it will influence who chooses to go to the countries/country to travel again.

Why do travellers avoid certain destinations are as relevant decision making? Why do they choose to go to the country(countries) to travel? Perceptions of risk and safety and travel experiences are likely to influence travel decisions; efforts to predict future travel behaviour can benefit to individual tourist's decision making. As Weber & Bottom (1989) defined risky decision is as "choices among alternatives that can be described by prodability distributions over possible outcomes" (p.114). Some psychologists judge subjective perceptions of physical reality, i.e. image of a particular tourist destination, whereas value judgement refers to the way individual rank destinations according to whose attributes. i.e. attractiveness, safety, risk etc. factors to form on overall image. So, if the individual traveler had unhappy and worried and unsafe experiences to go to where the place(country) to travel during whose vacation time before. Then, this negative travel experience will influence who is afraid to go to the place (country) to travel again. Risk of place, country, destination or region means the danger is relatively high to the place, ie. increasing in airplane accidents, crime or terrorist activity targeting citizens of potential traveler's nationality or the probability of occurrence is great , ie. recent occurrences involving travel regions/destinations under consideration or effective actions to control consequences exist. i.e. selecting safe regions and destinations, taking extra precautions when traveling to risky destinations. These risk factors will influence the individual traveler who chooses to cancel travel plan to go to the country again.

Another interesting research, how to predict behavioural intention of choosing a travel destination, which has focus of toursm research for years, but the complex decision making process leading to the choice of a travel destination has not been well researched. The planned behaviour model using its core constructs, attitude, subjective norm and perceived behavioural control, with the addition of the past behavioural variable on behavioural intention of choosing a travel destination.

Understanding why people travel and what factors influence their behavioural intention of choosing a travel destination is beneficial to tourism planning and marketing. Understanding travel motivation is the push and pull model. The idea of the push and pull model is the decomposition of an individual's choice of a travel destination into two forces. The first force is the push factor that pushes an indvidual away home and attempts to develop a general desire to go somewhere else, without specifying where that may be. The second force is the pull factor, that pulls on individual toward a destination, due to a region specific travel location or perceived attractiveness of a destination. The respective push and pull factors illustrate that people travel because who are pushed by their internal motives and pulled by external forces of a destination. Nevertheless, how push and pull factors guide people's attitude and how these attributes lead to behavioural intentions of choosing a travel destination have rarely been investigated.

The decision making process leading to the choice of a travel destination is a very complex process. The planned behaviour model is as a research framework to predict the behavioural intention of choosing a travel destination. The model based on the three constructs of attitude, subjective norm, and perceived behavioural control (Fishbein & Ajzen, 1975).

In conclusion, the factors can influence travelers who decide to choose to travel the country, which include personal safety was perceived to the highest motivation factors among the important factors which include, scenic beauty, cultural interests, friendliness of local people, price of trip, services in hotels and restaurants, quality and variety of food and shopping facilities and services. The factors include both push and pull. Push factors include knowledge, prestige, and enhancement of human relationship etc., whereas, the most significant pull factors include high technologic image, expenditure and accessibility etc. For example, Japanese travelers visiting Hong Kong. Push factors are such as exploration dream fulfillment and pull factors are such as benefits sought, attractions and good climate city. It will be the factor of future travel patterns and motivations of sub-cultural and ethic groups for Japanese choice to go to Hong Kong travelling.

Bibliography

Backman, K., Backman, S., Uysal, M. And Sunshine, K. (1995). Event Tourism : An Examination Of Motivations And Activities. Festival Management And Event Tourism, 3(1), 15-24.

Fishbein, M., & Ajzen, Z. (1975). Belief, Attitude, Intention And Behaviour: An Introduction To Theory And Research, Boston: Addison Wesley.

Hsu, C.H.C., Cai , L.A., Li, M(2010). Expectation,
Motivation And Attitude: A Tourist Behavioral
Model. Journal Of Travel Research, 49(3),
282-296. http://dx.doi, org/10.1177/004728750
9349266.

ICT Information And Communication Technology Switzerland, 2005. ICT Fakten (ICT facts).
Available from http://www.ictswitzerland.ch/de/ict%2fakten/factsfigures.asp(retrieved Dec.12, 2005) in German.
Lind, (2001): Befolkningen, Familjen, Livscykeln- Och Ekonomisk Tillvaxt. Institutet For Tillvaxtpo-litiska studier/ Vinnova/Nutek.
Lohmann, Martin (2001): The 31 st. Reiseanalyse-RA 2001. Tourism: vol. 49, no.1/2001;pp.65-67, Zagreb.
United Nations Population Division (2001). World Population Prospects: The 2000 year Revision, New York.
Weber E.U., & W, P.Bottom (1989). "Axiomatic
Measures Of Perceived Risk: Some Tests And extensions." journal of behavioral decision making, 2 (2): 113-31.

However, green or nature tourism strategy may include these elements : Quality, tourism should have an impact on the quality of life for all members of the tourist process, exploitation of nature resources should be optimal and ensure their generation, balance, distribution of benefits among participants in the tourist process must be fair. So, future any kinds of green or nature tourism will need have these features in order to attract many travelers to visit any countries' green lands, e.g. they may rent cars to travel to green lands. So, developing attractive green lands will be one kind new travelling trend for green tourism in global future travel market.

There are two types of models that contribute to the better understanding of future tourism industry development, explanatory model refer to factors that cause development growth. For example, whether the travelers feel necessary to travel to different destinations, very often nice landscapes and sightseeing, pescriptive modes (e.g. life clcle explanations, physical models) examines tourism from what appears on ground e.g. large hotels facilities etc. Hence, any kinds of tourism leisure must need build these both models in order to attract travelers to choose to buy the tourism package from the travel agent more easily. It is important tourism leisure element to any one travel agent's tourism service package if it hopes to develop its tourism service success. So, the expansion of the tourist region over the natural boundaries of the city centre that occured in the first place as a result of the growth of tourism demand, is the end causing this very expansion to continue.

Butler (1980) involves a six stage evoluation of tourism, namely explanation, involvement, development, consolidation, stagnation, and post-stagnation. The last stage is further characterized by a period of decline, rejuvenation or stabilization. The applicability of the model to a given area has been assessed and judged of a tourist destination's development matched the six phases conceptually described by Butler

reference

Butler, R.W. (1980). the concept of a tourist area cycle of evolution: Implications for management of resources. Canadian Geographer, 24, 5-12.

Hence, our tourism industry is facing decline life cycle stage because COVD 19 human mouth disease has influenced many travelers feel fear to catch airplanes to travel, even they also feel to contact the potential COVD 19 human mouth disease people when they arrive the country , they feel that they may contact these sick people, instead of airplanes. So, this kind disease had influenced many travel agents reduce tourism service package number , due to many travelers' tourism leisure activities will reduce, due to travelers number reduces, they only carry cargos to transport to replace travelers COVD 19 disease influence our tourism industry is experiencing decline life cycle stage nowadays. Unless, COVD 19 human mouth attacking to lung disease can be treated by new medicine invention . Otherwise, tourism industry can not re-grow to mature life cycle stage easily.

The most used framework for examing stagnation and possible decline in tourism destinations has been tourist area life cycle model (Butler, 1980). The model has been operationalized frequently in the tourism lierature. It includes series of stages in tourism development, leadning eventually to the stagnation and post-stagnation stages. When a nature destination can either decline, however, it does not offer a systematic explanation of hoe tourism destination might avoid decline . Such as COVD 19 human mouth disease may influence travelers feel fear to catch air planes. So, even the country has beautiful nature scene to attract people to travel, althoug it is a nature attractive destination, but due to COVD19 disease occurs, it may influence this country's this nature attractive destination to enter decline life cycle stage at this moment.

Hence, tourism industry's life cycle stage , sometime it can be influenced by non predicted factor, such as COVD19 disease factor, it can influence travelers' travelling desire to be reduced suddenly from 2019 , due to they feel afraid to catch air planes to avoid to get this kind COVD 19 human mouth disease to bring lung disease when they are sitting in closed window inside air plane environment. So, COVD 19 human counth disease causes global tourism industry is facing serious decline life cycle stage. The question is that any one does not know when this kind COVD 19 disease will be treated by new medicine invention, so if this kind COVD 19 disease still can not be killed by new medicine invention, then it will continue to influence global tourism development to be improved , even any nature attractive scenes, they can not persuade any travelers to catch air planes to visit any countries to travel easily. But, however, we still need to keep our natural environment to prepare future COVD 19 diease disappears , e.g. parks are important places for the protection of ecological systems and natural resources as well as for the provision ot recreational and tourism opportunities for the public. Then, nature or green tourism can be continue to develop to attract many travelers to travel after COVD 19 disease disappears in the future.

● What are the characteristics of birth life cycle stage to tourism industry ?

Butler , R.W. (1980)'s model begins with a discovery and exploration or birth stage in which a location is discovered by a small, select group of people as a place with desirable assets often, this discovery is nature population who may see the perceived assets. As just ordinary aspects of their environment or local culture. The early tourists have very little support in the form of amenities, and typically, this is preferred and is part of a location's of being undiscovered. The early tourists, therefore rely heavily on and interact frequently with the residents of the region. This small group of early tourists is largely in dependent and shares information about a destination by word of mouth or by select affinity groups. Over time, as more people are introduced to the destination, the number of visitors begins to increase. So " word of mouth" will be traveler information to persuade them to make travelling destination choices in the tourism industry beginning. It is tourism industry's birth life cycle stage characteristics . However, internet invention can let any one see any countries' scene photos, so it is one kind of good advertisement method to introduce any countries' scene, instead of travelling magazine in tourism growth and maturity life cucle both stages.

Moreover, space tourism is at the birth life cycle stage. It needs travelers feel interest to travel space, if this kind space tourism service providers hope to implement their any space journeys in success. These factors may influence its development succeeds. Nowadays, its target market is wealthy travelers group, wealthy individual are needed, as they serve as the main consumers for space tourism . For space tourism to succeed there must be enough demand from those who are able to afford to expensive ticket. To date there have only been seven commercial space travelers, or space tourists, although they prefer to be called space flight participant, as they see themselves as pioneers and adventers as opposed to ordinary tourists. So, any future space tourism that price must need to reduce to general public, e.g. ordinary income level people, they can spend, if space tourism hopes to reach from stage stage rapidly. So, space tourism is still far to mature stage.It depends on whether how long time its any space journey ticket price can be reduced to any one can pay. So, when its customer target is not only wealthy travelers, many ordinary or common income level people, they can pay to any one space jounrney. It may mean to reach growth life cycle stage.

● What characteristics to space tourism growth stage?

When human space tourism of commericalization of activities in outer space can bring these feeling to let any one space traveler feels then, it may mean that it can reach growth stage, such as they may feel their any space journeys may bring positive impacts that outer. Space recreation can produce, in order to come up with space tourism, exploring and untravelling the hidden anystories of the space are needed. Also they can feel need drastically broadens and enrichs human's technical awareness and constructive knowledge need from any one space tourism journey package.

When space tourism reachs mature life cycle stage? What its characteristics are? When any one space travelers can feel that not only earth based attractions that simulate the space experience , they must need to catch airships to experience this different tourism experience, such as space theme parks, space training camps, virtual reality facilities , space hotels (skotel), multimedia interactive games and tele robotic moon rovers controlled from earth, but also parabolic flights, lasting up to three days or week long stay at floating space hotel, including participatory educational ,as well as sports competitions (i.e. space olympics). Hence, above these will be nay space tourism development. It can reach mature life cycle stage characteristics when any one can feel the real travelling mouth to compare to travel our earth anywhere, they can not find that they feel space tourism may be same to our earth's holiday (need to rela) or cultural (know different places or specialized tourism, e.g. expectations of adventures , even space scientists discover new experiences to expectations of adventure or get more information, scientific interest feeling. Then, at this moment, we can call space tourism has reached the mature stage. However, I believe that to develop space tourism in success. We must need to control space tourism ticket price to be reduced to general low income people. They may spend budget level. So, ticket price may be one major factor to influence future space tourism growth when it can reach mature stage. Also, it mean that whether space tourism may become another kind of popular tourism lesiure activities to use. It depends on ticket price factor, instead of its any space tourism trip arrangement factor. So, any one space tourism service provider must need long time to spend in order to implement its different strategies, e.g. ticket price, space trip arrangemet to achieve its their space tourism to achieve its their space tourism different destination package in success if they hope their future space tourism business can grow up in short time.

Airport service life cycle stage improvement strategy

Any organizations will have life cycle stage from birth, growth , mature to decline. In airport service organizations have theis life cycle stages in service aspect. Airports organizatins aim to provide safe, comfortable , even shopping environment to let passengers to stay and to wait to transfer another air planes to visit another destination or arrive the country's airport to check out or check in to enter the airport to leave. If airports have life cycle stages, what the characteristics to every stage? How to improve airport service in order to reach mature life cycle stage rapidly? How to implement airport service strategy in order to reach mature life cycle stage to the aorport organization rapidly?I shall explain as below:

Any airports need to be planned in order to raise excellent service to let passengers to let any travelers choose to travel the country whether the country can provide excellent service and facilities. It will bring indirect emotion impact to influence the travelers chooce to revisit the country to travel again. However, soft or hard element or) staff service performance or airport facility), they will influence whether the different countries travelers to choose to travel to re-visit the country again. So, learning how to keep the mature or airport service life cycle stage to stay long time, it will be one important factor to influence any airport business in success.

In the birth life style stage to airport, airport organizations must maintain the capability to provide expert advice to airport owners an matters including operational safety, during construction, environmental compatibility, and airport development standards. No other private or public organization can be expected maintain this level of proficiency. These value-added services enhance public trust when assuring consistant application of standards for the nation's airport system. So, it seems that when the new airport is built if it hopes its passenger customers can consider themselves emotion need. So, it ought concentrate on nowadays airplane landing cunways or airport transfer free service transport etc. facilities can let them to feel safe when they were walking in any airport places. If they feel anywhere are dangerous when they are walking or staying in the ne sirport, then new airport non safe or dangerous factor may influence travelers to choose the country to travel again.

Any new airports will need have good new national airport plan in order to it might operate in the near future with respect to safety areas. The plan elements may include as below:

Achieving zero accidents aim, establish standard safety areas at all commercial service airports , achieving the most minimum 85% of all passenger flights operate on runways with safe feeling, increase measure to 100% of all passenger flight operating on runways with standard safety areas after three months. Within 5 years, 95% of all passenger flights begin and end on runways with standard safety areas.

On benefits aspect, aims to mobilize work force to improve safety area performance describes realistic investment benefits. So, in any new airports birth life cycle stage, they must need to consider safety and expenditure for repair aspect in order to keep its service performance to avoid passengers have dissatisfactory feeling when they are staying in their new airports.

When the country has many travelers travel to the country , then the country's new airport passengers number must increase. It is its the new airport growth life cycle stage. These are critical success factors influence the airport, whether it can improve service performance in order to excite different countries travelers visiting the country's airport desire or grow up the visitors number successfully. The critical success factors may include: Having necessary support from internal and externa stakeholders to implement and willing to share information and identify anywhere the total airport facilities of repair needs that are both reliable and feasible projections to let passengers to feel more safe feeling when they are staying in the airport, understand its future service vision and mission, set strategic direction and goals to process/product specific objectives and decision-making across and doen the organization, define, model and prioritize planning prcesses critical for mission performance, practice hand-on sernior management ownership of planning process and allow field, personnel flexiblity in performing jobs, adjust organizational structures , an essessment program to evaluate planning process and product management , e.g. national airport system performance, create organizational understanding of the value management to customer and stakeholder current and future expectations developing human resources management strategies to support new process that solves needs planners and engineers, building information resources strategies change, especially for entering data at the source and maintains data integrity and timeliness.,establish central support group to support reengineering efforts, outreach and training efforts across the organization, phase in short-and long-term results that achieve set goals and objectives over the next two years.

Thus, when one new airport begins to feel passengers number is increasing. It ought experience the growth life cycle stage to the new airport , if it hopes that it can reach mature life cycle stage rapidly as well as keeps its mature life cycle stage to stay in this stage long time or reachs the airport service performance to the most satisfactory level in this mature life cycle stage. It must need to attempt to plan these strategies to implement in order to avoid decline life cycle stage occurs in short time. So, it explains why some new airport can experience the development to mature life cycle stage from grow life cycle stage in short time,even when it reachs mature life cycle stage. It can keep to stay in this stage long time. The reason is that it had prepared effective strategies to achieve how to improve its airport service performance aim in order to satisfy passenger needs. When they are staying in the country's airport any time. Hence, every year revising service performance is needed to any airports.

Any airports must have development processes. The question is that whether the airport needs how long time to reach growth or mature life cycle stage from birth stage or decline life cycle stage will be delayed how long to occur. The development processes may mean that the airport development life cycle stages changes that had toard a particular result or even as a series of continuous actions or operations coducting to an end (Merriam-Webster, 2013).

reference

Merriam-webster (2013). On line dictionary. Available at:

https://www.merriam-webster. com/(last accessed July , 8 2013).

Hence, any airport organizations with experience development pricess. When the new airport is built, it must be in the birth life cycle stage. Its passengers number can not increase rapidly. It needs time to grow their number. But, when the new airport operates a period, many different countries begin feel this new airport is existence in the country. They will attempt to catch airplance to visit this country airport to catch airplane to visit tis country airport to travel. If they feel this country airport service performance can satisfy their short time staying feeling or its passengers or airports visitors number may increase rapidly. It meand that this airport is experiencing growth life cycle stage. So, if the airport can attract many visitors in short time. It will reduce time to growth life cycle stage from birth life cycke stage.

So , service performance may be one important factor to inflow the airport grows. When the airport develops to the period, passengers number can not increase rapidly, it may be the airport's mature life cycle stage. Due to it's passengers number can not grow rapidly, its passengers number also may reduce. When its passengers number has significant decrease, if its reduction number is increasing more. It implies that the airport is experiencing decline life cycle stage. All any country's airport may experience whole life cycle stages. If the country's airport can not implement successful strategies, it may experience birht life cycle stage in long time because it can not grow its passengers number significantly. So, any airports need to learn how to help them to change growth life cycle stage, even mature life cycle stage can stay in long time easily. If they hope to attract many different countries passengers to visit their airports or travel themselves countries or enjoy to stay short time in themselves airports in order to grow themselves airline industry development.

● How can processes improvement management strategy influence airport service performance?

Overall processes in an airport may involve passengers, luggage, cargo, aircraft movements, ground handling, and crews . All of these operations can be systematised into processes at airport terminal. Three main types of processes can be established departing , arrival and transfer . Departure consists in catching a flight to a final or intermediate destination, arrival consists in landing and leaving the airport, and transfer consists in landing at the airport only to catch another flight to a final or an intermediate destination. Airports also deal with cargo. It involves in the movement of cargo by air, cargo fies from the shopper to the consignee through one or more airlines. However, when the airport can let them freight forwarder, being familiar with the necessary procedures how permits the airline to concentrate on the provision of air transport and to avoid time consuming details of the facilitation and landside distribution system. It will raise efficiency and improve service performance. The services product by the ground handling are crucial to the success and efficiency of the airport operations.

These services are usually provided by specialised companies. Briefly, it includes the luggage treatment, passengers carrying from plan to terminal when needed and aircraft assistance. Also, focusing on crew, there are two majoe processes, one for departures and the other for arrivals. The crew members also have to pass the security and passport controls. However, they have special channels for this. Once they reach the aircraft, the similarities with the passengers' procedure stop. Hence, they have to perform a set of activities , such as check the aircraft load sheets and help passengers to name a few. Also airport terminal operations processes for passengers and luggage, typically for departures , passengers do the check on the airline area, pass security controls, proceed to the general lounge and lastly to the gate holding area. arriving passengers are able to immediately go from the luggage claim area, but the non-passengers have to pass the passport control at first. After this passengers have to decide if they need to declare goods or not as the paths are different . Hence, if the airport can reduce all of this service processes are less complex as immigration check in-out service, liggage claim can be efficient to carry when passengers need to find themselves luggage. Then, it will reduce waste time and let they satisfy airport service absolutely. So, reducing service process time amy also help the airport to increase customers number significantly. When airport role is the middleman between airlines , cargo transport service providers and passengers, e.g. short time transport cargo service and reducing passengers check in or check out service time. then, it will let them to feel more satisfactory service to the airport.

Hence, airport capacity is as a multifactor function leaves open the exact relationship between the factors but stresses that all factors are relevant to assess airport capacity . So , understanding airport capacity and what drives the capacity usage at airports may provide an insight in the set of instructments available to optimise the use of capacity. All of these factors may influence any capacity of an airport, they may include as below:

For example, technical constraints, e.g. ATM per hour service in a runway in a combined arrival and departure fashion, when many passengers are staying at the airport, they can withdraw money from ATM easily. So, ATM number facilities service supply number and location choice to the airport factors will infuence passengers ' satisfactory level, another factor is environmental constraints, it can directly offer the wellbeing of the communities surrounding the negative emotion to passengers and communities surrounding the airprt. For this factor, the change in technology and/or operational procedures can provide more capacity in the system.

Airline business models factor, it can affect the capacity spoke model when other under a point-point one ,these models directly affect the peak hour operational capacity, particularly in big international hubs. Airlines often compete with high frequencies between destinations, thus increasing the number of movements. In addition, conncectivity also has downsides for this model: the delays in one airport might be exported and sometimes in another, due to the connectivity influencing the real capacity. This factor has been setting economic incentives or pricing models. Furthermore, expanding information systems, from one airport to multiple airports gate-to-gate concept, and the use of larger airport to redcuce frequencies.

Hence, above these factors may influence whether the airport needs how long time to reach maturiry life cycle stage when it is staying the growth life cycle stage. It depends on how its strategies implementation and how environment influence its implementation , if it hopes to achieve to reach the maturity life cycle stage in success in short time.

Finally, I shall explain life cycle cst analysis to any country pavement strategy will bring what significant influential benefits to any airports continue to develop in order to avoid to reach decline life cycle stage time in short time easily , when they are staying in the mature life cycle stage. In the construction or rehabilitation investments of highway's pavements, it is already common to perform a life-cycle analysis or life cycle cost analysis for different alternatives to airport pavements. Becauae when any airport pavements are using for a long time, every day has many airplanes need to fly to land on the pavement. It can bring significant repace influence when the airport has many airplanes are needed to land on the pavements every day in the maturity life cycle stages.

Hence, how to evaluate the repair cost expenditure budget in order to satisfy every day air planes land on the airport pavement need. In the calculations are different cost factors (including direct and indirect cost)to any airport itself pavement. Direct costs are related to the critical construction cost landing on pavement activities and are calculated with information from the airport agency and constructors that work for them. The indirect costs are related with the loss of daily revenue of the airport during work activities, such as landing on the airport pavement.

Runways are the most critical pavements area of airport , so it is critical to ensure the quality of these pavement to let airplanes to land on the airport safety, e.g. they need to be constructed with sufficient strength to carry the moving airport and have a high resistance to skidding and aquaplaining. It is most of the time accomplished with reconstructions or deep rehabilitation. Hence, predicting how much will spend on airport pavement facilities expenditure must need in every day.

However, the life cycle assessment (LCA) is a mult step procedure for calculating the life time environmental impact of a product or service is needed to any airport organizations, when they reachs maturity life cycelt stage . The complex process includes goal and cope definition in inventory analysis impact assessment. The process is vaturally iterative as quality and completeness of information is constantly being testes. When the definition of the aim and scope of the study is done the next step is the development of an inventory, in which all significant environmental burdens during the lifetime of the product,, such as airport pavements or process , such as airplanes landing on the pavement or airplanes leaving from the pavement in the airport.

(Araujo, Oliveria & Silve) 2014 explained that life cycle snslysis of pavements are focused on the activities of extraction, production, transportation application of materials, concisely the construction of the road. Because its difficult to obtain other relevant data knowing that the use phase of the pavement is predominant with repect to energy consumption and also to gas emissions related to the atmosphere. One of the main factors for the use phase is the rolling resistance, this depends on the surface and structural characteristics of the different pavements.

Hence, , if the airport can have good repairment or renew skills to help its pavement to improve. Then, it may bring long time benefit, such as reducing airplanes energy consumption and also to avoid gas emissions or reduce gas emissions accident occurrene, even air plane landing on pavement accident occurrence chance can reduce to the zero. so, defining the expected pavement performance time improvement strategy can influence whether the airport pavement can satisfy all airplane users how long time landing on or leaving on the airport pavement. Also it is the major factor to influence airport main function success for any airplanes arriving to the country's airport pavement or leaving from the country's airport pavement. Hence, calculating any airport pavement life cycle costs factor. It is necessary to analysis and interpret carefully the results to identfy the most economic pavement strategy in any airport's whole life cycle development stages.

reference

Araujo, J.P.C. Oliveria, J.R.M. & Silva H.M.R.D. (2011) . the importance of the use phase on the LCA of environmentally friendly solutions for asphalt road pavements. transportation research part D: trasport and environment, 32(0), 97-110. Retrieved in March 2015 from://
dx. doi.org/10.1016/j.trd.2014.07.006.

Image

CHAPTER VIII

Factors influence oil industry life cycle stage

● How new economic development in oil industry

The future global economic growth, it will influence personal incomes and GDP rise. They would carry different weight in different countries at different times. Starting from low levels of incomer and economic development. Household consumption will change from being dominated by basic heat to rapidly rising energy use for higher levels of comfort in space heating and cooling (and large dwellings), and greater use of electrical appliances, finally to a degree of saturation influenced by the income distribution patterns of the country concerned. Income distribution typically changes very slowly, so that the technical market for heart will never be saturated because there will always be a proportion of poor people living in small spaces less comfortably than the average. Industrial energy consumption will be influenced by technical efficiency within each sector, and by changes in the structures of the economy, e.g. changing proportions of agriculture, heavy and light industry, and services. One may eventually see evidence of diminishing marginal returns to additional energy inputs compared to other inputs. Energy consumption in the energy transformation sector may be influenced by income, which drives the demand for electricity to influenced by income, which drives the demand for electricity to grow faster than the demand for heat, but is also subject to the chosen technology of transformation, which is influenced by the cost and availability of primary energy inputs (fuels) in new economic development environment.

IN new economic development environment, it will influences that fuels do not compete in all sectors; for example, the transport sector is dominated by oil. Nuclear and hydroelectric power (and most renewables) reach the user through electricity; electricity itself competes with the direct burning of fossil fuels. Electricity provides the means by which other fuels can compete with oil and gas in sectors, such as space heating and process heat. It also is the only means of powering applications such as motors, computers and lighting: these subsectors are difficult to analyze. However, there is strong evidence that higher incomes do not weaken the demand for electricity so much as the demand for energy in total (in contrast to the effect on the demand for non-electric energy forms).

Econometricians look at the historical record of change in fuel prices and quantities to distinguish several factors between the new economic development and old economic development to oil industry in the future. An income effect. Increasing (reducing) fuel prices reduces (increases) the purchasing power of consumers' income: higher incomes caused by lower prices will increase energy consumption; the consumers' allocation of the increased income to energy purchases may reduce as income rises. Thus income may be heading in a different direction from fuel prices that the effect of fuel price changes when incomes are rising means simply that rising incomes have increased demand. Reducing the cost of using energy through win-win efficiency measures causes a similar problem . On the consequence, in future new economic development environment, it may influence in both cases demand will be less than if the future oil price or efficiency has not changed. The other effect is that an efficiency or substitution effect. An increase in fuel prices may cause consumers to spend more on new equipment, building materials and management operations, which will reduce the amount of fuel required to give the same energy result to the user. The extent of the efficiency effect depends on what happens to the price of the new equipment or building: if those price s rise in line with the fuel price, changes in the balances between fuel and capital or management will not occur. A new user technology , such as the development of the combined cycle gas turbine generator may increase efficiency and thus greatly reduce the quantity of primary fuel needed to produce the required output in this case electricity. If electricity prices had remained sticky, and the electricity and gas markets were not competitive, some of this advantages could have accrued to the gas suppliers in the form of an increase in price, because th4 unit of gas produces more output of electricity, it would have a higher value. In reality, the development of new economic competitive environment in both gas and electricity has tended to ensure that the benefits of such technical advanced accrue to the consumer through lower final prices. The same many apply in the case of improved efficiency in future non-manual driving auto vehicle development: the consumer's cost of motoring is reduced in new economic non-manual driven auto vehicle (Artificial intelligent vehicle) can replace manual driven vehicle , even electricity battery can replace oil energy to be used in vehicles. So, oil price may be influenced to reduce in future new economic development environment.

New and old economic theories explain oil is not main factor to influence tourism income

● Can economic theory explain old price change to influence tourism income?

I shall attempt to apply old and new economic theory to explain whether oil changing price has direct relationship to influence global tourism indusry development or tourism income as below:

Is oil changing price the main to influence tourism income or tourism development or economic growth ? If oil price rises ar falls, it will or won't cause tourism income decreases or increases? If they have cause and effect relationship, what are the main factors to influence tourism income changes by oil price rises or falls ?

I aim to investigate how any why among oil price shocks will influence tourism income variables. We may distinguish between these oil price shocks: Supply-side , aggregate demand and oil specific demand shocks. I assume that oil specific demand shocks affect inflation and the tourism sector equity index. By constrast, I also believe that aggregate demand oil price shock exercisr an effect, either directly and indirectly tourism generated income and economic growth. So, in old economic theory, supply-side , aggregate demand view to oil specific demand shocks will influence tourism income varies. So, governments ought implement strategies against future oil price movements or plan for economic policy development.

In fact, instead of oil price changes will influence tourism income, it could also harm economic growth and tourism activities, due to the effect they expert on transporation, production cost, economic uncertainty.Because tourism activities is one important sector to influence any country's leisure consumption GDP income source. So, sudden fluctuations in oil prices may also influence economic growth. It is based a hyphthesis known as the tourism led economic growth. So, it seems that they have direct or indirect relationship to case effect between oil price and tourism activities and development. So, increase on tourism income, the called " economic-driven tourism growth". In addition, high oil prices are affecting certain tourism industry segments , e.g. airlines, cruises lines, hotel, rent travelling car services etc. for oil, importing countries example, with reference to macro economic effects, higher oil prices generally lead to higher inflation, when they negatively influence to country's income.

Hence, from a micro-economic perspective, positive oil price shocks lead to a decline in disposable income. for low income people, it will bring an immediate and negative impact on tourism, mainly due to they feel tourism leisure is regarded as a luxury good, when oil price shocks to rise suddenly . It influences any airline or cruise entertainment service providers' costs are influenced to raise. Then, they need to increase air ticket or cruise ticket price. It will bring on negative tourism leisure demands-side the oil price increases low income group, potential tourism leisure consumers. Hence, it seems that oil price may have indirect relationship to influence tourism leisure consumers' needs.

● How the price of oil changes influences global tourism industry growth or recession?

In macro-economic view, sudden mid and long term oil price shock can influence global torusim industry growth or recession. For example, a oil price of US$180 per barrel was considered only a few years ago, now this has a realistic scenario to which all plaers in the T&T sector have to adapt. At such a high level, the price of oil will become even more critical to almost every part of the tourism value chain. Although, weak global demand, caused by global economic recesson, resulted in a steep oil price decline to US$45 per barrel by the fourth quarter of 2008 in the past low oil price occurrence history, this won't change the mid to long -term oil forecast.

In fact, the past oil price occurrence history of the dramatic structural had changed a high price imposed on airlines, travelers, and destination countries, all of which will have to navigate through times of shifting or even declining travel demand. I assume that a high oil price scenario is assumed in the long term in order to highlight the changes , such a senario would mean for consumer behavior and the competitiveness of several destinations.

Low oil price in the 1970 and early 1980 did not bring significant growth of international air travel, but its growth has been strongest between 1980 and 2004, a period with stable and relatively moderate oil prices. Also, the rapid development of the low-cost carrier business model in the 1990s further fueled air travel growth by capturing tourism leisure demand , such as weekend leisure travel to cities using mostly secondary airports in any big area countries, such as UK, US . However, the tourism growth is whole influenced by high oil prices, due to oil price had been continue rising in possible.

Basis of oil is shortage supply product, oil is assumed to be the main energy source for the aviation sector for the nest 30 years. Although, second-generation biofuels seem to be on the horizon, the economics as well as the production scalability and aviation biofuel shortage will be a main challenge to airline industry. So, I assume that oil price will continue rise up, if there have none any aviation biofuel can be reflected to oil to use for air plane energy.

Until 2004, the only factors to have affected air travel growth, negatively were in external shocks , such as 9/11, causes catching air plane crisis or US regional geopolitical conflicts. It brings some travelers feel fear to go to US travel, as well as until recently 2019, human mouth disease can influence air to have disease to anyone from mouth. So, global travelers number had been continue decreasing, because they are fear to get disease by air when many themselves every stranger travelers are sitting on the without windows air planes. Although, mouth human and air disease and US 9/11 air attack both matters may influence oil price falls effect, because air planes flying times will reduce. They won't need frequent to fly, to cause aviation oil energy need reduce. Consequently, oil price will decrease, due to travelers number reduces and air planes flying times are also influenced to reduce. (oil demand decreases cause oil price decrease). Although, air lines ' cost will also be influenced reduce, but oil price decrease can not bring travelers number increase , when air ticket price reduce because global many leisure and business trip travelers feel fear to catch air planes frequently when human mouth air disease occured in 2019. So, oil price decreases can not grow up tourism industry growth or rise tourism income.

However, the obvious impact of a high oil price is an increase in the operating costs of airline. Moreover, fuel cost as a percentage of airline operating costs vary significantly based on the length of the flight. The longer the flight, the higher the fuel costs as a percentage of the airline operating cost. So, from an online's perspective, long -hauel flights represent the most criticial challenge to profitable operation because the share of fuel on these flights, compared with other cost items, is largest, because of the unfacorable fuel economics, due to fuel costs even at high-load factors. For example, Thai airways dropped its non-stop Bongkok to US flights in the summer of 2008 for commercial reasons, because fuel reached operating cost levels of 55 percent on this route, a cost burden that could not be passed on to their customers. So, the estimated price elacticity of passengers demand at this Bongkok to US flights route is high, if Thai Airways rises less air ticket price, it will influence many travelers to choose other airlines to catch air plan to fly. Hence, due to Thai Airways can not make decision to rise air ticket price, because it believes that it will lose many travelers, so it only chooses to drop this non-stop Bongkok to US flights to avoid fuel cost rising economic loss.

However, although micro and macro economic theories may also that oil price variable or change, it may influence global tourism income. But, recently, on 2019, human mouth and air diseases, it can influence global individual leisure and business trip travelers feel fear to catch air plans to avoid their bodies get this kind of death sickness when they sit in the no fresh air supplying air planes. They feel that they reduce leisure travelling flying times or business trip flying times with strange travelers to sit in crowd air planes together. Then, they must many avoid human moth and air disease to avoid death crisis. Hence, in this global human mouth and air diseases threat environment occurrence, even oil price sudden reduces to low price, it brings airline's cost reduces and air ticke price reduces. However, when air ticket price reduce to be very cheaper, it can not still attract global many leisure or business trip travelers to buy air tickets to fly frequently. Why does air ticket reduction, it can not attract many leisure or businee trip travelers to buy air ticket to fly ? The main reason is because human mouth and air disease influences global many travelers feel fear to catch air planes frequently. In psychological view, this kind of human mouth and air sickness will bring long time negative influence to global traveles do not want to catch air planes for business trips or travelling leisure frequently. So, it implies that oil price changing to influence air ticket price reduction factor ought not main factor to influence tourism income. It may include traveler individual negative emotion psychological factor, such as human mouth and air disease or 2019 9/11 attack both cases, they can influence global travelers feel fear to catch air planes to fly to avoid death threat. So, oil changing price ought not be only one absolute main factor to influence global tourism income significantly.

On conclusion, in economic view, it seems that oil chang price may have indirect or direct relationship to influence tourism income, instead of some unpredicted external environment factors influence, such as US 9/11 attack crisis and human mouth and air disease factors, they may be main factors to influence travellers number to reduce in non-economic external unpredicted environment view.

COVID 19 human disease how influences global airline fuel manufacturers to rapid reach decline life cycle stage

Recently, since 2019 end, COVID 19 human disease confirms that any one can be gotten this kind disease by the COVID 19 patient individual mouth or air, hand, even things contact. This kind disease may hurt the heath person individual lung to let him/her to feel difficult to breathe, even death. So, this kind disease had influenced many people feel fear to catch airplanes, because when many passengers are sitting in the airplane, if one or more is/are COV19 human disease patient, then the patient has possible to bring this disease to let the health passengers to get his/her COVID 19 human disease in the none window airplanes environment easily. SO, when this kind of human disease is threatening global travellers to avoid to catch air airplanes to fly to travel frequently. Then, airplanes won't need to fly often. When airplanes do not need often fly in sky. Then gas fuel demand will be influenced to reduce to airlines because airplanes won't need often catch many travellers to go to different countries, due to travellers number reduces as well as many different countries' travellers had begun to reduce travelling times frequently and their airports restrict any high body temperature people to enter their countries, because they will have possible to bring COVID 19 human disease when they arrive any airports. Consequently, airplanes do not need to buy and use any more gas fuel to provide them to fly any more since COVID 19 human disease occurs.

How COVID 19 human disease influences global gas fuel sale number? Because travellers number had been decreasing, airlines do not any airplanes often catch many passengers to fly to any countries again. Surely, gas fuel demand to airplanes may be also influenced to reduce and it can also influence whole tourism leisure industry development will experience to the decline cycle life stage absolutely. Before , due to global has many travellers feel need to travel leisure activity. So, global travellers increasing number impacted to global needs to have many airplanes to be provide to fly every day frequently. Before average per day had above 10,000 times of airplane flying times in our earth every day, so it implied that gas fuel need must be influenced to increase to airlines, because airlines must need to buy a lot gas fuel to provide their airplanes to fly to different countries every day , when any countries have many travellers need to fly to different countries to travel. It is sure that airline gas fuel product must reach the maturity life cycle stage in this airplane gas fuel manufacturing industry, because travelling leisure activities are accepted to be on kind of popular habit leisure to global travellers, when air ticket price had been decreasing, it can also attract many travellers accept to spend money to buy air tickets to go to different countries to travel frequently. So, cheap air ticket price and popular tourism leisure activity factors may influence global travellers number increases. When global travellers number increases, it impacts to global airplanes need to increase flying times to fly frequently and air tickets also increases purchase number. Consequently, airlines also are influenced to need to buy a lot gas fuel to provide to airplanes to fly. SO, due to gas fuel demand increases, but gas fuel supply number is not enough, then gas price can be influenced to raise, when airlines demand gas fuel number is more than gas fuel supply number. It is based on economic theory, when demand to the product increases in the market, but the product has shortage to supply, then price may be influenced to bring sale price increasing chance. So, in this airline gas fuel demand and supply case, due to airplanes need to fly frequently, so global flying numbers had been influenced to rise and global airplanes need to buy many airplanes to catch passengers or travellers to fly to different countries. So, airlines must need to buy a lot gas fuel to provide airplanes to fly to different countries every day in this airline industry mature life stage. Thus, before 1029, it is gas fuel manufacturing industry and airlines travelling transport industry and tourism industry their maturity cycle stage period. Every day, global gas manufacturers need to attempt to find any lands have gas and explore any gas lands, than using technology to manufacture gas fuel in order to supply and satisfy any airlines' gas fuel needs every day. But, since COVID 19 human disease occurred in 2019 end, it influenced many airlines lose confidence the travellers number will increase, due to travellers number had been beginning to reduce every day and airplanes' flying times are also influenced to reduce , these both factors must influence gas fuel need reduces to any airlines their airplanes needs.

Hence, after 2019 end, it may be global tourism leisure industry decline life cycle stage, moreover, it may also be global airline transport flying service industry decline life stage both. So, global gas fuel need on airline sector must be influenced to reduce, when global airplanes did not often fly and global airplanes flying times had been influencing to reduce to per day 500 flying times, even less from the top level per day 10,000 flying times. SO, it can prove that they have relationship between tourism leisure industry and airlines' airplanes transport flying service industry and airline gas fuel product manufacturing industry. It means that when any unpredicted factors influence tourism leisure industry's life cycle stage changes, then the unpredicted factors may influence airline transport flying service industry and airline gas fuel product manufacturing industry life cycle service or gas fuel product stage change suddenly , such as this unpredicted COVID 19 human mouth disease, it can influence global tourism leisure industry and airline airplanes transport flying service industry and airline gas fuel product manufacturing industry had been beginning to experience the decline life cycle stage nowadays.

What COVID-19 human mouth disease can let airlines transport service providers and gas fuel manufacturers and tourism leisure service providers to learn? Airlines clearly have a lot on their airplanes at the moment, but since COVID-19 human mouth disease occurred in 2019 end. Many airlines had brought many airlines to prepare to catch global different countries travellers to go to different countries to travel, but nowadays, they do not need to be driven to fly to countries per day. These airplanes are staying on any countries' airports, but per day airlines need to pay high rent to the countries' airports when they are staying on the countries' airports. SO, their airport airplanes rent expenditure must be high, but their airplanes do not need to fly to different countries every day again , because COVID -19 human mouth disease influenced global travellers number had been reducing continue. With unpredicted consequences, many airlines will choose to sell their airplanes later, it none any one medicine can be invented to kill this kind of human mouth disease later, because if some airlines did not make decision to sell their airplanes, then they may nor regrow to growth life cycle stage from decline life cycle stage easily, due to passengers number reduces and it can influence their income reduces. But airline staffs still need to pay , e.g. pilots, airplane front line staffs and airports front line check in service staffs. Hence, sale of airplanes their assets may be the final strategic decision, when any airplanes can not continue to fly every day after 2020 year. Due to COVID 19 human disease can not be killed by any new medicine. If this kind of disease can not be filled for two or more years, then I believe that there are many airlines will experience to death life cycle stage from decline life cycle stage rapidly, otherwise if they can choose to sell some airplanes , they may keep cash available to prepare to reduce expenditure more easily. Although, some airlines made decisions to dismiss some airline service staffs, even pilots to achieve reducing salary expenditure in this decline life cycle stage. But, it will raise unemployment rate to bring social negative challenge. If later airlines choose to sell airplanes their assets to raise cash available strategy. However, it implies that gas fuel need must be influenced to reduce, due to COVID-19 human disease will continue to occur. So, it is the right time, gas fuel manufacturers ought not only concern how to manufacture more airplane gas fuel product to satisfy airlines airplanes transport flying need in this COVID-19 human disease occurrence stage. They ought find any new gas fuel users in this gas fuel market, if these airplanes gas fuel manufacturers expect to re-grow their gas fuel manufacturing and sale business to reach the growing life cycle stage from decline life cycle stage again in the future. Otherwise, many of gas fuel manufacturers will experience the death life cycle stage from decline life cycle stage within one to two years soon as possible.

Hence, if the gas fuel manufacturers can attempt to find other new kinds of gas fuel users in this gas energy market , instead of airline airplane gas fuel market and vehicle gas market main both markets. I believe that they can re-grow to growth life cycle stage from decline life cycle stage again in possible. Although, gas price must be influenced to reduce, because excess of gas supply to airline markets before 2019 end, but when airplanes do not need to fly frequently in this COVID -19 human disease occurrence environment. The COVID-19 pandemic human disease had had a significant impact on the aviation industry, due to travel restrictions and a significant full in demand among travellers. Significant reductions in passengers number have results in airplanes do not need to fly , airplanes feel price must drop, due to oil price war occurred. Hence, due to airline fuel price falls down, it causes many gas manufacturers' gas sale number also reduces to airline market. So, it is right time , any gas fuel manufacturers ought attempt to seek other new gas users, instead of airplanes users or cars users basic both gas users market. If they expect that they can change to experience regrowth life cycle stage from decline life cycle stage again and avoid to reach the final death life cycle stage within one to two years, due to COVID-19 pandemic human disease external environment factor influence.

In fact, on early assessment of the impact of COVID-19 on airline industry, it seems to have a more serve and more rapid impact on air traffic of fuel (oil price plummeted during the first quarter of 2020). It implies that global airline fuel price had been falling down due to COVID-19 human disease influences to global airplanes' flying times reduce. Moreover, COVID-19 impact on Asia-Pacific Aviation worsens, we have seen that first airline casually in the region, such as China , Singapore, Japan, Taiwan aviation fuel need has been influenced to reduce much significantly. Consequently, Asia-Pacific Aviation fuel price had been influenced to reduce much significantly. Then, it also influences Western Aviation, e.g. US, UK etc. Their flying times are also influenced to reduce, then fuel price sale to western Pacific Aviation can also influenced to fall down. Hence, it seems that COVID-19 human disease may also influence global aviation fuel price falls down. If the fuel manufacturers still only depend on sale aviation fuel income. I believe that the fuel manufacturers may reach to the death life cycle stage rapidly in short time. So, seeking new fuel users market is real need to any one fuel manufacturers , because global medicine scientists still can not guarantee when the kind of new medicine can be invented to kill COVID-19 human disease successfully. So, In this COVID-19 human disease threat environment, many experiencing mature life cycle stage airlines, such as US airline, Cathy airlines , UK airlines , Australia airline etc. they may be influenced to experience decline life cycle stage , even death life cycle stage within two year rapidly. Also, this kind of disease can also influence many travel agents' travelling leisure business development to experience decline stage cycle stage as well as it can also influence any airplanes fuel manufacturers to experience decline life cycle stage from mature life cycle stage in possible. Hence, it is right time , they need to change any new market users or service strategies in order to keep their businesses can continue regrow to the growth life cycle stage again.

● Electronic vehicle invention factor how influences future gas vehicle market life cycle stage experience changes

Nowadays, since electronic vehicle invention, it brought competition to fight traditional gas vehicle martet. Electronic vehicle is only needed to be charged battery, then battery will bring energy to push the electornic car to be driven fastly. So traditional vehicle market is experiencing decline life cycle stage. When, electronic vehicle is popular to be accepted to every drivers. In fact, when we drive cars on the roads, our cars will have gas emission to polluate our sir. Earth warmth is dramatically increasing. The main reason is that global air is polluted, e.g. frequent driving activities will bring air pollution when gas emission is caused. Hecnce, environment vehicle is only needed to charged battery. Every time battery charged can bring one day driving time power or enerty to let drivers to drive . So, basing on environmental protection and battery long time driving both reasons, it brings strengths to electronic vehicle to persuade global any drivers to choose to buy electronic vehicle more than traditional gas vehicle.

I shall research these questions: These questions may concern: Will the gas vehicle be influenced to experience the decline life cycle stage rapidly when the electronic vehicle is accepted to be popular to drive ? Can traditional gas vehicle avoid decline life cycle stage comes as well as if traditional gas vehicle real prepares to experience decline life cycle stage ? Can it re-grow to change to enter growth life cycle stage again? Can new electronic vehicle market influence traditional gas vehicle market to shorten time to experience decline life cycle age rapidly?

In our driving history, cars invention had helped us do not need to spend long walking time to go to anywhere conveniently. In fact, due to technological limit, e.g. bus, taxi, tram, train must use gas to be energy to push them to be driven on the roads. When car invention period, or it may call car market birth life cycle stage period. In the 1800 year beginning , human does not know what car function or why we need car. When cars had been invented, it is global whole car industry borth life cycle stage period. This period its characteristics are: In societies , people accepted car tools to drive on the roads. Many people feel to spend money to buy cars, it is waste money, because they may choose to catch any kinds of public transport tools, e.g. bus, train, tram, taxi, ferry, undergroundtrain to arrive any destinations conveniently. So, from 1800 year to 1900 year, global whole car industy had been still keeping in the growth life cycle stage. Because in global society, many people hasd been general accepting public tranposrt tools, their fee are vey cheap and passengers can spend short time to catch them to go to anywhere, they can provide long transport service time for office working people, student from morning to evening time. Hence, this 100 years period, global car sale number could not significant increase, because public transport tools could bring convenience to any one when they needed to leave homes to arrive far away destination in short time.

Hence, global car industry ought not develop rapidly, because many peoplecould not accept to spend money to buy cars to replace to catch any public transport tools. But after 1900 year, global whole gas vehicle industry began to experience growth life cycle stage. Because global many people had jobs to do, unemployment ratio begain to reduce. In society, rich people number began to increase. It based on theseboth factors: families began to consider to attempt to buy any kinds of cars in order to attempt to buy any kinds of cars in order to let them to feel enjoyable to drive to go to anywhere. So, from 1901 year to 2000 year, it may be global whole gas vehicle market growth life cycle stage . In this period, global car buyers number had been increasing significantly . In average, global every family may own at least one car, even more. It depends on whether how many members number, the family has and whether the family has how many member(s), he/she has own one car licence. Moreover, in society, many people began to accept second hand cars, because second hand cars must be chaper to compare new cars as well as it is real one good choice for the low income car buyer social consumer groups in society. So, in this global vehicle market growth life cycle stage, instead of new car buyers number had been increasing significantly, the second hand car buyers number had also been increasing significantly in the same time. So, global new cars and secod hand car buyers number had increased rapidly every year, because global population is increasing. It also caused many working people did not like to spend long time to queue to wait public transport tools, it is another factor to persuade people chooce to buy cars to drive to go to offices or schools or anywhere in their relax time, e.g. holiday, sunday. So, this 100 year, may be global whole car industry growth life car cycle stage.

After 2000, it may be global car industy mature life cycle ctage , many car manufacturers begun to innovate any kinds of traditional cars to change to advanced engine function, auto-window, auto dooe functions , navigation road locaion search function, even non-manual driven artificial intelligent car invention. So, after 2000 year, due to global car buyers begun to pursue comfortable drivin feeling. They need to pursue comfortable driving feeling. They need to buy unique design of cars, or more functions of cars to drive on the road . Hence, global different unique function and styles of cars purchase needs had been significant increasing. Moreover, car prices had also been increasing more, due to more different unique functional and styles of car purchase needs had been increasing in order to satisfy the rich or high income car buyers group. So, after 2000, it may be global car market 's mature life cycle stage.

But, I believe that global car market's mature life cycle stage can not keep long time. The main reason is because the electronic car invention. After 2000 year, since one kind of new transport tool of electronic car invention, it influences many gas car owners or non car owners feel interesting to learn how to drive electronic cars and feel whether what advantages that electronic cars can satisfy their driving needs. IN special, environmental protection awareness drivers must believe electornic cars can reduce air pollution when they choose to drive them on the roads , due to none gas emission effect to pollute our earth air. When they choose to drive electronic cars, due to they only need to charge battery, then their electronic cars can be driven on the roads in short time rapidly. Even, report also indicated driving electronic cars accident occurrence chance may be also influenced to reduce to compare driving gas cars usually. So, electronic vehicle market may be future main competitor to global traditional gas vehicle market. May electronic vehicle invention influence future gas vehicle shorten time to experience to decline life cycle stage rapidly? How gas vehicle market may avoid the shorten time to experience decline life cycle stage if electronic vehicle market may influence its development in global car manufacture industry? I shall attempt to solve these challenges as below:

IN fact, electronic vehicle innovation is not long time , so the global electronic vehicle manufacturing and sale market is experiencing birth life cycle stage. Can electronic vehicle market reduce to shorten time to experience growth, even mature life cycle stages. It depends on these factors:

The factors may affect battery electronic vehicle energy consumption and driving behavior impact. They may include whether environment protection awareness will increase or decrease to global nay one gas car owners or non car owners. Because if global environment protection awareness increase, it will influence gas car owners or non car owners (potential either battery electronic vehicle energy or gas vehicle energy car choice buyers), begun to feel their frequent driving gas vehicle behaviors may bring air pollution or global warming, temperature rises weather disaster occurrence in the future. They alsoknow battery electronic vehicle energy consumption price may be cheap to same to gas vehicle energy consumption. Moreover, they may feel that if they change to drive battery electronic vehicles, it may help them to minimize environmental air pollution impacts of the end of life stage and brings positive impacts on improving climate change and air quality for our future. So, if many car owners or non car owners feel that they have responsibility to protect our climate environment pollution. Then, battery electronic vehicle buyers number will have possible to increase rapidly in short time. Due to the significant impact of gas vehicle and battery electronic vehicle their life cycle analysis can be utilized to analyze the advantages and disadvantages to cause car buyers make comparison between them and gas vehcile and battery electronic vehcile both kinds vehicles are highly complex supply chain choice in the automobile industry nowadays. Moreover, due to carbon intensity of this stage was calculated from emission factors at the global car manufacture industry. Hence, emission factor may be one important influential factor to influence any one makes car purchase decision or either gas or battery electronic car purchase decison.

For example , in our societies, if many peopl own environment protection awareness, then global gas vehicle buyers number may be influenced to reduce, even the owning gas vehicle families may be influenced to choose to buy battery electronic cars to replace their gas cars. They may sell their gas vehicles to any one, even to steel manufacturers easily. Hence, gas vehicle on steel existence number may also reduce ot they can disappear in our road in short time rapidly. If batttery electronic vehcile can be popular to accept to drive on the road to any one driver in our societies. Then, battery electronic cars may be influenced to increase driving needs to any one driver. it's sale number may also influenced to increase rapidly. Consequently, it may have chance to experience to growth life cycle stage from birth life cycle stage in short time rapidly in global whole electronic car manufacturer and sale market.

Then another influential factor concerns how owning car consumers feel the charge of the battery energy use of resources in comparison to conventional gas energy use of resources to driving cars. In combination with the regional electricity mix these factors influence the energy materials for a specific car market. For these first life cycle phases a range of values is possible to battery electronic car market. If in our societies, there are many people choose to use battery charge energy resource to drive electronic cars, their prices are very reasonable to compare gas vehicles or they feel gas will face rapid shortage challenge, if global any one only likes to drive gas vehicle. Then, they may be influenced to choose to buy the battery electronic vehicles to replace gas vehicles. Hence, enery resource used to car my also be one main factor to influence any one car buyer individual either battery electronic car or gas vehicle purchase choice.

Hence, it implies that the life style environmental impacts and energy resource used both impacts of battery electronic cars are a topic of increasing relative importance of the vehicle production stage and the maximum impact on climate change (ingc02/km) that is observed by many climate scientists, their observation to climate change good or bad change effect may influence global battery electronic vehicle needs. So, how clean are battery electric cars, it will be one popular topic for environmental scientists to environmental protection awareness car owners and non car owners. T o analysis hoe to cause electric car life cycle changes. The arrival of the electric car has brought with it an array of life cycle factors that influence the carbon emission level to any one country's environment.

Influence of national electricity grid over the use phase, so it implies that if the country feels carbon emission level is high , due to gas vehicle may bring carbon emission to pollute air to the country. Although, factory's carbon emission or airplane carbon emisson may be one factor to influence the country's air pollution level to be increase. The year has high carbon emission level, it considers gas vehicle air carbon emission level whether it is high or low in the year. So, if the country's gas vehicle car owners number is sudden increasing rapidly. Consequently, it will evaluate that the car increasing number may influence the country itself carbon emission level to be high and it may cause air pollution seriously.

Hence, battery electric car industry life cycle whether when it can experience growth life cycle stage or mature life cycle stage from birth life cycle stage, it depends on what carbon emisson level to any one country. If this year has many countries believe their high carbon emissin level is due to gas vehicle 's carbon emission causes. Then, this high carbon emission level report factor may raise many car owners or non car owners consider environment protection awareness and it may also influence many car buyers choose to buy battery electric cars to replace gas cars to drive on the road frequently in this year.

Also in order to avoid themselves countries' air pollution is more serious. Hence, global carbon emission rise or fall level and any one environmental protection awareness psychological both factors may influence future battery electric car market development. They may have close relationship to influence any one traditional gas vehicle owner to buy one new battery vehicle vehicle to replace it to drive on the road, or any one potential car purchaser makes final battery electric car or gas vehicle decision absolutely.

On conclusion, above these factors may explain whether it is possible that battery electronic vehicle invention may influence future gas vehicle market changes to decline life cysle stage from mature life cycle stage. It depends on whether environmental protection awareness to car owners increasing or decreasing number , carbon emission level whether it is high or low, gas energy resource facing shortage factors to influence future electronic vehicle need.

MTR transport electric energy need factor

Nowadays, transportation and economic development have close relationship. Economic development stimulates transportation demand by increasing the numbers of workers commuting to and from work, customers traveling to and from services areas, and products being moving by lorries on the roads between products and customers. According to Bailey, Mokhtarian and Little (2008) indicated "transportation route is past of distinct development pattern or road network and mostly described by regular street patterns as an important factor of human existence, development and civilization. The route network combined with increased road transportation investment result in changed levels of conveniently reflected through cost benefit analysis, savings in travel time, and other benefits. " These benefits are noticeable in increased catchment areas for services and facilities , shops, schools, offices, banks and leisure activities.

What are the crisis of neglection to care transporation system ? Why do any countries need to design road transportation system? Can MTR transport be popular to be accepted to cause transport electric energy need increases? For example, the Japan country lacks design road trsnaportation system effectively. So, the crisis of road traffic fatalities will raise and the econominc influence will be changed. The crisis indicates more than 7,000 people die annually as a result of motor vehicle crashes in Japan. Driving when under the influence of alcohol is the leading cause of motor vehicle crash fatalities in both developed and developing countries. So, alcohol is the most serious factor to raise personal risk when drivers are driving in Japan. However, a number of studies have shown that deterring drink driving is an important way to cause fatalities. There is a demonstrative need for social change in Japan.

Japan has recently strengthened its already strict laws in order to reduce the number of alcohol related road fatalities. Those deforms lowered the legal blood alochol contant limit increased, the penalties for offenders. The Japan road traffic legal needs. Any driving a motor with a alcohol limit of 0.03 or higher Japan's maximum sentence is up to 3 years imprisonment or a fine not exceeding 500,000 yen dollars. Is law impact to reduce drinking alcohol to drive in Japan? What are economic influence of the crisis of road traffic fatalities in Japan?

The rational choice theory of offending suggests that offenders are active decision makers who influence a large number of variables into decision whether or not to commit an offence. On the cost-benefit analysis, it is the punishment a possible jail, large fines worth is the reward the convenience of driving home without the expause of a taxi and innovenience to the alcohol drivers in Japan. Instead of law reforms when it detects alcohol in the air exhaled from the alcohol and other offenders and it educates children about the dangers of drinking and it also explains why alcohol driving can also threaten drivers' life when who are drinking alcohol and driving behaviour in the same time in Japan.

On the economic influence hand, implementation of the policy deregulating alcohol sales and alcohol production did not appear to increase traffic fatalities among adult or teenage males or females in Japan. We found that male adult fatalities demonstrated a statistically significant decline following enactment of the deregulation policy in 1994 year. So, Japan implement law to threaten alcohol drinking behaviour is useful. It can influence the alcohol availability and consumption, alcohol production and sales, the 24 hours operated convenience stores or liquor discount stores incomes to be reduced. Even, Japan overall GDP is also reduced from the deduction of liquor alcohol production and sale, also the occurrence of traffic accident fatalities chances will be also reduced.

The Japanese economy has entered a rapid process of liberalization since the mid-1990 year. Many sectors previously under direct government control are now regulated by the competitive market place. The Japanese alcohol beverage market has changed. The entry of cheaper import alcohol products resulted in a encouragement of alcohol consumption to Japan drinking drivers and an raising of increasing of more import alcohol products supply to Japan. Although, it is beneficial to Japan GDP growth. But it also raise the occurrence of chance to traffic accidents rate to cause alcohol drinkers to be death or hurt when who choose drinking alcohol to drive at the same time in Japan. So, alcohol import can bring more consumption, but it can also raise many traffic accidents occurrence in Japan in the same time.

In conclusion, alcohol is not good for health to drink when the consumer often buys alcohol at drink habitually. So, if many Japanese, including the alcohol driving consumers and the alcohol non drinking consumers both who often buy different countries alcohol to drink daily. It will cause their bodies to be unhealth for long term in Japan. It is possible to increase Japan's government's medical expenses to assist the low income or poor people in the future. So, although alcohol import can raise Japan GDP growth in the short term, but it also raise Japan government's medical expenditure to the low income or poor Japanese long term in the future, So it's economic benefit will not good in the future if Japan still import much alcohol to sell in its country.

Many commercial users depend on road transport facilities, with movement of products and services from place to place on the roads, aspect of global and urban economic survival. Hence, developments of various transportation modes have become important to physical and economic developments. For example, urban locations with such relative advantages are found where different transport routes with high degree of connectivity, within the intra and inter urban road networks. On similarly, commercial activities like banking, retail/wholesale businesses and professional services can take advantage of nearness to concentration of activities attracted consumers service providers. This partly caused increase in demand for commercial space and its effects on commercial property values along commercial roads can be rose. However, some countries' roads need to provide pedestrian movements more than the businesses activities, e.g. shorten the time of lorries parking on the road to let pedestrian movements on the narrow road. If the country government did not consider the roads need to let more pedestrian movements or shorten the time of lorries parking on the road. It will cause traffic jam or traffic density of the individual roads. Hence, governments need to concern the locations of commercial property buildings and the relationship between the explanatory variables of the design road networks.

What are construction of roads design networks benefits? In fact, construction of roads increased substantially with the opening up of residential environments that also is getting much benefits from increasing demand for spaces in commercial properties. Many private companies, retail stores, commercial banks aggregate in the main roads of cities, which get advantage of opportunities afforded by locations near central of cities to attract many pedestrians concerning their businesses existence. This led to high concentration of vehicular and pedestrian movements. Specially along the access main roads in the central of cities. The main roads exhibits linkages to form networks of minor routes along which commercial properties locate. If commercial users are displaced residential users, causing sites to be at the highest and best uses with increases in the values of commercial properties. However, it seems road network development is affected by the compact nature of various routes that sometimes causes volume of traffic jam. Thus, demand for transport can't be treated solely as a derived demand road. Improved main and minor roads access an city or rural areas is a necessary (but not sufficient). Precondition for increased productivity, the UK Standing Advisory committee On Trunk Road Assessment (SACTRA, 1999) noted "various ways in which transport can affect economic growth, for example benefits include through reorganization and rationalization of production, distribution and land use: reducing labor costs by expanding catchment areas etc."

What is land use and road transport design system relationship? Land use refers to the whole range of human activity and of the built environment, and to some aspects of the natural environment. This is a way relationship between land use and road transport. Governments need to design how to use land and how to design road transportation systems. e.g. where are built the main roads and/or where are built the minor roads are the most suitable locations in the cities or rural areas ? If the main roads is located in the not suitable locations at the centers of the cities or rural, it will case the increasing traffic volumes and levels of congestion, including air pollution, noise, ground water pollution from run-off , loss of soil functions and loss of bio-diversity to natural environment. By influencing the spatial structure of locations in the urban environment, so land use planning can help to mitigate any negative effects resulting from land use changes.

Modelling and land use transportation interactions has become an important aspect of road design transport planning. On the one side, for example, design roads in urban centers, it can increase land use and it can also reduce employees or students catching buses or driving cars' time spending to go to workplaces or schools users. Hence, the land use and roads designing transportation can give benefits to residents and employment people to reduce time to wait buses or taxies etc. public transportations to go to workplaces or schools or shopping centers etc. anywhere. It seems to assist bus companies or taxi drivers to earn more income, On the other side, designing urban transport systems is also important . Increased densities mean more destinations become within convenient walking and cycling distances and consequently the use of these modes tends to be higher. Also in dese cities public transport systems are able to offer higher levels of service and operate more economically, when the provision of sufficient road space to meet potential demand becomes impractical. It aims to reduce the danger of driving or walking in urban areas. The transport modes (that is walking, cycling, public transport) and the extent of car dependence is less, due to driving users dependency is less on rural roads. Hence, building main roads can concentrate on designing convenience to pedestrian walking to close to their houses on the streets. However, poor transport design and land use can cause to spend too expenditure not only transport costs on governments and transport users both and also the costs of providing other services. These include the usual utilities and also education and health services as well as negative externalities , such as greenhouse gas emissions. Most such studies concluded that there are significant financial and economics cost advantage of inner city redevelopment compared with fringe development.

However, such policies won't necessarily be successfully, in particular because of the two ways road problem, they may result in additional private investments and employment opportunities flowing into the region, buy may equally result in population and employment opportunities flowing out of the target region because of the improved access to other centers. Hence governments need to analyze how to arrange the land use to assist the property developers to choose where are the suitable locations to build offices or factories or shopping centers or houses at capital or urban cities to adapt to whose the growth of living population. For example, to judge where the land use whether where main roads or junior roads are built where are the suitable locations to satisfy the lorry drivers to park their lorries are the safe locations ; to design the minor roads to let the pedestrians to feel no danger to walk on the streets when the cars are driven to near to the streets on the minor roads. Thus, the factor of choosing where the land use to design the main or minor roads areas, sizes and lengths and of the minor or major roads can influence the drivers and pedestrians feel safe or dangerous when who are driving whose cars on the roads or who are walking on the streets to arrive the offices, schools, cinemas, church, houses etc. destination.

Designing road transportation networks how to assist economic growth ? I feel it is not all transport investments will be equally effective in enhancing economic growth. Designing road transport investment is a necessary, but on its own not sufficient requirement to earn significant economic growth at either a national or regional level. There are conditions under three categories: economic conditions, investment conditions and political conditions. In fact, although in some circumstances, transport investment may be a necessary condition for enhancing economic growth, it is rarely on its own a sufficient condition. Other factors including the broader policy environment, need to be present if the investment is going to be successful in addressing regional economic objectives. My some suggestions the following key aspects as being most relevant including:

a. Scale economies for example, where these dominate, lower transportation costs through improved accessibility may encourage increased concentration of firms in core regions, until the point that diseconomies set in.

b. Size of the local market.

c. Local land and labor conditions.

d. The nature and scale of transport improvements.

e. The nature of backward and forward linkages

in the country 's local economy.

In any countries, road transportation improvements don't guarantee increased economic development. To increase economic development, an improvement needs to assist any lorry drivers to drive in short trips to reduce transportation costs and shorten time driving on the road or to make transportation more reliable, e.g. reducing the numbers of traffic jams on any roads. A proper economic climate must also exist as well as other support services. With these factors to influence transportation improvements can become catalysts for economic expansion. However, road transportation improvement that intends to induce job creation, when employers need many lorry drivers to help them to transport products and to move products on the roads often. So, the employers need to employ many transportation workers and lorry drivers to help who to transport their products to send to clients, due to the transportation time is shorten and work efficiency is rasied, so the transportation times are also increasing every day when the road transportation roles are improved. On the other side, improving transportation can raise productivity when many customers need to buy many products and the lorry drivers may drive whose lorries to transport many products between factory and office or between factory to the client's home or between the shop and the client's on the road in the short time fast.

I recommend one model links in an overall road transportation network includes these four modes.

I. Maximizing use of the existing road highway system.

II. Extending or improving the multi-lane divides system local roads and connectors.

III. Continually improving the entire road highway network in response to business activities demand.

The improvement of modern road transportation successful factors include:

● How to improve the highway network

modernization includes obsolete interchanges and other segments of the road, transport network of new designs to improve the life and service of pedestrian walking streets, rebuilding certain in main or minor roads. To the extent that labor markets operate more efficiently and more jobs are created to raise economic expansion if our governments can improve road transportation system to design to satisfy business users demand when lorry drivers need to move or transport whose products on the streets, but who will not influence pedestrian are walking on the streets. Hence, excellent transportation design network can subsequent plan efforts, it can also rise economic efficiency, community and social effects, it can also encourage transportation users to attempt to drive lorries to transport products a lot of times in one day fast and who can also avoid traffic jams occurrence on the road easily. On the one side, economic development is a concept referring to the material aspects of community welfare. There are numerous factors need of development: growth in income and wealth, equitable distribution of income, decreased infant mortality rates, increased literacy rates. On the other side, economic growth means which is sustainable increase in community income and /or wealth. (wealth is the net of resources that generate income). It seems the link between transportation facilities and economic growth has close relationship. Good transportation facilities support economic growth by lowing the transportation costs of users of the transportation network, such as roads. Direct users benefits are reductions in travel, times and fuel consumption, increased reliability and increased safety in the movement of people and products, users' transportation costs are reduced, resources are used for other purpose.

The relationship between transport and economic development occur in two directions, in the sense that (i) land use and economic development are major drivers' of demand for transport (in terms of quantity , type, location and mode); and (ii) transportation investments and other initiatives (such as regulations, pricing) can influence levels, patterns and locations of economic development. The principal role of road transportation is to provide access between spatially separated locations for the business and household sectors, for both commodity (lands transportation) and person movements. For the business sector, this involves connections businesses and their input sources between business factories and other business shops and between business and their markets. For the households sector, it provides people with access to workplaces and education facilities, shops and social recreation, community and medical facilities etc. on the roads. I feel different countries' road transportation system can be self funded in the sense that the majority of the costs of transportation system investment operation and maintenance are either paid directly by users (for example, through car operating costs) are funded initially by governments and recovered from transport users (for example, through petrol duties and road user charges). Governments' road transportation system and their use also give rise to some external costs(externalities). These include global environmental impacts (greenhouse gas emissions) and local environmental and health impacts (for example, noise partial pollution and road accident costs). The direct effects of transportation investments are to reduce road transportation time and costs through reducing travel time, decreasing the operating costs of transportation and enhancing access to destinations within the road network. A good road transportation network also needs to reduce any economic disbenefits, for example where projects reduce congestion or the risk of injury. These incremental benefits of transportation investments may be measured through commercial cost benefit analysis. Other indirect consequences of road transportation network should also be considered when evaluating effects on productivity and the spatial pattern of economic development. Good road transportation design network benefits can include lower costs and enhanced accessibility, due to better transportation links and services expand markets for individual transportation using business and improved access to input.

The economic contribution of road transportation policy can be assessed from various perspectives. These include:

● Effects on aggregate economic welfare (e.g. the sum of consumer and which is the times of cost benefit analysis, as linking to transportation productivity effect.

● Micro economic, for example, enterprise or household level productivity effects.

● Macro economics, for example, contributions to GDP investment or employment and the spatial patterns of economic activity.

One key characteristics of road transportation is split between infrastructure and operations. Infrastructure refers to the right of way on which vehicles operate, which may include ancillary facilities to ensure efficient and effective operations (for example, traffic signals, railway stations). In developed countries, are in most transportation is operated by the private cars, road trucks, the majority of bus and coach services. In long term , overall purpose, to ensure transportation system helps to develop that maximizes the economic and social benefits and minimizes harm. Hence, governments need to concern who are their main target users to use every road. Such as the road is used to near to park and leisure, or local and national economic conditions, keep clean natural environment etc. facilities to provide different benefits to different target users to enjoy to use. It seems that good transportation networks designing can influence economic activities, shopping convenience or business convenience etc. activities to cause whether the country's economic behavior to achieve close relationship successfully. Possible relationship between road networks, location attribute, demand and supply and accessibility and commercial property values of these factors which will influence different countries' concerning to choose where to build main roads and sub minor roads in different cities and rural locations. However, I shall suppose hypotheses how governments to find the most suitable places to build main roads and sub minor roads to whose cities and rural. There is no significant relationship between commercial property values and individual contributions of explanatory variables to variability in commercial property values in whose countries.

In conclusion, I suggest methods how to design suitable transportation networks to governments to build, such as it is essential to establish a technique that may be useful for determining relative accessibility of locations in the network of main roads and sub minor roads. Even, when relative advantages are determined, there is need to develop models that will be useful for predicting commercial properly values. The model may become tool for professional estate surveyors and values to change their practice of using intuition to determine relative access of locations in a road network. Similarly, there is the need to predict the supply of, demand for, and fair market values of commercial properties by developers. Hence if the cities or rural locations can attract many businesses to build commercial properties, governments can build the main roads in the locations. Otherwise, if the cities or rural locations can not attract many businesses to build commercial properties, governments can build the sub minor roads in these locations. Hence, the main roads must have high transportation valuation to let big lorries to drive and park in these main roads easily and conveniently. It seems capital cities may not influence to build the main road factors. Natural environment, commercial properties values, the lands areas size and shape and pedestrian walking numbers on the streets and lorries available numbers on the areas will be other factors to influence where to build main roads in any cities or rural in the country.

In road concept, the route network consists of primary and secondary roads, known as main roads and minor roads respectively. Main roads are usually moderate or high capacity roads that are below highway level of service, carrying large volumes of traffic between areas in urban centers and designed for traffic between neighbors. They have intersections with collector and local streets and commercial areas, such as shopping centers, petrol stations and other businesses are located along such roads. In additions, main roads link up to expressways and freeways with inter-changes in cities or rural. Road network constitutes an important element in urban development , due to urban areas have many farms, gardens, forests , so roads and building needed to provide accessibility required by different land uses and the proper functioning of such urban areas depends an efficient transport network existence. In computing des, the network indicator are used to partition road network into different parts in reasonable way. The results in number of connection to describe density differences in road networks. The parameter records how many roads connect to each road in a network. For two roads with the same length, the ones in the dense area will connect to more roads than that in a sparse area and the connection differences will indicate the density differences to some extent, so road density can also be calculated as the total length of all known roads divided by the total land area in a road divided by the total land area in a road network. Hence, governments need to consider road length to decide how to build main or minor roads to design its transportation systems for businesses activities , such as driving lorries and parking lorries and products are been moving on the streets from roads easily and conveniently. As Wikipedia Contributors (2008) indicate that "transport networks are spatial structures designed to channel flows from the points of demand to points of supply and to link the points together in a transportation system. They are useful for transport network analysis to determine the flow of people, products, services and vehicles." Hence, governments need to research whether where the shopping centers, cinemas, houses, hospitals, schools, offices, factories etc. are located, then, which need to follow these location datas to predict the cars, lorries, taxies, buses etc. of the demand numbers of transportation users to design the lengths, width and distances and the construction of main and minor roads locations and their supply numbers in different capital cities or country roads. It aims to reduce traffic jams and shorten time and air pollution as well as increasing the available spaces to let the lorry drivers to move their logistc on the road easily and reducing the accidents occurrence when the pedestrians are walking on the streets. If the vehicles can be moved on the roads easily. It will also increase time efficiency and productivity to any businessmen. Hence, how to design of the main roads and/or minor roads in any capital or country cities. It will influence any country's economic growth long time in the future.

● Underground train transportation tool is popular needed to influence transport electric energy need trend incrseases more than transport gas energy need

Understanding individual passenger behaviour is essential for the design MTR transportation, because who can choose to catch bus, taxi, tram, train ferry etc. different kinds of public transportation tools. Individual traveler who decides to catch which kinds of public transportation tools, it depends on whether the public transportation tool can provide real time travel information, liking link travel time schedule. So, MTR underground train needs to understand where it has terminal to give convenience to the local living areas of time travelers to choose to catch MTR easily. Although, MTR ticket fare is one factor to influence any passengers choice. But, those other factors can also influence them to choice. e.g. MTR any terminal location of convenience, short time travelling, none crowding in busy (peak) time, MTR platform waiting arrival time, none sudden MTR engineering machines broken accident events occurrence frequently etc. different factors, any one of these factors which can influence passengers who choose to catch MTR or other kinds of transportation tools.

Why route choice can influence passenger behavioural choice ? Usually, the busy time passengers will regard the route choice as a coordination problem to influence them to choose to catch which kinds of transportation tools. The route choice is as an opportunity costs to influence any busy time passengers to decide to choose to catch which kind of transportation tool which is the best right choice in the right time among of them. In the short time, for example, it seems any busy time passengers will choose to catch bus to substitute MTR underground train transportation tool, due to who feels the bus can arrive any destinations to compare other kinds of transportation tools in the most short time. However even if the MTR can either charge cheaper ticket fare to sell full day or charge discount ticket fare to sell in the busy (peak) time to compare to bus fare. It is possible that the busy time passengers will still choose to catch bus, if between the bus terminal and the another bus terminal that distance is the shorter time route to spend time to arrive destination to compare between the MTR terminal to the another MTR terminal arrival time . Also, although the busy time passengers will feel to enounter traffic jam to influence sitting or waiting bus time to be longer time in possible and who also feel MTR can avoid traffic jam problem. However, usually any busy (peak) time passengers will feel the chance of traffic jam occurrence will be less. So, the short bus route choice is more potential factor to influence the busy (peak) time passengers still to choose bus to catch.

However, if anyone wants to investigate results of day-to-day route choice which can be transferred to more realistic environment. It is necessary to explore individual behaviour in an interactive experimental set up to ensure busy (peak) time passenger transportation behavioural choice. For example, a passenger has a choice between a main road (M) and a side road (S) for travelling from (A) to (B). (M) is faster if (M) and (S) are chose by the same number of passengers. So, this method can be researched whether MTR terminal station is located at the main road (M) or the side road (S) where is more suitable to accept to passengers generally.

Why trip time reliability and crowding factors can influence MTR passenger choice? Other problem is MTR busy (peak) time's crowding in public transportation occurrence of MTR underground train transportation tool is becoming a growth to concern as MTR demand growth at a busy (peak) time. To capture the MTR passengers benefits with reduced crowding from improved MTR public transport service and image. It is necessary a identify the relevant dimensions of crowding that are meaningful measures of what crowding means to MTR passengers. Two main influences on MTR model choice that are growing in relevance are trip time reliability and crowding. It represents a benefit-cost framework. In fact, MTR passengers can be willing to pay more expensive ticket fare, it MTR can avoid crowding and short and the accurate arrival trip time between terminals is reliable to occur. How to measure of MTR crowding, e.g. weighting the gap between the busy time, the standard (i.e. objective) and the perceived (i.e. subjective) metrics. We are not in a position to definitely map the two dimensions, which is a crucial requirement for translating objective improvements into equivalent subjective gains that then can be applied, willingness to pay estimates MTR ticket fares to obtain the additional MTR passenger benefits of MTR public transportation investment to any terminal stations. Because MTR crowding has a negative impact on passengers in terms of psychological on emotional distress. MTR passengers are willing to stand for up to 20 minutes of the service is fast and reliable. However crowding outweighed these benefits from a MTR passenger's perpective, experienced crowding leads a increased dissatisfaction. e.g. stress and less privacy during who needs to stand up in MTR. Due to there are no enough places to supply to them to stand up in MTR. If the MTR trip time was longer time between the passenger's terminals, who will feel more dissatisfaction and it will cause who feels whether who ought need to choose to catch other transportation tools to substitute MTR next time. e.g. bus, train, tram, ferry, taxi etc. So, from an operator's perspective, the MTR service frequency or MTR size is significantly influenced by the level of ridership, which sends a signal to respond if the monitored crowding level exceeds the benchmark standard in the busy time. e.g. in the morning time or at the night time, the students or employment people who need to go to schools or offices (working places). The locations of different places between MTR terminals and crowding are regarded as a key service attribute for MTR pubic transportation along with other factors, such as travelling time and reliability, e.g. service quality, none engineering machines are broken to cause MTR stops suddenly.

Given the increasing importance of crowding on both the disutility to existing MTR public transportation users and the influence to it. MTR passenger can choose to use either the MTR public public transportation or other public transportation. It is timely to review the MTR current measures of crowding defined by transportation authorities. MTR operators ought evaluate whether they apporpriately reflect MTR each traveler experiences and perceptions of crowding in busy (peak) time. I suggest that MTR needs to buy other underground trains to supply to the busy (peak) time passengers to let them have enough seats to sit down, so who do not need to stand up in any MTR underground trains when they catch MTR underground trains in busy time. It aims to let who are willingness to pay the estimation of reasonable ticket fares to compare the other kinds of transportation tools in the busy (peak) time.

What is the crowding difference between train and MTR underground train? In fact, crowding won't be happened to brother these transportation tools easily in the busy time and non busy time both. e.g. bus, taxi, train, tram, ferry. Because passengers can not choose to stand up in these transportation tools easily, due to these transportation tools have no enough areas (spaces) to let them to stand up easily . So, the crowding will be avoided to occur in these tranportation tools usually. Otherwise, MTR will have many passengers who can choose to stand up because MTR design of length is very long and it has enough areas (places) to let passengers to choose to stand up, even there have none any seats are provided to let them to sit down. So, MTR passengers will feel more dissatisfaction and crowding easily, especial in any peak (busy) time every day.

Comparing to bus, much more diverse crowding measures are defined in the passenger rail industry. For passenger, different specifications for measuring crowding are found across countries and even within a country. For example, rail crowding measures in the UK, the passengers in excess of capacity is crowding measure that applies to all London and South east operators weekday train services at a London terminus during the morning peak from 0700 to 09: 59 , and those departing during the afternoon peak from 16:00 to 18:59 (office of rail regulation 2011 year). The overall PIXC figure is considered the planned standard class capacity of each train service as well as the actual number of standard class passengers on the service at the critical point. i.e. the location on a trains of standard class passengers that surpass the planned capacity as the difference between the number of actual passengers and the capacity of the train divided by the number of passenger is within the capacity . So, it seems train and MTR underground public transportaton tools had been encountering the crowding problems in peak time, the difference in train passengers need to wait next train or more train arrival is who doesn't plan to enter the train, when who discovers the current train has no seats to provide to them to sit down in whose trip. Otherwise, MTR passengers can choose either to stand up within the large areas (places) if who discovered there are no any seats to provide to them to sit down or who can wait the next MTR arrival in order to who can sit down. It seems MTR transportation tool crowding environment includes in waiting platform and inside of the MTR underground train. Otherwise, train transportation tool crowding environment only includes the waiting platform and the passengers will not have crowding feeling inside of the train, due to none of passengers choose to stand up inside any trains because any train inside has no enough places to let them to stand up.

How MTR can attract many passengers. On the commuter departure time choice of any reference point researching hand, the departure time decisions of communters are of fundamental importance of peak period MTR traffic congestion. However, whether on the demand side, MTR underground train congestion relief measures, such as MTR ticket fare to every terminal station needs to be charged cheaper fare or discount fare in the peak (busy) time every day. To aim to attract many passengers to choose to catch MTR Underground train public transportation tools, substitute to choose other public transportation tools in the peak time.

Over the past decades, there have been very active research efforts in the departure time problem, both in econometric modeling and dynamic user equilibrium fields. Although, these works provide valuable insights into dynamic commuter decision making, they do not identify the commuters' response to gains and losses related to whole actual arrival time to reference points who may have relative. The appliability of the reference point hypothesis of prospect theory to the commuter's departure time decision making to obtain a better understanding of how departure time choice in MTR platform during their waiting underground train arrival time. However, every MTR underground train actual arrival time and deviation variables related to reference points (gains and losses) are the key factors in the departure time choice model. How the MTR underground train of every communter's daily departure time decision can be modelled when the reference point hypothesis of prospect theory. The MTR underground train's schedule delay is defined as the difference between the preferred arrival time (PAT) and the actual arrival time (AT) for a given MTR communter. In a daily MTR commute, a commuter in the indifference band actual arrival time is an essential feature of MTR schedule study. Two reference points are the earliest acceptable arrival time and the work starting time for a given MTR platform waiting passengers. In psychological view point, prospect theory proposes that the displeasure of a loss is perceived or greater than the pleasure of a gain of the same attitude and therefore, the value function is stronger for losses than gains.

To conclude, it seems that if MTR waiting passengers need not spend long time to wait underground train arrival in platform and it can provide seats to let them to sit down in the busy (peak) crowding time. It will make them to feel pleasure, even the MTR ticket fare is not fair and reasonable to charge higher fare to compare other kinds of public transportation tools fares. So the peak waiting time factor can influence the passengers to choose other kind of transportation tools to catch easily. Moreover, MTR's two reference points are the earliest role. Similarly a loss is observed when the MTR platform waiting commuter experiences or actual arrival time which is beyond that the MTR schedule time. Due to that a MTR waiting commuter is as an early side arrival of whose actual arrival time is earlier than whose preferred arrival time.

Reference
Bailey, L., Mokhtarian, P.L. Little, A. (2008). The broader Connection Between Public Transportation, Energy Conservation And Greenhouse Gas Reduction, Report Prepared As Part Of TCRP Project J-11/Tasks Transit Cooperative Research Program, Transportation Research Board Submitted To American Public Transportation Association in http://www.apta.com/research/into/online/land_use.cfmi, accessed 17 April 2008.

The UK Standing Advisory Committee On Trunk Road Assessment (SACTRA) (1999). Transport And The Economy (Report To UK DETR). Retrieved From: http://webarchive.nationalarchives.gov.uk/20050301192906 ; http://dft.gov.uk/stellent/groups/dft-econappr/documents/pdf/dft_econappr_pdf_022512.pdf

Wikipedia Contributors (2008). Arterial Roads In Wikipedia, The Free Encyclopeda, http://en.wikipedia.org/w/index.php?title=Arterial_road&oldid=212832640(accessed May30,2008).

● Why electric transport tool service increasing causes gas enery to transport needs decrease

Any countries must need road, sea and air transport to assist businessmen to transport products in local or overseas. If the country's road , sea or air transport system service quality is poor. It will influence any products transport time, speed, inefficient transport to anywhere.

How to raise the country's transport system in order to improve efficiencies to let any businessmen can deliver their products to anywhere easily,e.g. warehouses, client homes, supermarkets destination in the most short time to avoid delay occurrence to let clients feel unsatisfactory or complaint their perform their delivery services poorly. I shall discuss the factors how to improve any countrues' transport systems to achieve the most efficient way as below:

Any countries' transport systems will create economic value, e.g. demonstrate value for money, economic worth, viable commercial worth, financial affordable worth, achieveable worth. Any countries' transport systems can bring welfare value by economics. It has direct relationship to take the form of measured economic activity, i.e. GDP. The form of measured economic activity can impact on any countries' economic economic geography, locally , regionally and nationally's local GDP impacts. The welfare impacts may include: leisure time savings, e.g. the local people drive cars or catch any public transportation tools to go to any geogrpahical location's shopping centers, big gardens, swimming pools, cinemas etc. places to carry on any kinds of leisure activities.

Environmental impacts may include avoiding noise, air pollution on road transportation aspect , when the main road is only on on focus on the main city, but the city lacks other roads to let any drivers can choose them to drive, instead of the main road in the city. Then, when many cars are driven on the busy transport

time, e.g. morning working time or night busy time between 6:00 and 9:00 AM, between 6:00 and 9:00 PM. When either many working people need to catch public transport or drive themselves cars to go to offices to work or they need to catch pubic transport tools or drive themselves cars to home. Then, the only one main road problem will need them to stay themselves cars on roads, due to traffic jam or traffic accidence occurrence problem causes when many cars are driven on the road in the busy transport time. It will influence they can not go to offices or homes easily daily, even in the busy transport time, their cars' gas need to be used much to cause air pollution and traffic noise is easily caused easily in the busy transport time on the road. When the city has only one main road for drivers in the busy transport time. So, poor road transport system can bring poor impact on economic welfare benefits arising from proved labour supply from commuting, time savings, including exchequer benefits. Consequently, the county's GDP will be fallen down, due to labour market effects which do not add to welfare value.

Whether can poor transport system impact indirectly on GDP or not on local, regional , or national economic geography impacts? Does transport lead to greater economic activity i.e. higher GDP? DO they lead to change in economic activity location? Does transport impact the existence of business location and new economic activity opportunities? The measurement on every country's transport how impacts on economic change, facilitating geographic division of labour and specialization. It can be analyzed on these general aspects:

Costs and speed of travel time (Economic value of travel time savings) . Travel time savings to users from improved transport is a key of economic value, but it has only less influence,journey time reliability is more important to business frieght as well as business travellers, network connectivity enhancements as well as business travellers, network connectivity enhancement can help people and goods travel more quickly (i.e. linked to jounrey time and journey time reliability, as well as opening new destinations and new journeys, comfort and quality service provision is relevant to public transport, e.g. detering jounreys at particular times or by certain modes (e.g. overcrowding), impact on productivity at work for commuters, safety and security , due to loss of output from workers, transport accidents occur easily. All of these issues will impact any countries' standard of living to local people (geography) , even GDP income.

Why does the direct and indirect effects of transportation have a positive impact on the economic growth and development of a country? Does it influence acccess to goods, services and

employment opportunities in any regions? Underdeveloped countries must need to consider how transport system influences their economic growth. For example, the costs of transportation and production are reduced through timely delivery and enhancing the economies of scale in the production process, when the road is often traffic joam, gas cost, time waste , air pollution cost, noise has many roads, but if one lorry drivers needs drive more than one day to day to deliver goods to another city's warehouse every day. It will bring psychological pressure in terrible, when they need long time to drive on the road. They can not sleep easily because road accident will occur easily when they need to spend long time to drive lorries on the road.

So, how to solve the long driving time on road transport problem will be one issue concerns human life welfare benefit aspect, instead of economic benefit aspect. The transport system welfare worth needs to include human life worth. It is a valuable insight into the causality (ot lack of causality) between transport and economic growth and will serve to compare to any countries' national level and local geographical location level both.

In special, underdeveloped countries' public transport time whether it is long or short factor, it will influence workers their going to offices to work time. If they often need spend long time to catch buses, due to traffic jam,then it will influence their efficiences to be reduced, productive number is influenced to reduce also, because traffic jam causes they often go to offices too lately.It can influence workers' bad emotion to work every day. So, traffic jam will bring negative relationship between low efficiency and bad emotion to the workers, because they need to spend long time to wait, public transportation tools and traffic jam also influence their working emotion. Consequently, service and working performance will be influenced to poor, because long time traffic jam problem causes their bad emotion to work. It is one critical factor in the path of more widely spread economic growth and urbanization for traffic jam problem to underdeveloped countries.

However, transport system can also influence developed countries' economy. How does it influence on environmental impacts aspect from mature stage. Its business activities must raise, dramastic expansion during this period, such as underdeveloped country, US, UK. In order to acheive long term sustainable development , new demands are being placed on transport sector, such as underground mass transit rail transport , ferry, local air frieght transport, train , e.g. Japan, Fance, US high speed prior rail. Because their developed countries , business and entertainment activities needs increase, it influences high time efficient and rapid speed public transportation tools needs are also needed in societies. These new technological public transport tools invention will impact on climate, noise, human health, land use and damage to ozene layer, acidification aspects, instead of economic beneficial aspect. For long -term sustainable development to be achieved, the various activities within developed and underdeveloped societies must be adapted to what can be tolerated by humans and by the natural environment. Transport is an activity which affects humans and the natural environment for both the development of society as a whole as well as for the mobility for the individual. For Swedish underdeveloped country example, air pollution in Swedish urban areas has beed reduced, but in many places concentrations of certain substances deiving from transport activities are still at unacceptable levels and much more has to be done. Carbon dioxide emissions and noise are examples of environmental problems demanding further efforts. Measures to limit the exploitation of valuable natural and cultural environments to protect biological diviersity are also needed. So, if Swedish still hopes to develop its tourism industry to attract many travellers to choose to travel itself country. It needs to solve environmental problems from different modes of transport are of different dimensions, such as improving its air transport to avoid cause different problems and rail transport differs in turn from road transport.

The transport problem to Swedish may include poor technological communication information to its public and purchasers of transportation and communication services as to the environmental effects of different solutions is significant in creating the demand for environmentally sound public transport service concepts. It is therefore important that such lacking high technological communication and information system is presented in as completem accurate and clear way as a method for non-monetary comparison of the environmental public transport service system aspect.

In real, it's public tranport service system is needed to be improved and upgraded in order to let travellers feel Swedish's any rail, underground train, ferry, bus , taxi etc. different public transport travelling service can provide excellent performance to serve their travelling passengers, when they need to catch any kinds of public transport tools to go to travel. They can feel convenient and comfortable to attract them to visit Swedish to travel again. Then, its tourism industry GDP income will be raised, if Swedish government can innovate any new kinds of purchase ticket equipment to install in and public transport stations to let travelling passengers feel that they do not need to spend long time to queue to buy tickets to catch ferry, train, underground mass transit rail on stations conveniently. Because long time purchase ticket queue waiting will cause travellers feel its public service performance dissatisfaction and they will complain , even they won't choose to catch the kind of public transport, even the travellers won't choose to travel Swedish again, if they feel Swedish is one developed country, but it neglects to take care about travellers' catching public transport travelling service needs.

It is one poor or bad feeing to let travellers choose to Swedish again. Hence, Swedish needs to improve its public transport service performance in order to achieve to raise their comfortable and satisfactory catching public transport tools needs to let travellers to feel. They may include efficient land use for transportation tools, comprising issues concerning natural and cultural environment, natural resources, biological diversity and aesthetics, noise reducing, public transportation energy consumption and time consumption reducing, raising public transport service facilities performance functions and other issues concerning the model. For example, Swedish government can facilitate the public transport price conparison and journey time spending comparison information gathering enquiring machines public transportation selection method of public transportation services to let every travellers can evaluate different modes of public transport when they are staying in ferry, bus, train, underground mass transit rail, taxi stations.

A travelling family can seek its sustainable transport selection system for passenger transport tool. When they touch the enquiry machine, they can compare busm ferry, train, underground train, taxi price and journey spending time from their transportation stations to another destinations. Then, travelling passengers can compare these public transport tools ticket prices, journey spending time immediately when they touch the public transport enquiring machines in stations any time. Then, they can make the most righ choice to decide whether they ought catch which kind of public transport tool to arrive the another journey destination. It is one every attractive high technological enquiry method to help any travelling passegners to choose which kind of public transport tool, it can be the most cheap transport tool at the moment in any public transport stations. So , for developed countries innovative its public transport service performance will need future passengers' journey needs daily. Hence, they can not neglect how to improve public transport service needs to satisfy passengers to feel satisfaction, if Sweden government hopes its tourism industry can raise GDP income in long time.

- How underground train MTR can let passengers to feel catching time reducing

It has close relationship between globalization and global tranport development. How globalisation impacts on the environment via changes taking place in the transport sectors. In fact, it is not clear how the relative price changes that result from openness will affect the environental composition of economic activity. For example, some countries will produce more environmentally intensive goods, others will produce fewer. On the other hand, liberalisation will raise incomes, perhaps increasing the willingness to pay for environmental improvement. These potential income effects increased outweigh the negative scale effects with increased economic activities. When combined with the positive effects with technology transfer, the net effect on local pollutants could be positive . Hence, we need to find methods to solve the problem of raising transport economic activities and serious environmental pollution creating as the same time occurrence.

Globalisation helps to facilitate greater division of labor, and to exploit its comparative advantage more completely. In longer term, globalization also stimilates technology an dlabour transfers, and allows the dynamism that accompanies economic activities to stimulate the development of new transport technologies and short time transport processes that lead to global welfare improvement.

On shipping transport industry aspect, shipping will increase ocean pollution, when international shipping activities are increasing. Trade and shipping encourages energy use in shipping is coupled with the movement of waterborne commerce. The estimates depending on the transport goods number of at-sea or in port days much increase globally every day. The energy demand of international shipping fuel sale number and domestically assigned fuel sales number also increases for global fuel usage. Estimates of ocean going ships now consume about 2% to 3% and perhaps even as much as 4% of world fossil fuels.Hence, when global shipping energy fuel usage number increases, because global shipping trading activities number increases. It will bring the environmental pollution to ocean level increases.

On air transport industry aspect, their travellers' catching air plans travelling needs and businesses' goods transport air delivery service needs are increasing from the requirements for high quality , fast and reliable international transport. Moreover, the networks that airline companies operate have changed often to hub-and spoke networks, many new often low -cost companies have entered the air freight market, any long time air journey is needed, e.g. Australia airline expands its one new air journey flies to UK, it needs two days flying time. It means that every flight to UK from Australia , it needs to use more fuel to fly. Then , air pollution will increase also.

On road transport industry aspect, global road transport cost and transit times, traffic jam occurrence chances also increase because when the road building number is increasing globally. So, it will cause traffic jam and long journey time spending , even fuel usage spending number is also increased. Then, accident occurrence chance is raised. Hence, global business or entertainment transport activities number increasing , it will bring much negative impact on environmental pollution, traffic jams number increases, long journey spending time increases, fuel usage number increases. Although , frequent transport activities may bring GDP income.

On transport service industy aspect, but is also brings negative influence to standard of living. It means that when transport fuel demand increases, transport activities number increases, GDP income on relative any transport activities needs industy , e.g. logistic demand needs, when lorry drivers need to drive lorries to deliver goods from one warehouse to another warehouse or supermarket or office etc. different business places on the road driving activities increase. But, it also bring air pollution , traffic noise and traffic jam etc. transport problems to road and natural environment and raises worse standard of living , bad emotion to working people or learning emotion to students , due to frequent traffic jam causes , low efficiency and productivity to workers, even student individual learning time can be reduced if they need to spend long time to wait bus, ferry, rail, underground train to go to schools , due to frequent long time traffic jam occurs on the roads to influence they can not go to schools on time often when they are catching buses to go to schools absolutely in busy transport time.

Thus, although any countries need to consider how to design their transport system, e.g. how to e.g. how to choose the right locations to build roads to let many cars can be driven available easily when the morning and evening (office and school transport busy time, e.g. 6:00 to 9:00 AM morning, 6:00 to 9:00 PM in the evening transport time usually because these two transport periods are usually , there are many students and working people need to catch any public transportation or drive cars tools to go back homes. So, enough roads number and long and not narrow road area must be needed to design in order to let enough cars be driven on the roads in the transport busy times to the countries have many big cities or have high population , such as UK, US, China, India, Hong Kong. They have many people , but drivers and cars numbers both are increasing. So, efficient road design and road number are also needed to increase in order to let drivers can transport goods to deliver, students and working people can catch any public transport tools to arrive any destinations on reads in the short time rapidly in order to avoid to spend long time transportation time and late to arrive any destinations in possible occurrence. So, any sudden traffic jam is not hoped to be caused by easy traffic accidents occurrence any time.

Hence, global efficient road transport system is needed, when global transport activities are increased, because any road logistic transport activities are increasing, they will also influence the students and working people when they also need to catch any public transport tools or drive themselves cars to go to working places or schools on the roads at the same busy transport time between 6:00 to 9:00 AM morning busy transport time and between 6:00 to 9:00 PM evening busy transport time. Because these both times will be have many students, working people , they need either go to offices or schools or go to homes. Hence, if the country had many lorry drivers need to drive their lorries to deliver goods on the roads in the transport busy morning or evening time in the same driving time on the roads. It will increase the risk to cause frequent traffic jam or traffic accident occurrence easily in possible in the country. So, any countries' governments can not neglect how to design roads and choose anywhere are the roads suitable locations to be built as well as anywhere land useful number to build road location choices in order to solve geographical traffic jams occurrence chance.

Hence, globalization of transport activities may bring geographical GDP growth, but it also bring traffic jams and traffic accidents occurrences, hearing impairment due to traffic noise, air pollution, traffic crashed, bad working emotions to workers and bad learning emotions to students, due to spending long transport time when traffic jam or traffic accidence occurs more easily.

However, transportation is an important tool if a country's progress. Rapid economic growth and increasing level of urbanization enhances a person's living standard have, it leads to a greater travel demands. Hence, governments ought not neglect have to design its roads , measure every road's length or width whether it has how many cars need to drive in morning or evening transport busy time for students, working people and delivery goods drivers of public transportation tools or private transportation tools easy driving needs in order to avoid frequent traffic jams or traffic accidents occurrences in possible.

Moreover, any governments also need to solve these issues, if they hope to develop their transport system successfully. These issues include : What mode of transportation to cost-effective in meeting a region's transportation needs to the country? How should a state department of transportation prioritize its highway delivers to maximize economic growth? What is the trade-off between additional growth in urban area and the cost of expanding transportation systems to accommodate greater growth? What effect does the expansion of transportation systems have on the need to invest in other types of transport modes? For example , the transport expansion may include the construction of additional highway segments, rail lines, runways, or additional sea, air, rail or bus terminal capacity using traditional technology; highway may include the additional of lanes to an interstate highway system; the conversion of an existing two-lane road to a four lane limited access highway, replacement or widening of bridges, and the extension of an existing road. Airport examples, include runway lengthening, apron expansion, and additional terminal gates.

On the other hand, enhancement to new transport technologies may bring efficiency of the existing highway system, examples may include intelligent highway systems, congestion pricing, intermodal freight facilities, geographic positioning systems, and instrument landing systems to mention of a few major transport innovations. So, transport policy makers need to understand the effects of these new transport mode innovations on economic development or GDP growth on transport activities growth transportation services and a more efficient use of limited land supplying scarce resources , air quality ,and noise pollution, traffic jams, long spending transport time to students, working people, entertaining people, even deliver goods lorry drivers their every day essential driving activities or catching public transportation tools needs problems. For example, the concept of intelligent highway systems needs increase trend. In simply , vehicles are being linked to each other and to traffic control devices to improve the efficiency of the total highway system. Similar types of innovations in intelligent traffic management are increasing needs for air, sea, and rail systems. The question is that whether intelligent highway systems can attribute of highways on economic development, raising on productivity of reducing highway congestion or improving pavement condition.

In fact, many developed countries' transportation system is mature. The nation has gone beyond the frontier of building, the interstate highway system and connecting most cities (markets). Tweaking the system with additional lanes and the new intelligent highway systems are useful in China, US, UK, because they have many cities. SO, road efficient traffic congestion control is needed when many students, working people, delivery goods transport people need to drive cars or catch cars on every city's roads in the transport busy time between 6:00 to 9:00 AM morning transport busy time as well as between 6:00 to 9:00 PM evening transport busy time.

However, transportation investment must be needed, if the country hoped to have good economic productivity, efficient transport service can bring good effects on the flows goods and people on roads every day when they use the country's transport system. So, any countries need to collect data, they can not be lack of enough transport information in any time that links anywhere locations of any drivers to the locations of the transport system that provide them with services in any time, e.g. every day morning and evening transport busy time, radio can report the real transport time of any roads traffic jam or traffic accident message to let drivers to listen to know whether anywhere roads are occurring traffic accidents or traffic jams or when the road traffic accident or traffic jam is solved to let the drivers can know whether when the roads can be opened to drive again. So, real time road transport message information is needed to report by radio, in order to let any drivers to know whether they ought choose to drive themselves cars on the road when they need to choose anywhere road to drive to the destination if they can know when the road has traffic accident or traffic jam occurs. They won't drive their cars on the road in the moment immediately.

On conclusion, globalization can being frequent transport economic activities. So, road , air, sea, transport service users' transport service needs are also increased. Every country ought not neglect how to innovate their transport service in order to satisfy their transport needs to achieve economic growth, efficient and short transport time spending, productivities increase, reducing air pollution, traffic noise , raisins standard of living on transport influence aspect to satisfy working people, students, entertaining people, delivery goods transport users' efficient road transport time behavioral spending aspect.

On conclusion, when one country's electric public transport tool service increases, it may cause gas need decreases and gas business will experience decline stage cycle stage rapidly.